The Politics
of Early Childhood
Education

Rethinking Childhood

Joe L. Kincheloe and Janice A. Jipson
General Editors

Vol. 10

PETER LANG
New York • Washington, D.C./Baltimore • Boston • Bern
Frankfurt am Main • Berlin • Brussels • Vienna • Oxford

The Politics
of Early Childhood
Education

Edited by
Lourdes Diaz Soto

PETER LANG
New York • Washington, D.C./Baltimore • Boston • Bern
Frankfurt am Main • Berlin • Brussels • Vienna • Oxford

Library of Congress Cataloging-in-Publication Data

The politics of early childhood education / [edited by] Lourdes Diaz Soto.
p. cm. — (Rethinking childhood; vol. 10)
Includes bibliographical references.
1. Early childhood education—Political aspects—United States.
2. Child development—United States. 3. Critical pedagogy—United States.
4. Multicultural education—United States. 5. Minorities—Education (Early
Childhood)—United States. I. Soto, Lourdes Diaz. II. Series.
LB1139.25.P65 372.21—dc21 98-38989
ISBN 0-8204-4164-3
ISSN 1086-7155

Die Deutsche Bibliothek-CIP-Einheitsaufnahme

The politics of early childhood education / ed. by Lourdes Diaz Soto.
–New York; Washington, D.C./Baltimore; Boston; Bern;
Frankfurt am Main; Berlin; Brussels; Vienna; Oxford: Lang.
(Rethinking childhood; Vol. 10)
ISBN 0-8204-4164-3

Cover design by Lisa Dillon

Cover art: Dori Lemeh, *The Key,* © 1995.
Collection of Mr. and Mrs. Charles Dumas

The paper in this book meets the guidelines for permanence and durability
of the Committee on Production Guidelines for Book Longevity
of the Council of Library Resources.

© 2000 Peter Lang Publishing, Inc., New York

Printed in the United States of America

DEDICATION

To early childhood educators toiling in the
fields of postmodern America.

ACKNOWLEDGMENTS

We would like to thank our children, our students, our families, and our colleagues who have encouraged, supported, and nurtured our work. To them we owe any semblance of balance we may have in our daily "muddled" postmodern lives. Gratitude is especially expressed to Joe Kincheloe, Shirley Steinberg, and those at Peter Lang Publishing whose support helped to make this project possible.

Are Disney Movies Good for your Kids? Approximately 14 pages from *Kinderculture* by Henry Giroux. Copyright © 1997 by Westview Press. Reprinted by permission of Westview Press.

Hedy Nai-Lin Chang, Amy Muckelroy and Dora Pulido-Tobiassen, *Looking In Looking Out: Redefining Child Care and Early Education in a Diverse Society*. San Francisco: California Tomorrow, Reprinted by permission of California Tomorrow, 1996.

True peace is not merely the absence of tension;
it is the presence of justice.

Martin Luther King, Jr. (1963)

CONTENTS

LIST OF FIGURES

FOREWORD

Peter McLaren
University of California-Los Angeles

Childhood and adolescence in the United States are rapidly disappearing. Children on the road to adolescence and young people on the road to adulthood have decided to take their own detour. The exit ramp is well traveled by an increasing number of youth who have discovered that schools and society have not only failed them, but were never set up to address their needs in the first place. In other words, they have learned that they don't possess the necessary requirements even to be failures, and hence have no identities. Instead, they remain invisible, as if they were never born—*Je ne suis pas encore né.* All that remains, it seems, is to steal an identity, to become an imposter, always to let somebody else sign their name in the place where one's own signature ought to be.

In May 1998 an Oregon high school student murdered his parents, then carried three guns into the school cafeteria and fired on hundreds of students, killing 2 and injuring 22, 4 critically. That same year a Tennessee high school senior shot and killed another student in the school parking lot; a 14-year-old Pennsylvania student opened fire at an eighth grade graduation dance, killing a teacher and wounding 2 students and another teacher; a 15-year-old Houston high school student was shot in the leg in her classroom; and a 15-year-old Washington State student returned home from school carrying a gun and shot himself in the head. In 1997, a Kentucky high school student sprayed gunfire into a high school prayer circle, killing 3 students and wounding five others; a Mississippi student killed two schoolmates and wounded seven more; in Arkansas, an 11-year-old student and a 13-year-old companion killed four other students and a teacher and wounded 10 others. Don't you remember carving your initials in the desk with your penknife, stealing an extra dessert from the cafeteria cart, dipping the pigtails of the girl in front of you into the ink jar, and the laughing eyes of the boy with the face full of freckles and the strange popping sound his hunting rifle made just before you lost consciousness and woke up in the hospital on a life support system?

As educators within a neo-liberal capitalist regime, we too often fail to see the connection among youth violence, capitalism's law of xvi The Politics of Early Childhood Education

value, and the constitution of subjectivity. As capital reconstitutes itself, as factory work is replaced by McJobs, as the disadvantaged are cast about in the wind of world commodity price fluctuations, as the *comprador* elite expands its power base, as the middle-class fades away, and as the White House redecorates itself in the spiraling patterns of neo-liberalism, capitalist hegemony must extend to the structure of subjectivity itself. Communication networks, with their explosions and fluxes of information that have grown apace with capitalism make this hegemony not only a possibility but also an inevitability as they promote forms of exploitation so furious that every vulnerability of the masses is seized and made over into a crisis. The global death rattle that announces this *fin-de-siècle* moment alerts lost generations, whose subjectivities are molded into capitalist forms of such pure intensity, that time and history do not seem necessary. We are always already shaped by the labyrinthine circuits of capitalist desire.

This volume is about the condition of adolescence in present-day late capitalist society. Apart from being one of the few collections that addresses early childhood education from the perspective of critical social theory, what is especially compelling about *The Politics of Early Childhood Education* is the breadth and scope of the terrain that it contests and the vigor of its contestability. Developmental theories of early childhood and adolescents do not exist in a realm of their own, in some protected scientific enclave detached from the sociopolitical milieu in which they are generated. They did not suddenly appear on the educational firmament fully formed and accompanied by celestial fanfare. The sovereign epistemes and scientific practices that guide them could not have emerged from precincts of neutrality, but instead were dragged through the murky waters of history by forces of human interest. Recognizing the ideological dimensions of developmental theories that purport to be underwritten by politically neutral "objective" science, Lourdes Díaz Soto set out to create a volume that, among other things, uncovers the particular ideological practices and functions of dominant ideas, values, beliefs, and sensibilities that present themselves in the field of child development as nonhierarchical and interest-free.

This book raises the question of what constitutes the ideological functions of conventional research in early childhood education and seeks to identify those particular interests that remain cloaked by the status of empirical verifiability. In other words, how has the claim for uncovering the necessary conditions of early childhood education made by developmental psychologists actually made invisible the contingency of conditions and changeable circumstances behind such a claim. Rejecting claims for immunity from prosecution on the grounds that it constitutes "hard science," the authors of this volume press their case against early childhood development education's overreliance on child development paradigms, cognitive psychology, and exclusive western ways of seeing the world, which in turn promotes a particular "psychodynamic" description of truth, reality, and knowledge that appears to be independent of the cultural practices and conventions of social agents. This book provides alternate possibilities for the field from proponents of early childhood reconceptualization (Mimi Block, Shirley Kessler, Sally Lubeck, Beth Blue Swadener) and critical theorists (Henry Giroux and Joe Kincheloe).

More specifically, the authors in this volume have brought early childhood education into conversation with social theory and in doing so have located the formation of childhood subjectivity within relations of power and exploitation and not simply as a cluster of cognitive characteristics and psychological traits captured in a web of dependent and independent variables in the universe of Cartesian consciousness.

Recognizing that the field of research has been politically bankrupt for decades, Lourdes Díaz Soto and her colleagues take the issue of early childhood education beyond the dead facts of conventional empiricists, facts that remain divorced from the contingencies of history and that are propagated by those who refuse to acknowledge the transient character of knowledge claims and that who fail to locate behavior as internal to the exigencies of politics and power within late capitalist society.

Treating youth culture prismatically—as a site of conflict, as an arena of competing discourses, as a social text, as products of social relations of production and patterns of consumption—helps to maintain the horizons necessary for a critical interrogation of dominant systems of intelligibility and classification within the field of early childhood education. Early childhood education is refracted through lenses that bring into focus multidimensionality and context rather than the monolithic dreariness of dominant models.

The Politics of Early Childhood Education is an important volume that offers educators a critical vernacular and language of analysis that will enable contemporary childhood to be understood within the context of cultural commodification, contemporary capitalist social relations, and popular culture. It is a book that will share with educators some approaches that can be taken to give contemporary youth a chance to survive the new millennium and to dream a new history.

INTRODUCTION

Lourdes Diáz Soto
Pennsylvania State University

The purpose of this book is to critique the field of early childhood education for its overreliance on child development paradigms, psychology, and the exclusive western ways of seeing the world. This book provides alternate possibilities for the field from both the proponents of early childhood reconceptualization and contemporary critical theorists. The basic premise for this book is simple—it brings together early childhood and cultural studies professionals who are willing to provide a kaleidoscope of views capable of challenging the sanctity of the single early childhood western lens. The idea is to continue the dialogue initiated by early childhood reconceptualists (Kessler & Swadener, 1992) and to propose "the intersection of educational/childhood studies and cultural studies" referred to in *Kinderculture* (Steinberg & Kincheloe, 1997).

In many ways we are fast becoming explorers venturing into new areas and new spaces that Homi Bhabha might call the "third space of translation." McLaren (1993) notes that the third space of translation requires that identities—especially cultural identities—be seen as "decentered structures." The "third space refers to a condition of hybridity in which the essentialism of origins and the discourse of authenticity are challenged" (p. 22). In our case, the third space of translation becomes a journey leading us closer toward a critical early childhood multicultural dreamspace of social justice and equity.

This volume is presented to you, the reader, as a promise and with the hope that we can continue to travel together and in solidarity in uncharted paths and newly evolving possibilities. The hope includes the idea that as you read our contributions you will not only further analyze but explore your own role in the collaborative third space. This is a call for alternative research and pedagogical practices in the field that move toward the critical, toward the multicultural, toward the dialogic, toward the feminist, toward the personal—with the others, with the silenced, and in solidarity with multiple players.

The field has continued to cling to outdated and unrealistic constructions and representations of childhood. Who stands to benefit from the elitist early childhood western canon? In whose best interest are the existing socioculturally embedded child development and psychologically driven views of children and families? How can we address issues of power as we critically examine the historically situated politics of early childhood education?

As we examine the prevalent child development, psychologically driven perspectives in early childhood education, we begin to notice multiple forms of oppression that are rarely uncovered, examined, or addressed.

The scholars and practitioners contributing to this volume reach out to the reader in ways that can guide us toward a liberating third space. In this book we will first examine the overreliance on child development by the field; second, we will critically analyze young children's daily realities in a postmodern society; third, we will share evidence reflecting the need for the field to embrace critical multiculturalism. We will view examples of how the ivory tower continues to influence the field of early childhood education, and finally we will relate a critical early childhood multicultural dreamspace of social justice and equity.

Marianne Block and Thomas Popkewitz begin the dialogue by examining the child, parent, and teacher discourses of child development. Why are questions being raised about the relationship between child development and early childhood education? Sally Lubeck continues to encourage us to explore the notion of "developmentally appropriate," which is advocated by professionals in the field and she asks us to critically reflect on "Who stands to benefit?" Shirley Kessler analyzes the existing perspectives on young children's play and how these specifically relate to issues of class and gender in our postmodern condition.

Young children's daily realities and contemporary constructions of childhood are examined in the second section of this volume. These scholars call for the deconstruction of taken-for-granted experiences and activities that currently influence children's everyday lives. Joe Kincheloe, for example, asks us to step outside the boundaries of formalism in order to construct a postformal vision. In "Take the Money and Run," Glenda MacNaughton and Patrick Hughes examine the commodification of early education by professional organizations while Henry Giroux asks, "Are Disney Movies Good for Your Kids?"

The need for a critical multicultural perspective in early childhood education is discussed by Beth Blue Swadener, who asks us to replace the deficit constructions of the "other childhood" with authentic alliances with children and families. Nila Rinehart describes the very real needs of young Native American children as she examines the politics of language and culture. The "California Tomorrow" researchers and practitioners studied immigrant children's experiences in childcare settings while recommending dialogue and reflections. The contributors in this section call for a move toward the dialogic, toward the critical, and toward alliances.

How institutions of higher learning can affect the field of early childhood education is highlighted by Amos Hatch, who traces his experiences as an early childhood teacher educator attempting to introduce postmodern thought, while Jan Jipson relays the multiple and the complex experiences discovered in early childhood research and scholarship. How can we move the field beyond existing child development and scientifically driven epistemologies? How are the early childhood reconceptualists and proponents of cultural studies providing hope for the field? In the concluding chapter we ask the reader to envision the field moving toward a newly evolving liberating "third space."

As we envision the possibilities let us first begin by problematizing the existing child development discourses and the multiple issues that we refer to as the politics of early childhood education.

Part One

Child Development Paradigms in
a Postmodern Society

CHAPTER ONE

Constructing the Parent, Teacher, and Child:
Discourses of Development

Marianne N. Bloch and Thomas S. Popkewitz
University of Wisconsin-Madison

Introduction

In a recent issue of the American journal *Early Childhood Research Quarterly (ECRQ)*, a special section of articles discussed the "importance of child development knowledge in teacher education" (Goffin, 1996; also see Polakow, 1982; Kessler, 1991; Mallory & New, 1994; Swadener & Kessler, 1991). The responses to the basic question posed in the *ECRQ* articles (see Goffin, 1996)—What is the importance of child development knowledge in early childhood education teacher education—represent, we believe, one paradigmatic approach to think about the practices of education, teacher education, and educational research. The idea of childhood is accepted as a given principle, with the question of research as how best to understand patterns of development in order to improve teaching, teacher education, *and* childhood while most current research does challenge the idea of child development as a universal or natural/biological phenomenon; it marshals its multiple arguments to understand the mediated meaning of development through ideas that examine, for example, "development-in-context" (e.g., New, 1994) or the social, cultural, and economic factors that influence development (e.g., Lubeck, 1994).

While this chapter responds, in part, to the same issue as the "importance of child development knowledge," our interest is on the ways in which the idea of *development* is embedded in a system of reason that shapes and fashions how educators "see," think, talk, and act toward teaching, children, and schooling. This chapter places the idea of *development* in a relationship among science, child development knowledge, and early childhood teacher and parent education in the twentieth century. This relationship entails considering first how child development knowledge has been inscribed in a broad, diffuse, and complex form of governing of the *soul*; that is, the governing of the inner dispositions, sensitivities, and capabilities of the child's being. This governing idea in the nineteenth century was to produce a child who would develop into the new liberal, democratic citizen who acted as a responsible, self-motivated individual. This linking of power and knowledge, we argue, is produced through the sets of categories, distinctions, and divisions that organize the principles of action and participation, what Foucault (1979, 1991) has called a *governmentality* (see also, Burman, 1994; Cannella, 1997; Hultqvist, 1998; Polakow, 1982; Popkewitz & Brennan, 1998; Rose, 1989; Walkerdine, 1988). By the end of the chapter, we present a preliminary exploration of current relationships in light of changes in the discourses, knowledge, and power relations that govern the child and parent/teachers in the late 20th century. In each instance, our concern is the effect of the knowledge of *development* on generating principles of action and participation that exclude as well as include.

Child Development and the Problematic of Governmentality

We can think of child development knowledge as emerging within multiple discourses that were characteristic of modernity in the nineteenth and the first part of the twentieth century. This is exemplified by the growth in discourses about science and progress, and growth in the belief in the methods and logic of science that were paralleled by a growth in political discourses about the liberal democratic citizen during this period (Popkewitz, 1998a). The interest in the adult who could participate in the new political orders of liberalism also reached down into the problems of family and childrearing. It became possible to think about the possibility of socially administering the child in order to produce an adult who acted and participated in the new social, cultural, and political institutions.

One way to consider the new patterns of social administration of the family and the child is through the idea of *governmentality*. Foucault used the concept of governing that organizes this concept in two ways; first in relation to *governance of others* and second in relation to *governance of the self*. This understanding of governance refers to all those ways of reflecting and acting that aim to shape, guide, manage or regulate the conduct of persons—not only other persons but also one's self—in light of certain principles or goals. This sense of government is most closely aligned with a sense of the political in terms of the rules of *reasoning* mentalities that order the affairs of a territory to ensure citizens' well-being rather than the more conventional notion of the political as a domain or aspect of the state, or particular political acts or actors. It is this focus on rules of reasoning that discipline action and participation to which the idea of *governmentality* gives focus (Foucault, 1979/1991; Foucault, 1980; Foucault, 1983).

The new patterns of governance through the rules of reasoning tied the individual, the "family" to liberal and democratic philosophies in Western Europe. According to Hindess, "liberal or representative democracy, as the former name suggests, ...can be seen as an uneasy compromise in which the institutions of representative government are supposed to play a major part in satisfying the demands of both (collective and individual) positions. Liberalism, representative government, and the rule of law might be described as containing the influence of the people within strict limits. Against the tyranny of majority or minority factions, they could be said to secure defenses of a kind ...to balance the needs of individuals and groups in civil society with the well-being of the whole" (Hindess, 1996).

The ideas of liberalism, while balancing the needs of society as a whole with the protection of the individual, his interests, liberty, and opportunities, were also a governing practice. But this governing operated on a different layer from the legal and administrative rules of the institutions of the state. It operated in a way that facilitated the governance and creation of "autonomy," or a certain type of freedom, an ability to care for the "self" (Hindess, 1996, p. 68). This personal independence, rationality, responsibility, and care for the "self" and "others" embodied a new set of relations between the State and individuality. A liberal society was to construct the individual who was a productive and (self- and other-) disciplined citizen within the new social and political arrangements. Thus, while a philosophy of welfare emphasizes the joint rights of individuals and the collective, perhaps through a philosophy of liberalism, the philosophy was a way of reasoning that was broadly diffused in society.

Thus, liberalism, as one example, was a form of thought or political rationality concerned not only with the affairs of state but with the affairs of the individual. The knowledge of a political community was based on the individual who acted within the rules of liberalism itself. Governance became both a macrosocial problem of administration as well as a microgoverning of the "self." Thus, a liberal philosophy of welfare accepts the concept of *limited* government; activities of a liberal welfare philosophy involve a reasoning that supports laws and regulations that ensure the maintenance of the community—especially those who cannot act independently, while providing limited regulation of those who are autonomous or independent, who can act for themselves, in economic, political, religious, or social spheres. The reasoning traversed institutions and could be found in rules of law, reform policies, media texts/statements, and through statistical reasoning that organized the administrative practices of the State (Hacking, 1991), *or* through the knowledge promoted by pedagogical experts in child development in scientific institutions and universities (see, e.g., Wittrock & Wagner, 1996).

The social administration of the child inscribed norms of reasoning about the child that were the effects of power. The very knowledge taken as "natural" to the development of the child was built upon notions of stages of development, norms of achievement, and growth that inscribed certain ways of thinking about children and their parents that tied the new political rationalities of governing with the self-governing principles that ordered individuality.

Thus, it is possible to think of the idea and theories of child development that were constituted as part of the new ways of governing and socially administering the child at the turn of the century. Development as a principle of social practice was embedded in a system of reasoning (governmentalities) that ordered how difference was to be understood, classified the normal and that outside of normalcy, what care for children came to mean, and principles of "childhood" that shaped and fashioned the "education" and "care" to take place (Rose, 1989; Foucault, 1979, 1991). These principles guided with whom care occurred (mother versus others), where children and others were to spend time (at home or elsewhere), and how we conceive and construct our identities of self (see Bloch, 1987; Polakow, 1993; Popkewitz & Brennan, 1998).

By relating liberal principles to the problem of social administration and governmentality, we are suggesting that scientific knowledge about families, schooling, and the child were part of a broad and complex system of governance that linked power with the knowledge or the truths constructed about the child, his development, and nature. We argue that the power/knowledge relations historically embedded in the discourses of education are obscured when the subject of a child's development is assumed and naturalized.

The social administration of the child inscribed norms of reasoning about the child that were the effects of power. The very knowledge taken as "natural" to the development of the child was built upon notions of stages of development, norms of achievement, and growth that inscribed certain ways of thinking about children and their parents that tied the new political rationalities of governing with the self-governing principles that ordered individuality.

Welfare and Childcare

The larger changes of social planning and welfare obligations had particular historical trajectories within the field of the family and childraising toward the turn of the century. The new constructions of the child were produced through an overlapping of various institutions. At one level was the formal State legal administrative apparatus that produced child labor laws as well as an extensive social organization related to care of the home, health regulations to prevent the spread of disease, and urban planning to rationalize and order urban existence. At a different level were the invention of the social and psychological sciences as special institutions concerned with producing knowledge that would describe and order the reforms considered important to the modernization of the family.

By the early twentieth century, the rise of science, changing demographics, and new institutions and affiliations resulted in varying government rules and social science initiatives that were designed to insure social welfare practices were to help families develop "autonomy." New notions of the liberal welfare state that would identify those in need of government intervention or assistance were developed. The discourses of policies and science focused on the male breadwinner as the target for welfare-related employment insurance if the family was judged to be nonautonomous. Dependent nonautonomous females would "need" temporary or emergency non-employment related welfare assistance in order to be at home with children, or temporary assistance to send children to a day nursery (Bloch, 1987; Fraser & Gordon, 1994; Gordon, 1994). Childcare in settlement houses was run by social workers from the newly established professional field of social work; childcare workers as well as trained Froebelian teachers ran day nurseries and kindergartens for children in the morning, for example, and the teachers visited homes in the afternoons. The specially trained social workers and teachers educated parents about hygiene and "good" parenting skills using a burgeoning field of "scientific" child development, health, and social welfare knowledge to communicate knowledge about what the good parent would do.

The Profession Expert and Professionalized
Knowledge as a Strategy of Social Administration

The social sciences were active factors in the re-envisioning of the principles through which individuals were governed and were to come to govern themselves. The new disciplines of the social sciences were expected to spread modernity by giving focus to the micro-processes by which individuals became self-motivated, self-responsible, and "reasonable." Where this governing had previously been the domain of spiritual advisors who elaborated on the norms of conduct, criteria of self-judgment, and techniques of life conduct for the individual, now this spiritual salvation of souls was administered through scientifically guided self-betterment (see Popkewitz, 1998b). The social sciences generated principles for a particular type of childhood, family, citizen, and worker who could operate with the dispositions deemed necessary for liberal democratic societies. It was in this institutionalization of the social sciences during the decades after the turn of the century that the domestic sciences and educational sciences became recognized as disciplines (e.g., home economics, and educational psychology departments). While forms of scientific reasoning were contested, social betterment was viewed as dependent upon the rational (re)construction of the family and the child who would become "citizens" who could act progressively to control their own circumstances and environment.

The modern social sciences were made possible within a particular overlay of ideas that made progress a key concept of social administration. It became possible in the nineteenth century to reason about modern institutions as having movement, development, and progress through the application of rational systems of thought and scientific knowledge. This belief about planned change-as-progress also moved into the idea of individual change—progress of the individual involved thinking of the development of humans as gradual, linear, and the product of scientific evolution—constantly making progress, and improvement in life and development as the problem of scientific knowledge.

In this context, we can view the sciences of early childhood education as involving more than the organization and the interpretation of social life. Achievement, moral deportment, and development (progress) of the "self" in childhood were envisioned through the new classificatory systems of scientific reasoning. Ideas of children's development in the kindergarten, for example, linked the physical, moral, and intellectual through concepts such as "joyous" learning, and teaching cleanliness and tidiness, with ideas about intellectual and social development. Children's play and the development of organized playgrounds and equipment were part of a social welfare surveillance system that also used G. Stanley Hall's conception of evolutionary stages to portray play as the natural stage of development for primitive, relatively uncivilized young children, something to grow out of or to evolve from; in these ways development, competence, and salvation were combined (Gould, 1977; Bloch & Choi, 1990). Thorndike's educational psychology guided the new social administration through educational psychology by examining the developing "nature" of the child through the measurement of his natural tendencies, impulses, and social needs in order to bring progress; progress, however, was now in the changes in the individual rather than in social institutions.

The disciplinary qualities of the social and educational sciences, then, can be understood as having a double meaning. The systemic, professional knowledge about society functioned as a guide for thinking about institutional reforms and social policy. But the disciplinary knowledge also generated governing principles that related the new political rationalities of a liberal democracy to the construction of individuals and individual subjectivities. Psychology and child development were an important part in the new disciplinary strategies of governing, and the production of the "individual." The theoretical systems of these and other social sciences entailed a profound shift in how consciousness was ordered and action generated at the level of an individual's 'being'.

While the beliefs in science as a bearer of social and personal progress only became dominant in the twentieth century, it is also critical to understand that the rationalities about the relation of social administration and individuality—political rationalities of the different ideological strands of change—came to govern mentalities of the self through a number of historical movements. Further, the social sciences merged what was thought to be separate (Scheler, 1980), that is, the interests of power/knowledge, achievement, and salvation.

Populational Reasoning and Governmentalities. One strategy in the social administration is *populational reasoning.* Thinking of the *child* and *childhood* is one such invention of populational reasoning. Populational reasoning emerged with state reform tactics concerned with administering social welfare. Hacking (1991) called the use of populational reasoning the "taming of chance" because it provided methodological strategies in which to order the present in relation to the past and uncertainties of the future. It appeared as a way to deal with the challenge to certainty that existed as the beliefs about natural laws and theological destiny became undone. Populational reasoning introduced(es) a probability into thinking about how to control change in a world of *indeterminism.*

Populational reasoning provided an important innovation in the social administration of individuals. People came to be defined as populations that could be ordered through the political arithmetic of the State, which the French called *statistique*. State administrators spoke of social welfare in terms of biological issues such as reproduction, disease, and education (individual development, growth, and evolution). Human needs were conceptualized in instrumental and empirical terms in relation to the functioning of the state.

The notion of population produced a new form of individuality that is subsumed within *developmental thought*. The individual is defined normatively in relation to statistical aggregates from which specific characteristics can be ascribed to that person, and according to which her growth and development can be monitored and supervised. Assessing intelligence and developmental stage, as these emerged during the early twentieth century, are principal examples of such statistical ascription.

Populations, once established as a concept of development, can be measured, organized, divided into categories using statistical techniques, and dealt with through techniques of power-knowledge. Applying this calculus of probability, populational reasoning constructs our understanding of the way in which children learn, grow, achieve, and of the social and psychological attributes presumed to cause school failure. Individuals and events of a child's development are organized and reclassified in a manner that separates the particular event from its immediate historical situation. Populational reasoning normalizes by creating the normal/abnormal.

Populational reasoning performs as a system of social administration through the inscription of norms that exist as the average. There is the average or normal state of affairs according to which all children are to be understood and evaluated. This is what the pedagogical theories and psychological studies of the child have provided since the turn of the century. Thus, it is possible to talk about child development, about the urban or rural child, or children who are "at-risk" (see Castel, 1991). But also present in the discourses that are to rescue the designated populations of children are the norms of the future from which progress and amelioration can be obtained. The norms of pedagogical practices produce a composite figure of perfection toward which children may progress. It is in this combining of averages and progress where education links the "is" and the "ought" into a seamless line.

Defining how people "fit into" a group as defined by particular sets of characteristics, then, is "more" than just a way to classify. It is also a system of reasoning that normalizes, individualizes, and divides. Reasoning about children as populations makes possible a particular type of governance. The reasoning secures individuals' identities.

According to the calculus of probability, individuals and events could be administratively organized and regulated, and classified through physical and mental development, level of income and employment, and achievement and skill levels. We can think of the modern propensity to place individuals into groups defined as populations, and its reverse, as defining individuality through deriving particular and discrete characteristics of individual well-being from probabilistic reasoning (e.g., children learn to read better through having parents read stories to them; single mothers "need" to be taught mothering skills). Populational reasoning produces the taming of chance and thus makes possible the administration of social life and the ordering of identities.

Gender, Poverty, and Race: Constructing the Good Parent and Family. Feminist scholarship has enabled us to recognize that liberal notions of political theory discursively normalize a gendered division of labor where some autonomous individuals (typically "male") are assumed to be responsible for the others (typically "women and children") (Hindess, 1996). What is less discussed is how a particular "populational reasoning" becomes part of the social administration of gender, poverty, and ethnically "different" groups in the discourse of pedagogy and childhood, especially for poor families with young children, single parents (primarily women), and children in the U.S. in the early twentieth century.

If the "reason" of the family and parents that dominates many contemporary discussions about enabling children to be a success in school is examined, it immediately becomes evident that the organization of problems and problem solving is bounded by notions of the normal that reside in populational and probabilistic reasoning. When one assumes that the normal family is considered to be an independent unit led by the responsible autonomous male "head," that unit is built on norms of autonomy (ability to take care of one's self and one's family) that function to administer populational groups that are considered outside the normal—people of color who are defined as dependent or single low-income mothers. Families are statistical units that are judged as to whether they are headed by an autonomous male father, even though using such statistics would produce a different composite of a "family" if the norm were a family headed by a grandparent, a single mother, a nonbiologically related adult, groups in collective living arrangements, etc. These "other" populational or statistical groups (including children) become, relationally, constructed as abnormal and in "need" of monetary and/or social, psychological, or educational intervention, assistance, or redemption (Popkewitz, 1997).

It was in these ways that the growth of the social sciences as well as professions, and specifically, early education and child development professionals, were linked to state governing techniques. Through the complex weaving of beliefs in modernity, progress through science, salvation of those "in need" or who were abnormal, psychology, child development and early childhood social scientists and professionals participated actively—being administered and administering in the limitation of freedom, and the construction of normalities and differences.

Transferring the Soul to Science: The Invention of Psychology

The psychological sciences, including child development, were examples of the multiple attempts in the nascent social sciences to spread modernity through a revisioning of individuality. The construction of modern psychology, and child psychology within it, embodied a commitment to reconstruct society. Psychology would transform Enlightenment beliefs into practical technologies that would construct people's understanding of experience and form the norms of conduct. Subjectivity was one of the most important sites of struggle.

The Soul as the Site of Struggle. Emerging as an academic discipline during the U.S. Progressive Era (see, e.g., O'Donnell, 1985), psychology was largely conceptualized and given moral justification by the project to construct the self-governing individual (Herman, 1995). Psychology sought to produce the disciplined self that embodied an ethic of self control and the extension of processes of rationalization into personal conduct (Lears, 1981). Demands for social amelioration incorporated the Victorian ethic of self-control and the extension of the processes of rationalization into personal conduct. Industrialization involved a call for "systematic methods of self-control beyond the work place into the most intimate areas of daily experience—perhaps even into unconscious wishes, dreams, and fantasies" (Lears, 1981, p. 13). The presidents of universities, especially private East Coast institutions, embraced psychology as a way of reconciling faith and reason, Christian belief and Enlightenment empiricism (O'Donnell, 1985), it would also differentiate the universities from other knowledge bearers, including the church, grandparents, and other community elders.

The development of psychology and, later, child psychology and development, was heavily supported by new school administrators centralizing the organization of teaching and increasingly required to sort and group students from diverse backgrounds. This was true in the elementary school and was important for kindergartens and nursery schools as they came to be affiliated with public schools and/or became age-graded (Bloch, 1987; Bloch, Seward, & Seidlinger, 1989). Psychology and child psychology provided a new form of *expertise*, experts in the selection, organization, and evaluation of institutional and personal knowledge (Danziger, 1990).

Psychology was to administer the new institutions of governing, and simultaneously to provide for individuality and reason. The formation of the kindergarten and the field of early childhood drew on psychology to unite pedagogical ideas in the tasks of dissemination and advancement of practical knowledge that used logic, rationality, and science as its hallmark. While the disciplines were not monolithic in their outlook, the various approaches shared a goal of organizing liberty and progress through the construction of a child who could contribute productively to the transformations (development) of their 'being' through their own self-discipline. Faith was placed in the rational individual as the locus of change, whereas earlier conceptions of the child in infant and primary school movements in the nineteenth century placed more emphasis on faith and self-governed morality for stability as well as change (Bloch, 1987).

The disciplinary processes made individual desires, affects, and bodily practices objects of change, and subjects of scrutiny to observe for "development." This decentralization and individualization of subjectivities can be referred to as *the governing of the soul*. By soul, we mean that people's desires, attitudes, and bodily practices were made the focus of scrutiny and administration. The church's pastoral concern with saving the "soul" was transferred by the pedagogical and psychological sciences into the secular confessional practices that rescued the person through the social planning of the State (see Foucault, 1979, 1991, 1983; Rose, 1989).

The conviction that truth can be discovered through the self-examination of consciousness and the confession of one's thoughts and acts now appears so natural, so compelling, indeed so self-evident, that it seems unreasonable to posit that such self-examination is a central component of a strategy of power. This unseemingness rests on an attachment to a repressive power hypothesis; if truth is inherently opposed to power, then its uncovering would surely lead us on a path to liberation (Foucault, 1983, p. 175); the relationships between power and knowledge that we are discussing here, in contrast, point toward conceptions of truth being at the core of power/knowledge relations and their diffusion (see also Foucault, 1980).

Psychologists believed that they had sufficient knowledge and disinterest to promote institutional change. Acting as "an evolutionary cadre," psychologists "asked the public to have confidence not merely in their knowledge and skills but in their ability to construct a better world as well" (Napoli, 1981, p. 41). There was a belief that science was the "mainstream of inevitable progress" and that man "could make and remake his own world" (O'Donnell, 1985, p. 212). Promising what utopian thinkers had long sought, G. Stanley Hall (1911, 1969), for example, saw psychology as the means to overcome the problems of urban life, family, and inadequate social development.

Philanthropic Groups and Change of the Soul. To consider the new governing strategies of the child and family, however, we need to examine a particular U.S. institution, the philanthropic groups that emerged to promote social and personal change.

The rise of philanthropic groups, often funded by men and directed by university-educated women, were influential in developing day nurseries, kindergartens, and settlement house childcare centers that were run for children of poor urban families, offering temporary childcare. By the early twentieth century, philanthropists also established important foundations to support the growth and involvement of the social sciences in welfare policies. The Social Science Research Council was one such example.

Through support of research and theories about the causes and solutions to problems of poverty, immigration, and family, the philanthropic agencies practically were part of the mobilization of the welfare strategies that ordered social policy. The dilettante philanthropist of the late nineteenth century, acting on his/her own, however, had given way to other expertise and experts who often acted for the interests of the wealthy in the early twentieth century; these included the Ford Foundation, The Rockefeller Foundation, and the Laura Spelman Rockefeller Foundation that sponsored many of the first laboratory child development research nursery schools and institutes during the early twentieth century. The nonautonomous family would be rescued through new scientifically trained social welfare experts and workers, new regulations that limited employment, and experts who could teach parenting. By the early 1920s, nursery schools for the children of the growing middle class and elite would also emerge to expand governing through scientific and medical expertise to middle-class parents, their children, *and* through training provided in home economics departments and teacher education training programs, to nursery and kindergarten school teachers (Bloch, 1992; Sears, 1975).

The philanthropic focus inscribed an important shift within religious groups and social policy about the causes of poverty. Whereas the early part of the century maintained a Protestant view of poverty as a consequence of individual sin and thus failure, the end of the century focused on the cause of poverty as related to the social conditions in which the poor lived.

The Growth of Scientific Child Development Knowledge

The new governing practices involve a complex amalgamation of institutions, ideas, and technologies. The philanthropic foundations overlayed with other institutions, such as school administrators in the NEA, and the national parents association, to make possible the assumption of social administration of individuality and child development. Research and teaching laboratory schools developed in many major universities around the nation by the 1930s and "scientific journals" to promote child development. Female undergraduates (future parents and future teachers) were trained by the 1930s, as they are today, in domestic sciences and, if in teacher training, to imitate laboratory teachers who were "scientifically trained," and to use the best new information from research (Burman, 1994; Cannella, 1997; Rothman, 1980; Rose, 1989, 1996; Sears, 1975). By the 1940s, science and the measurement of ages and stages of development had become part of general knowledge, repeated in parent magazines, included in parent education classes, taught in college child development classes in home economic departments, and incorporated into teacher training classes as part of the required educational and psychological knowledge base; teachers were told to individualize by "knowing" the child.

The growth of social sciences, the struggle for professional status, and the growth of universities as sites within the U.S. for social policy, joined with ideas of statistical reasoning and social Darwinism to speak to the intertwining of practices embodied in child development. Where the children of the late twentieth century could be constructed in terms of their family background, the church they attended, and from the way their conduct deviated from the hypothetical "rural" child that Hall and Froebelian kindergarten teachers mythologized, or by the children that town doctors saw (a more locally contextualized knowledge base), in the early decades of the twentieth century a universalized, generalizable scientific knowledge governed the "good" parent and teacher. Early childhood education teachers did required child study observations on single children (following Hall's initial ideas) to incorporate ages/stages of development into observations and conclusions of the individual child. Parents met with similar information, the science of child development in doctors' offices, where ages and stages of development from the Gesell Institute (Gesell was a student of G. Stanley Hall) were markers of normality/ abnormality for the doctors as well as their patients and their parents.

A particular discourse of childhood was developed through observations, tests, and measurements done in laboratory schools around the nation drawn from a particular populational group of middle-class white nursery school children attending the schools. These discourses of development—that the normal one or three year old would be able to do "X"—constructed the normal as well as the biologically natural, the abnormal, and the gifted (see Danziger, 1990). That the norms, the natural, and the biological were those of middle-class, white, young boys and girls (typically including gendered norms as well as those reflecting class and racial constructions of ethnic background), as observed by "scientific" methods used by white, middle-class, "scientifically trained" men and women, was, in the 1920s–1940s, rarely discussed, and with some likelihood, rarely recognized. Nonetheless, these norms created a universalized girl or boy, what was normal and what was deviant, who was advanced, which children were retarded, in short, what normal childhood versus adolescence and adulthood were, what normal stages of progress were, what backwardness looked like, and what evolutionary ideals or "norms" for childhood should be.

Adding a sense of naturalness to the divisions about "the being" of childhood that were fabricated was the "scientific" belief that IQ was a fixed and stable characteristic, that teachers were more likely to affect physical or socioemotional development than mental development, and that biology determined many of the important aspects of development, including intelligence. Inherent in these beliefs were assumptions that racial biology heavily influenced heredity and, especially, intellectual capability (see Danziger, 1990; Gould, 1981).

This normalization of dispositions, sensitivities, and awareness produced a particular form of inclusion and exclusion. Children qualified or disqualified for participation through the ideas of "development" that classified them as belonging to populations that moved along a continuum that divided the normal from those outside of the norms. The normalcies focused on inner senses of being—the skills, cognitive, and emotional qualities that were to distinguish and differentiate the space of childhood. When children were "abnormal," deviating from the observations and tests of middle-class nursery school children, the home became deviant and abnormal; the abnormal home created "different" children.

Normalizations were, therefore, not only of the child. Normalization was applied to new constructs of "the parent," and "the community," words that entered into policy and science to administer the subjectivities of different populations. Parents, associations in schools were developed in the early twentieth century to provide opportunities to educate parents about school processes and about what was "normal" (see, for example, Schlossman, 1981). The "good parent" and the good and normal child, as constructed through the burgeoning scientific research on parenting and child development, constructed a group of parents and their children as normal/abnormal. The discourse constructing normality was also gendered and had racial and class divisions when classifying the characteristics of the child. Community groups were also constructed through probabilistic reasoning that divided and differentiated the individuals through sets of norms about the normal/abnormal. Urbanness or ruralness, for example, came to have certain meanings; in the early twentieth century, Hall used images of the "rural" to contrast with the abnormal urban; later in the twentieth century, both rural and urban came to take on constructions in education that placed the urbanness and ruralness of the child as having capabilities and dispositions that were outside of normalcy (see Popkewitz, 1998b). "Community" in education became a term to construct the otherness of individuals' identities.

The complexity of the ways in which scientific knowledge of child development became an aspect of governing parents' and teachers' mentalities and, through them, children, is what is even more fascinating. The growth of new professions and groups of professionals, increasingly bolstered by scientific information as well as the authority of "scientific expertise," framed the complexity of the new ways of governing. The emergence of professional status and expertise within the psychological and educational sciences was matched by the growth in communications (parents' magazines) and new local and national organizations (e.g., the Parent Teacher Associations or the National Association for Nursery Education— forerunner to NAEYC) that could spread conceptions of normality and, by relationship, difference. Through these various technologies, the theories of child development that emerged and that were communicated to teachers and parents inscribed normality. In addition, the new theories from Hall, Freud, Erikson, and others inscribed principles of action through discourses about stages of childhood (early, adolescence) as well as how to think about "childhood." Finally, the new space for children involved distinctions that divided children, this time in which the category of groups were reinscribed as categories that related to the "inner" skills, cognitions, and feelings of the child—the being of childhood. Whether one spoke of the "whole child" or of individual skills and capabilities, the whole child was now investigated in parts (see Bloch, 1987, p. 54).

Child Development Knowledge and Teacher Education

Teacher education was one of the institution sites that changed the "nature" of the family and child through the use of scientific discourses. As teacher education moved from teacher institutions to normal schools and to universities and their laboratory schools, teachers and teacher educators incorporated the latest scientific discourses from the psychological, educational, health, and social welfare sciences in their work and both groups gained status as scientific professionals by doing so (Bloch, 1987). The governance patterns assumed that as a society, as professional groups, and as independent individuals, "we" could learn how to be better parents and teachers with better knowledge. "We" also came to believe that scientists, including those in the health, educational, and psychological sciences, could make teachers and parents, eventually children and childhood, better (Baker, 1998). Thus, these were models for education that were to change the broader society through linking liberal democratic rationalities to *the soul* of the child and the parent.

G. Stanley Hall at Clark University, known as the father of "child study" and child development, was one of the first self-proclaimed and acknowledged child development experts of the period. He used teachers to test children in Boston schools to determine what was normal and nonnormal knowledge, what was normal/nonnormal "development." This knowledge was inserted directly into teacher and parent training courses. By the early 1920s the Laura Spelman Rockefeller Fund, under the direction of Lawrence Frank, financed the child development research stations that appeared in university laboratory schools across the nation (Sears, 1975); these were funded and sponsored to (a) develop more scientific knowledge about the child, (b) establish child development as a professional and scientific field, and (c) teach undergraduate women, future mothers, and teachers scientific knowledge about child development.

The construction of child development intersected with two other discourses that gendered the production of education. Child development related to ideas about the family as a divided system of labor in which mothers would be supported and "helped" as they were principally responsible for reproduction and education of children within homes; other "different" mothers would be helped through other interventions by teachers and other scientifically trained experts. The growth of university educated women, along with a rise in turn-of-the-century feminist discourse, promoted the old idea that "professional, and *scientific*, mothers" was a noble career path for university educated woman (Rothman, 1980), while scientific interventions to save the child were appropriate in other families.

This idea of professionalism had a dual quality: it provided a legitimating discourse for women to participate in a world that had excluded them. But at the same time, the discourse of professionalization inscribed particular rules of social administration that revised the "nature" of womanhood as it did the "nature" of childhood and constructed women who had various degrees of professional and scientific knowledge, in contrast with others who were unprofessional, or less scientific/scientifically knowledgeable. It is easy to move from this point to the assumptions underlying parent education programs, and differentiations between university-educated teachers and mothers and "others."

In addition to constructing differences and hierarchies, the professionalization of the teacher embodied particular systems of "problem solving." Scientific discourses maintained principles that children's *souls* could be improved by the administration of disciplinary knowledge. But to change the *souls* of the child also embodied a reconstructed parent and teacher. Knowledge was administered by teachers and parents such that teachers would use this knowledge with children in schools while parents, especially mothers, would organize the lives of children in the home so that children could learn appropriate self-motivation and responsibility. Mothers who could not educate children properly and "autonomously" in the home were constructed as abnormal; they required different mechanisms for governing, scientifically guided parent education in the home, and interventions through home, school, or welfare agency-provided "parent education." The middle-class mothers needed other interventions—to be trained in scientific mothering—but the mechanisms with this group involved new university disciplines, new media sources, even new communities.

Governing discourses then traversed multiple sites and institutions with similar messages about childhood, the good child, the good parent, mother, father, and family, and what the good scientifically educated teacher should be. The governing strategies used in the early twentieth century settlement house day care centers included teacher visits to parents' homes in the afternoon, kindergartens run by scientific and "professional" teachers (Bloch, 1987), and trained child development and educational researchers and professors who would communicate findings to teachers and parents through physicians, parenting magazines, and new organizations (e.g., the PTA).

The normalities inscribed in the discourses of the mother, the child, and biological/social development had a particular social location and sets of distinctions. As we can see from the above, the principles of classification that ordered the actions of the female teachers were envisioned through the burgeoning scientific knowledge about health, hygiene, social welfare, and child development. That knowledge separated the family into related obligations and responsibilities through which a gender aware citizen was created. Further, as we argued earlier, these ideas linked gender, class, and racialized discourses through the distinctions and differentiations that normalized childhood.

The overlapping of discourses about biology/evolution, science, professions, and political rationalities of liberalism established certain norms of individuality, action, and natural progress as legitimate. These norms were projected as universal and natural. But these universal and natural norms were neither universal nor natural. They emerged from the particular social practices and sensitivities of particular groups within society that had the power to affect their knowledge as that of the society as a whole. But by projecting the knowledge of development and learning of particular groups as universal, the new scientific organization of the child functioned to exclude by placing those outside categories and distinctions of "childhood" as also outside the range of the normal and reasonable.

In summary, our argument here is that the liberal welfare "model" used at the turn of the century in the United States intersected with multiple discourses that governed action. This governing was through the ordering of "reason" by which principles of action and participation were generated. Although the "reason" seemed universal and involved with natural forces of "child development," the knowledge of pedagogy and childhood was in fact, historically constructed and functioned to produce an intersection of gendered, classed, and racialized[1] divisions and distinctions. While there were overt exclusions through formal mechanisms of group segregation and discrimination, there were also more subtle forms of inclusion/ exclusion through the patterns of differentiation and division. Children were compared along a continuum of values that ordered identities through the normalization of sensibilities and dispositions.

These distinctions moved across institutional boundaries of welfare institutions and schools and day care programs.

Comparing the Discourses of the Past and Present

The previous sections of this chapter have focused on the complex patterns of governing through which child development knowledge and teacher education (as well as parent education) came to be related, the primary issue in this chapter. In this section, we examine some of the ways in which the governing practices of the past are changing as new relationships of power, knowledge, and individuals are produced today. Here our understanding of the history is that it exists within an amalgamation of ideas, institutions, and technologies that change over time, even if the words of "childhood" and teaching remain the same (Popkewitz, 1997). Therefore, while an issue of child development knowledge governs the questions and programs of early childhood teacher education today (e.g., in the special issue of *ECRQ* referred to earlier), that issue embodies different systems of governing teachers, parents, children, and child development than found at the turn of the century. Our concern here, then, is to explore briefly the discourses of development that circulate about the child, parent, and teacher as not only an intellectual but also as a historical trajectory that moves among multiple institutions in the production of systems that govern individuality.

Turn-of-the-century discourses about childhood, the family, and schooling, we argued above, were based on a concept of social administration of freedom, and, as expressed elsewhere, cultural redemption (rescuing) of the soul (Popkewitz, 1998a). Pedagogy would rescue the child so that the child could be an adult who is self-disciplined, self-motivated, and would function as a productive participant in the new collective social projects of the day. Similarly, today's pedagogical practices involve the social administration of the child through the inscription of calculated systems of self-inspection and self-consciousness (e.g., "the reflective teacher" and the child with "positive self-esteem," and the parent who practices the "proper" upbringing habits). However, while current discourses maintain the ideas of social administration to rescue the "soul" of the child, today's child, teacher, and parent are based on an argument of "constructivism" in which the "reasonable" person finds his or her own solutions through flexible, independent problem-solving strategies.

As we look at contemporary pedagogical discourses, the language of child development appears within particular educational discourses. The image of the child and childhood is still one of dependency, with children being constructed in hierarchical, developmental relationships with adults. In addition, a picture is still painted that the renewal of interest in children's development is part of the evolutionary development of scientific knowledge that will lead to child, school, and societal improvement. But the discourses of development, in contrast to social science thought at the turn of the century, which assumed a certain fixed set of relations between identities and institutions, embody today an individuality that is presumed to be less stable. *The image is of the citizen (adult and child), worker, and teacher as* "problem solving" *and flexible in responding to multiple and contingently defined contexts.*

A strategy through which this image is constructed is, in part, embodied in discourses of "parent involvement" and "community." Today we speak of the importance of parent education in the home, as in the early twentieth century. Now, that parent is also to be involved in the school "community" to be "good," as well as to be "good" parents at home. While scientific research embodied images of the good parent in earlier years, and to teach parents directly as well as indirectly (for example, through parenting magazines), now governing discourses construct the good parent as one who participates in meetings, as one who volunteers in schools or classes, as the parent who regularly attends teacher-parent conferences, who is flexible in time and space, as well as responsive, supportive, and "involved." The construction of the good parent, again, uses a gendered, classed, and racialized discourse that defines these "involved" parents as normal and others as "outside normalcy"; special "invitations" and programs to participate also signals difference—the construction of a marginalized parent, family, child, or group who needs special interventions to behave normally. It is in this way "inclusion" that is at the same time "exclusion."

To illustrate different historical discourses in another way, a particular type of *child* and *teacher* appears within pedagogy. The imagery is of the teacher (and the child) who is expected to collaborate, reflect, and "construct knowledge" in a decentralized system of education. The "new" teacher (and the child) is an "empowered," problem-solving individual capable of responding flexibly to problems that have no clear set of boundaries or singular answers. The teacher is assumed to possess a pragmatic individuality that is tied to the contingencies of situations in which problems arise. Knowledge seems uncertain, context seems as all that is important. In this sense, the sense of evolutionary linear child development is also insufficient in the current world; children, parents, and teachers need to be ready for new worlds, new problems, and crises without a promise of certainty and linear progress.

The questioning of child development knowledge as a base for early childhood teacher education is also an excellent example of this discourse of uncertainty as the social administration of change. Lubeck's call for reflective, problem solving teachers ready to work with diversity also reflects our collective immersion in this broad discursive construction of reality (Lubeck, 1996). Child development, in its sense from the early twentieth century, then begins to pull apart; in the last part of the twentieth century, children's dispositions rather than development are key—with the constructive, reflecting, inventive, and problem solving child being key to an envisioned future. Now the social administration of the child is located deeply in the soul of the child at the level of problem solving and dispositions toward action.

Reconstitution of Governmentalities and Other Social Fields

The revisioning of the images of development and the child occurring in early childhood education are related to other changes in multiple social fields. If we examine the changes in the conceptions of political participation and the identity of the worker, there is a more local, pragmatic orientation to participation and its image of individual capabilities. While nineteenth-century projects of modernity were concerned with social and the collective social movements and a "Fordist" model of production, contemporary discourses use local and communal metaphors. Today's social, economic, and political landscape, with different ideological agendas, calls for reforms that emphasize the community, community health, community schools, community-based welfare systems, and local control (Rose, 1996).

The Changing Subjectivities of the Political Actor. The focus on "community" and multiple identities is embedded in current discourses about multiculturalism and the canons of university teaching. The discourses construct society as being composed of different and disparate groupings of people that are located in the "community." The rhetoric of inclusion relates to ideas about the knowledge of diverse "community" groups in our understanding of child development and in the recognition of diversity and developmentally appropriate practices (Bredekamp & Copple, 1997; Mallory & New,

1994, the 1996 special issue of *ECRQ*). While one can laud the efforts to include different knowledge, the discourses of inclusion are built upon the principles of populational reasoning that reinstitutes the problematic of social administration and normalization, but in a different layer of governing than found at the turn of the century. Thus, the construction of groups as different is a normalizing/non-normalizing practice that excludes while trying to include (see Popkewitz, 1998b).

The pragmatic, communal, and local outlook for change is embodied in current school reforms including calls for standards and professionalism as ways of building strong U.S. government monitoring and steering systems, new methods of measurement such as portfolio assessment, national teacher tests, local decision making, site-based management, "reflective teachers," and "action research." These provide localities, teachers, and parents with a sense of autonomy and responsibility to identify appropriate strategies to improve teaching, while at the same time embodying discourses of choice and autonomy that are part of a broader global and national governance.

These contemporary educational reforms entail a more pragmatic outlook about state governing patterns and the capabilities of the citizen—the skills, attitudes, and attributes of the individual who participates in the modern state. The reform discourses, for example, are based on the concept of a "teacher" who is personally responsible for "problem solving" in a world that is personally unstable. The professional teacher is "self-governing" and has greater local responsibility in implementing curriculum decisions.

A new sense of displacement and the new calculus of intervention reconstitutes the principles of the participatory citizen (see Rose & Miller, 1992; also Popkewitz, 1996). The centralized/decentralized organization of teacher and child seems not to have any single center, as all is negotiated within fluid boundaries. Yet again, in these reform practices as in earlier twentieth-century ones, the governing of the individual is not through the explicit defining of procedures but through the deployments of "reasoning" through which the teacher and child construct their capabilities and actions. The pragmatic outlook of social reform utilizes and instrumentalizes new experts and expertise: management/financial experts, experts of parenting/family life, of lifestyle. Experts have proliferated in the late twentieth century in intersections between sociopolitical aspirations and private desires for self-advancement (Rose & Miller, 1992).

The Production of Identities in the New Work. The revisioning of work and the worker in the world of business provides another homology to educational constructivism. According to the business pages describing the structuring of the new workplace, a new corporate structure is being formed that is less hierarchical and pyramidal than it was in the past. Furthermore, mass production instituted in the first half of the century has been challenged because mass production no longer provides an efficient scheme in modern technological industries. Business literature no longer speaks of stable "roles." The new business entails an individual who is "enterprising," with certain problem-solving capabilities—where highly variable customer demands, new technologies, multicentered business structures, and horizontal structures organize workers into groups concerned with specified projects that do not have the older layers of management. Self-managing teams and individual participation have been given priority in the reorganization of industrial production. The worker is "empowered" and develops flexible, responsive environments that can respond quickly to customer demands. The desirable worker is conceptualized as one who is not solely competent in skills but one who has the appropriate capabilities and dispositions (see Gee, Hull, & Lankshear, 1996 for further discussion).

This new worker is reminiscent of the constructivist teacher and child who problem-solves in a pragmatic way to find contingent solutions. It is the capability of the child, the work, and the parent that is the site of struggle in the new pedagogies of work, social movements, and schools. The new focus on capability revisits the turn-of-the-century concerns with the social administration of governing the soul. But this governing is different from that period. The focus on capabilities and dispositions of the worker breaks the psychological ties that previously defined individual identity in terms of fixed roles of work and production. The new approaches accent relationships between an individual's autonomy and the capacity to adapt, the agency of change in a changing world, and his or her self-fulfillment. "Instead of defining the individual by the work he is assigned to, (the new psychology) regards productive activity as the site of deployment of the person's personal skills" (Donzelot, 1991, p. 252).

The identities discussed are not universal as the world of business involves different capabilities of workers. The desirable worker described above differs substantially from the worker constructed within the schemes of mass production, workers who still dominate a substantial part of the labor market. Furthermore, not all workers have equal access to the capabilities or competencies associated with, or required of, the new worker citizen. In fact, these are not universal traits, but are specific norms produced within particular social groupings.

Our purpose is pointing to the relationship between the subjectivity to govern the worker, or the citizen, and constructivist pedagogy is to provide homologous changes that enable us to think about the shifts in identity that are embedded in the new discourses of childhood and child development. The emphasis on flexibility, problem solving, and contingent, personal, or interactional communication embody an amalgamation of changes that are occurring to signal, we believe, different patterns of governing that cannot be assumed but need to be explored as different from those of the turn of the century. These different patterns of governing are called into play in an unequal playing field; the rules for participation are different for different groups.

We End Almost Where We Began This Essay

It is easy to laud the conceptual changes in contemporary educational reforms and to accept rhetorical strategies about saving or rescuing the child through paying attention to the varied but unique qualities of development. The rhetorical claims of redemption in contemporary research capture a populist, democratic appeal. The reforms, including adding new knowledge and ideas about different groups to early childhood teacher education programs or to revise conceptions that reference a revised and more inclusive Developmentally Appropriate Practice are posited as strategies to make schooling more democratic, more progressive, and socially responsive. But if we follow the previous analysis, the making/remaking of the teacher, the child, and the parent that are embodied in these pedagogical discourses are, following Rose (1989), ways to "govern the soul" and are effects of power.

These effects of power need to be continually scrutinized and examined historically as to their paradoxes and ironies. Further the effects of pedagogical practices to open up spaces for individuals to act cannot be assured. In fact, educational research needs to examine efforts to develop social inclusion as also maintaining its opposite, the systems of exclusion. What appears to be a widening of opportunities simultaneously functions to divide and normalize. This inclusion/exclusion is historically tied to the social administration of liberalism but given a particular form in contemporary educational reforms.

Using the field of early childhood and its psychologies to develop a historical and comparative perspective, we argued that there are certain continuities between current and past movements toward the governing of the soul. The discourses about the disciplined, self-motivated, independent, and responsible individual have persisted and become part of our current unquestioned assumptions about reforming the home, the (welfare) parent, the school, and the child. The site of power remains the individual's productive activity and capabilities—the child's potential for development. However, our focus on the homologies between pedagogical reforms, the political governance of the citizen, and the economy explored the complex relations in which contemporary governing patterns are being reconstituted as the effects of power. When the words "community," "parents," "parent involvement," "diversity," and "local control," or the words "child" and "development," appear in current reform texts, these words have no meaning outside of current sets of relations.

This brings us to two related points about educational change and *development*. First, the governing patterns that organize the construction of the child and parent circulated among multiple institutions, such as the growth of science, the practices of the modern school and university, the processes of professionalization, as well as the welfare practices related to a participatory democracy. The governing practices also crossed labor practices, such as the emergence of categories of employment and unemployment within the administrative apparatus of the State. Governance was also embodied in the philosophy of liberalism and the liberal democratic welfare philosophy that included a sense that scientific information represented important knowledge, our best approximation to *"truth,"* and that we could modernize, *progress*, or *develop* through the proper social administration of society and individuals. To talk about a centralized (or decentralized) system of governance or an individuality that does not take into account the problematic of *governmentality* is to obscure knowledge of the child, teacher, and parent as an effect of power that circulates through multiple institutions.

Second, our arguments about the pedagogical discourses are intended to historicize the systems of reasoning through which the parent, teacher, the child, and her development are constructed. We suggest that while the governing principles in current teacher education are neither bad nor good, they also cannot be taken unproblematically. At this point, we return to the earlier paradox and irony of modernity that reappears in educational reforms. The social administration of the individual was to produce a particular type of disciplined subject who was free from external policing. The situating of recent educational discourses in contemporary reforms points to the reconstitution of that paradox. Rethinking of childhood and child development in early childhood education is to produce a greater range of possibilities for teachers and children. But ideas are not only logical principles; they produce reasoning that differentiates, distinguishes, and divides.

NOTES

1   See Gordon (1994) for more documentation for the historical references that document the class- and race-based discourses and policies that contextualize the history of the development of U.S. welfare policy. See Polakow (1997) for discussions of current discourses in new U.S. "welfare-to-work" reforms.

CHAPTER TWO

Creating a Head Start Community of Practice

Sally Lubeck and Jackie Post
University of Michigan-Ann Arbor

"Realizing that no metanarrative can offer guarantees, educators may come together in local spaces and struggle to create humane communities, playful communities, at once beautiful and just." (Greene, 1994, p. 459)

Start and other Great Society programs had their origins in an era dominated by the "metanarrative" of human progress (Lyotard, 1984), a belief that science and rational planning would inevitably improve the human condition. As the nation's major early childhood initiative, Head Start has served nearly 17 million children, across the span of seven federal administrations (U.S. General Accounting Office, 1997, p. 3), and, throughout this time, the vast majority of research on the program has been done in accordance with the tenets of positivist social science. Schubert (1986) writes that

Quantitatively expressed data were seen as the prime source of truth and the only avenue to credible reports of accomplishments...and statistical virtuosity became more politically persuasive than did careful argument and interpretation of experience as a basis for funding. (p. 173)

In a political climate dominated by the language of accountability, program advocates and planners have also had to formulate clear-cut procedures to ensure program improvement. For example, in the *Final Report of the Advisory Committee on Head Start Quality and Expansion* (USDHHS, 1993), as a first priority for improving the quality of services, the committee advises expanded emphasis on management training, the development of performance measures, a strengthening of Head Start monitoring, and "prompt action to deal with low performing grantees" (p. vii). [1]

Certain commonalities are thus apparent in the logic that has undergirded Head Start research and program improvement efforts. It has been assumed (1) that programs and people can be objectively studied and assessed; (2) that a treatment will have an identifiable outcome and a policy its intended effect; (3) that the primary focus of attention should be on products or outcomes, with less attention paid to the processes that lead to particular results; (4) that program efficacy is demonstrated because of its effects on individuals (e.g., children will score higher on achievement tests or teachers will show improvement on a performance measure); and (5) that program improvements should apply generally across the population of Head Start centers and children.

It is understandable that policymakers and program planners would be concerned to demonstrate that Head Start is having an impact.² However, one of the drawbacks of measuring and monitoring is that an ethos of accountability can be created that has deleterious social consequences. People may be reticent to speak about concerns or problems, or they may feel demeaned by evaluations that focus only on what is wrong. Moreover, if all improvement initiatives are top-down and across-the-board, attention is diverted from the ways in which people in local settings face different challenges or may have a different sense of what a situation requires.

In this chapter, we endeavor to provide an alternative way to think about research and program improvement within Head Start. In doing so, however, we provide only a single and evolving example of one type of "improvement" research, staff development, and we make no grand or sweeping claims. Our intent is mainly to make a case for looking at new ways in this complex and multifaceted social program. To that end, we provide a contrastive example, one that functions according to a different logic. It is an example that is based in large part on the *subjective* experiences of teachers and researchers, for we believe that research is always a human construction, presenting a particular point of view. It is also an example that is *dynamic* and *in process.* We could not—and cannot—predict what the outcome will be, but the process itself seems to be an important one for all of us who are involved. It is also an example of a *group* working and learning together. And, finally, it is a *specific* example, drawing on the perceived needs and interests of one group of teachers who expressed an interest in interacting more with one another. Head Start is unlike other social programs in the United States in that it was deliberately structured to bypass the states (Zigler & Muenchow, 1992), and it functions to this day as a unique blend of centralized governance and local decision making. To date, however, useful ways of representing change processes in the many and diverse settings that bring Head Start to life have not been developed. This chapter is a small step in that direction.

Specifically, we describe how teachers and administrators in one Head Start program (here called Labardie Head Start) worked in concert with university educators (Post and Lubeck) to create a "community of practice" (Bourdieu, 1972). To provide a context for reconceptualizing change processes and research efforts, we discuss, in the next section, new approaches to knowledge, and call attention to work on communities in general and communities of practice in particular. This is followed by a brief overview of the research study in which this work is based. We then turn to a description of the Labardie Head Start program and a discussion of how the project came into being. The section on "Mutual Mentoring Project," then describes the key features of the program. In the conclusion, we suggest that a priori assumptions about how change is to be effected and represented has constrained our ability to imagine other ways in which practical concerns might be addressed. Drawing instead from "the hermeneutic dimension of science" (Bernstein, 1988, p. xiv), we detail numerous ways in which learning within this community differs from conventional staff development activities. Finally, we address some of the concerns of recent scholars who consider the formidable challenges we face in establishing dialogic teaching communities. We now turn to a discussion of new approaches to knowledge.

The "Refiguration of Social Thought"

Perhaps what most distinguishes Enlightenment thinking from contemporary philosophy of science is the idea that there is one fixed, essential, and irreducible reality. The consensus view of knowledge, based on value neutral science and shared understanding, pivots on modernist assumptions of equivalence, generalizability, and rationally planned and progressive change. When the world is so objectified, human relations likewise become governed by taken-for-granted social practices (Lubeck, 1998).

In the latter decades of the twentieth century, deep rifts have appeared in this consensus reality. Interpretive, phenomenological, hermeneutic, feminist, and postmodern approaches to knowledge instead call attention to the socially constructed nature of reality and to situated—as opposed to totalizing and decontextualized—knowledge.[3] For example, Rorty (1979) argues that there is no common ground from which all human phenomena derive meaning. And Thompson (1990) challenges epistemological criteria that privilege monologic representation. With his principle of nonimposition, Thompson distinguishes between justifying an interpretation and imposing it on others:

> To justify is to provide reasons, grounds, evidence, elucidation...to treat the other as an individual capable of being convinced...to impose is to assert or re-assert, to force others to accept, to silence questioning or dissent...to treat the other as an individual who must be subjected. (p. 321)

> For Thompson, the justification of an interpretation requires "the suspension of asymmetrical relations of power" (p. 321).

Social theorists have also become skeptical of metanarratives (Lyotard, 1984), encompassing paradigms that serve to legitimate both science and the social order. As Marcus and Fischer (1986) explain "the problem of the moment is less one of explaining changes within broad encompassing frameworks of theory...than of exploring innovative ways of describing at a microscopic level the process of change itself" (p. 15). And Greene (1994) writes:

> For all the skepticism with regard to possibilities of general agreements and rational consensus, there remains the need to move from particular standpoints to shared commitments, especially if reflectiveness about knowing is linked to a concern for democracy or some sort of humane normative community. (p. 452)

Head Start is uniquely structured as a large, federal bureaucracy deeply rooted in local communities, but to date research on the program has not adequately represented the diverse and innovative ways in which Head Start matters in specific settings. In their book, *Building Communities from the Inside Out* (1993), Kretzmann and McKnight distinguish between two ways of getting things done: systems and associations. Systems (bureaucracies or institutions) developed out of the Industrial Revolution as a way to put many people under the control of a few. People are paid to do work, and the criteria for performance are explicit. It is a production model that serves important purposes, ensuring, for example, that cars will have a certain uniform quality or that airplanes will take off on time and land safely. Associations, by contrast, are distinguished by the fact that people willingly come together for their own benefit and that of others; members choose to be involved—and they don't get paid. Arguing that associations are the fundamental building blocks of American communities, Kretzmann and McKnight maintain that communities cannot be created or rebuilt by focusing on people's needs or deficiencies. Rather communities are assembled from the strengths and capacities of people who come together willingly to make changes they perceive as important.

While most program improvement initiatives have been based on a "systems" model, we have seen the creation of the Labardie Head Start "community of practice" to offer an alternative way to think about program improvement generally and staff development specifically within Head Start, one that highlights teachers' strengths, builds on their eager and willing participation, and is fueled by the dynamic interchange between and among group members. Although teachers are paid, we have been struck by how their involvement seems otherwise to clearly be, in Kretzmann and McKnight's terms, "associational."

In recent research on communities of learners (e.g., Brown, Collins, & Duiguid, 1989; Salomon, 1993), intelligence is seen not as something that exists "in the head" but rather as something that exists in the group. Brown and colleagues (1993) have illustrated in classroom-based research how knowledge is "distributed," with both teachers and learners contributing ideas that are appropriated and transformed by others. More recently, Matusov (1996) describes how interactions among people who think and do things differently provide the impetus for changes in cognition as well as in the nature of joint activity. Teachers and parents learn new ways of teaching and learning through participation in educational settings where people have the opportunity to share and discuss their differing views and practices (e.g., Rogoff, Matusov, & White, 1996). Our own work in Head Start has focused on the interpretive worlds of local Head Start programs (e.g., Lubeck, deVries, Nicholson, & Post, 1997). The next section provides a brief overview of this work.

The Social Context of Head Start

Head Start was originally administered by the Office of Economic Opportunity and, over time, has undergone numerous changes. Most recently, it has been governed by the Administration for Children, Youth and Families (ACYF) of the Administration for Children and Families in the Department of Health and Human Services (DHHS). Grants are given to approximately 1,400 local community agencies, school districts, and private nonprofit organizations. Grantees may sponsor centers or subcontract with delegate agencies that run them. DHHS has authorized 10 offices to oversee grantee agencies within their geographic regions, i.e., to process grants, monitor programs, and provide technical assistance (Washington & Bailey, 1993).

For the last several years, we have been involved in a study of "the social context of Head Start." The study was aimed at understanding how Head Start works on the ground. However, it was not conceived merely as a bottom-up study of a top-down federal program. Rather we sought explicitly to understand how Head Start takes shape in local settings, and how people in different places work together in context and over time to make sense of what they are doing. Richard Harvey Brown (1978) clearly states our view of Head Start as an organization: "Organizational realities are not external to human consciousness, out there waiting to be recorded. Instead the world as humans know it is constituted intersubjectively. The facts (*facta*) of this world are things made" (p. 369). We thus saw Head Start as an interpretive enterprise, or more precisely, as interpretive enterprises that would, to some extent, be constituted differently in different places.

We undertook case studies of four Head Start centers that were selected to maximize variability. Bushnell is located in an industrial township; Labardie in a rural area, and the Heights and Crossings in a large, metropolitan area. Each of the programs has distinctive constituencies. Bushnell serves approximately equal numbers of African American and European American families; Labardee serves European American families; the Heights serves African American families, and Crossings serves a multicultural, multilingual population that includes many recent immigrant families.[4] After piloting the work in an urban and rural site in 1995, members of the research team worked in each of the four programs initially for periods of four to six months, assisting in classrooms, attending staff and parent meetings and special events, making home visits, and speaking with staff and family members both formally and informally.[5] We also interviewed program administrators across a broader range of programs.

In this work, we have observed how Head Start is constituted locally by people who interpret the Head Start Performance Standards and other policy mandates in the light of community needs and resources, local/cultural understandings, and established institutional practices. Changes in federal policy have a pronounced impact on what is done in local settings, and yet virtually every facet of the program is interpreted and reinterpreted in the light of personal experience and shared/cultural ways of knowing and doing. For example, programs often seem to amplify one particular approach to family involvement (e.g., parent education, family support, two-generational programs that provide employment assistance, etc.), to meet the perceived needs of families in local communities (deVries & Lubeck, 1998). As we have worked with staff in different sites, we have thus come to appreciate how change initiatives take root when they are built on what Rogoff (1990) has called "local norms and goals." In the next section, we describe the creation of a Head Start teaching community.

The Labardie Head Start Teaching/Learning Community

Labardee is a large, rural county located in a midwestern state. The county intermediate school district (ISD) serves as the local Head Start grantee agency. It sponsors 11 classrooms serving approximately 300 children. The classrooms are located in churches and elementary schools, in a community center, and in an ISD building where space is shared with other programs. Because classrooms are dispersed throughout the district, staff members reported feeling isolated, typically seeing other teachers and assistants only at staff meetings or inservice workshops.

From our early encounters with this agency, however, we were impressed by the warm and caring relationships that existed among the women. Some staff members had lived in the community all their lives, and there was a sense of shared values and easy familiarity. Not insignificantly, the director, Jane, encouraged open discussion at staff meetings, and staff were not reluctant to express views that differed from those stated by administrators. We have heard Jane referred to with affection and with humor, both as "Mom" and "the budget police." The educational coordinator, Doris, also was a woman whom the teachers liked and respected.

After we had worked in Labardie for more than five months in conjunction with the Head Start Context Study, we began discussions with Jane and Doris about how we might continue to collaborate on projects of mutual interest and concern. Doris noted that a number of teachers had mentioned in their final evaluations that they would like more time to talk about what they were doing. We suggested that teachers might benefit from visiting one another's classrooms, and Jane enthusiastically agreed, stating that she had wanted to do exactly that but that she had not yet been able to figure out the logistics. We offered to facilitate this process by having one of us (Jackie Post) visit classrooms on a regular basis, either to collaborate with teachers in their classrooms and to talk afterwards or to substitute for them so that they could visit other teachers. We talked about some of the recent work that was being done in K-12 schools to establish teacher communities and networks and also about Reggio Emilia, the exemplary early education program in Italy that involves teachers and parents in active and ongoing collaborations in support of children's learning. Ultimately, the project we came to envision involved two forms of collaboration: a collaboration between university and Head Start educators and between and among the teachers themselves. For logistical reasons, only 8 of the 11 teachers participated in the project during the first year. Nonetheless, project teachers visited the other teachers, and they presented at a staff meeting in the spring so that everyone would know what was happening.

Thus it was that the "mutual mentoring" project was born.[6] We recognized early on that the support and encouragement of key administrators was crucial, but equally important was the way in which people who played different roles within this Head Start program spontaneously endeavored to diminish status differentials. The previous year, administrators had worked with teachers to change evaluation procedures, and it was then decided that both Doris, the educational coordinator, and the teacher would fill out the same forms and meet to talk about their respective evaluations.

Our own role was clarified at the outset. We agreed that, when the teacher was visiting another classroom, Jackie would be assisting the teaching assistant, who would assume the role of lead teacher—and receive lead teacher pay. Doris, the educational coordinator, made this very clear at the first meeting: "Just to clarify: If the teacher is gone, the assistant takes over, and Jackie is the sub. Some people are not sure of that and, because she is from U of M or whatever, expect her to take over and run the classroom." Over the year, teachers repeatedly commented that the assistants rose to the challenge of taking on more responsibility.

At the end of the first year, plans were made to continue the program and expand it to include all of the teachers. The liaisons were to replace Jackie in most of the classrooms (her role in the project is described in more detail below) so that the project could be self-sustaining. In an unrelated administrative reorganization, each of the[7] coordinators has been acting as the "liaison" for particular centers. By having the liaisons in the classrooms once a month (Jackie had been in twice), teachers could continue to work with a visiting collaborator or to visit other teachers' classrooms. Jackie would then function as a liaison for three teachers, and both of us would continue to meet with the group throughout the year.

As plans were shared, the group began to discuss whether the assistants would be intimidated working with the liaisons/coordinators in the classrooms. It was a crucial concern, for coordinators would be expected to be "in charge" and to evaluate the assistants' performance. One teacher, Rachel, mentioned that her assistant appreciated getting lead teacher pay when she visited, and she thought that being trusted in this way had greatly increased her self-confidence. Four of the liaisons attended this fourth and final meeting, and Lisa, the health coordinator, addressed the concern in the following way: "That's fine with me. I don't need to come in and do it. They're the ones that know your kids better than anybody." One teacher commented that the liaisons were so supportive, that it wouldn't bother the assistants to have them helping out in the classrooms. And Doris commented: "They'll probably be happy, if we have the same problems that they have." Everyone laughed, but what had happened was important. There seemed to be an intuitive understanding that this was not "business as usual." Through the transformative power of language, people had committed themselves to working with one another in new ways.

The Mutual Mentoring Project

The mutual mentoring project—establishing a Head Start community of practice—came to have three key features: (1) classroom visits twice a month by Post; (2) teachers' visits to one another's classrooms; and (3) group meetings five times during the school year.

Classroom visits. Jackie visited four teachers each week (eight over the course of a two-week period), so that each teacher in the project was visited twice a month. During this time, Jackie assisted the teacher in various ways. For example, some teachers would ask her to do specific projects with children (e.g., making Playdough) or to work in certain areas with them (e.g., computer, small manipulatives). Sometimes teachers would use this time to make observations of individual children, while Jackie and the assistant "covered" the classroom. Jackie and the teacher talked at the end of each session. Early conversations dealt with practical issues such as how best to arrange the space in the classroom. Sometimes teachers found it helpful just to honestly talk about things that were bothering them. One, for example, vented about being "bombarded with paperwork and meetings." Teachers often talked about what didn't seem to be working, what they had observed others doing, and what they wanted to change.

Teacher visits. Teachers could also decide to use this time to visit other teachers. Over the course of the year, teachers made 30 visits to one another's classrooms. A "web" of these visits is represented in Figure 1.

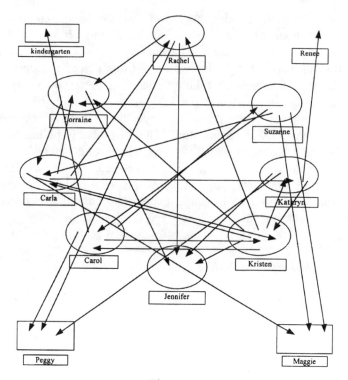

Figure 1.
"Web" of Labardee Teacher Visits

In this figure, the names of the eight teachers participating in the project are arranged in a circle; the three who did not participate, but who were visited by project teachers, appear in the corners.

Teachers often used the visiting option as a way to address problems they identified in their own practice. For example, Kristen felt that her classroom was "too unstructured," so she opted to visit teachers she perceived to be more structured. Carla felt that she didn't handle transitions well and thus was eager to see how other teachers managed them. It was striking to us that problems that a teacher might well try to hide from an evaluator or a supervisor were repeatedly identified by teachers themselves as aspects of their teaching in need of improvement. As Carla voiced at a group meeting in February:

> I found that sometimes teachers are reluctant to talk about things that aren't so great, because they never want anybody to think that their classroom isn't going really, really well. Sometimes it's nice to talk honestly.

In a supportive environment, this kind of learning did not seem threatening, and it encouraged teachers not only to zero in on things they wanted to improve but also to gain insight into their practice by engaging with others who faced similar challenges but had resolved them in different ways.

Sometimes teachers wanted to learn from others who were in a situation similar to their own. For example, Carol wanted to visit Peggy, because they were the only two teachers with combination programs. Kathryn wanted to visit Laura, the "sub" for Renee, who was out on maternity leave. Kathryn herself would soon be on maternity leave, and she hoped to get ideas that she could share with her own assistant who would be taking over.

Teachers also gathered specific ideas for such things as Playdough recipes, transition activities, songs and fingerplays, and clean-up strategies, including the more traditional job charts. They observed how each other managed both space and time by looking at room arrangements and talking about how to reorganize the day when things weren't going as they wanted. Sometimes visiting caused teachers to make changes that were related to things they had seen. Kathryn reported that she liked the way Peggy helped children understand where to sit on the carpet by using taped signs on the floor, and Carla borrowed ideas from Kathryn to help children learn about the rain forest. At other times, what they saw sparked a new idea, such as when Carla thought of making a "stop" and "go" sign to more safely move her children from inside to outside for bus line-up. She had observed that Kristen used signs to help children know when clean-up time was approaching, but she put signs to a new and unexpected use.

Group meetings. The third feature of the project was five group meetings, scheduled in August, October, December, February, and May. The initial organizational meeting was held briefly after a long day of meetings. It was used primarily to handle logistics and to answer questions. At this meeting, we found that two of the teachers were new to the system, and they appeared quiet and even a bit wary. There was also some anxiety about the idea of teacher presentations that Jackie had proposed. Some felt that a half-hour per teacher seemed too long a time for them to talk. Someone asked whether they needed props for these presentations. All agreed to meet with Post after each session, however, and the mood was generally positive as they asked "When can you start?" Rachel, a veteran teacher, nonetheless confided after the meeting that she wasn't sure what was expected of her if she participated in this.

At the second scheduled meeting in October, one teacher shared a copy of her journal. Kristen had decided to keep track of her thoughts by taping on a small recorder as she drove a considerable distance back and forth to work. Teachers seemed to like this idea, and fully half of the group said that they too wanted to keep dialogue journals. They would write down their thoughts from day to day and give Jackie the pages when she visited. She, in turn, would write comments and return them. Although this seemed like a terrific way to encourage "reflective" practice (Schön, 1983), teachers got busy, and journaling came to be perceived as just another chore. For better or for worse, journal writing petered out after a few weeks.

During lunch that day, teachers were encouraged to talk in pairs about what was going on in their classrooms. This seemed to work for some pairs better than for others. Two teachers were able to discuss what they had gained from visiting others. For example, Lorraine mentioned that, when Suzanne was visiting her classroom, children were roaming about and not cleaning up as they should. Suzanne then showed her something that she does in her classroom, and it worked like a charm.

> Lorraine: At clean up, half of the kids won't clean up. No matter what you do or say to them. "I'm not cleaning up." "I didn't make that mess." " I already picked that up." [Suzanne] has children put on these Martian ears and run around going 'bee-bee-bee-bee' looking for mess. And here they all go [laughter] picking things up off the floor! It worked beautifully. The next day they said, "Where are your Martian ears?" and they did it! It was a new idea. It was helpful.
> Jackie: Do you think that worked because she was able to be there when it was happening? Would it have been different, would there have been an opportunity for you to have asked people, "I'm having problems at clean-up time. What do I do?"
>
> Suzanne: I think being involved with them [makes a difference].
>
> Doris: Being on the spot.
> Lorraine: She could show it to me, too. She doesn't just tell me what she does; she modeled it. She did it.
> Doris: She models like the good teacher she is!
> Lorraine: That was really helpful to me. It was quick, and it was at the moment. Like she [Suzanne] said, she might not have thought of it if she wasn't in my classroom, and we weren't at clean-up time.
> Suzanne: I might have started thinking about other ways, too.
> Kristen: Well, that's not what you do in your class, but it just happened to work for her at the moment.
> Suzanne: No, I do it, but it's not every day. And it works different.
> Doris: Martian ears. Can everybody do that? [laughter]
> Jackie: Everybody is now writing down Martian ears.

This led to a brief discussion about other methods teachers use to get children to clean up after free play. For example, Rachel commented:

> A lot of times when there is stuff left, I'll say, "OK, can everyone find five items to pick up?" They'll go, "I found six!"

Teachers then requested directions to each others' sites and copies of each others' classroom schedules. Then, per schedule, Kristen shared some information she had gotten from a class on encouraging children's prosocial development. As the meeting drew to a close, teachers also shared transition ideas with each other.

At the third meeting in December, Jackie used photographs and video footage to show how teachers addressed similar topics but in different ways. For example, the photographs showed how children across the classrooms worked at problem solving; used tools; explored with Playdough, gak and other materials, learned how to use scissors; played games; counted; used computers; built with blocks; and engaged in literacy activities and dramatic play. Significantly, however, it was evident that teachers were very often doing *different* activities in each of these areas. This was even more apparent in the video, which provided a window on Head Start classrooms throughout the district. The video showed children and teachers engaged in literacy experiences, games, dramatic play, etc. For several of the teachers this was the first time they had ever seen what other classrooms in the district looked like. An animated discussion ensued, sparked by exclamations of surprise regarding obvious differences in the physical characteristics of the spaces: "Your room seems much bigger than mine!" "Where did you find those large, cardboard blocks?" or "That's a great rug!"

The teachers expressed avid interest in the activities that other teachers had done and eagerly asked one another for more details. Those being asked seemed delighted that others were interested. The conversation was relaxed, an animated give and take. Later, teachers who had not yet visited now signed up to do so.[8] Rachel seemed especially pleased that two teachers were eager to visit her classroom. The teachers also decided that they wanted to do a conference presentation at an upcoming local Head Start conference and chose (by drawing lots) which teacher would represent them at the conference. Kathryn was selected, and others, including Rachel, offered to help plan the session.

During the fourth teacher meeting, teachers considered how the program was working so far. Doris, the educational coordinator, had suggested that videotaping might be a way to include those who wanted to participate in the conference, at least in spirit, and the tape subsequently became a part of the conference presentation. Through this medium, teachers were able to share their thoughts about what it meant to them to be able to visit one another. A few examples from the tape indicate how they found that the visits helped them to feel better about themselves as well as to strengthen the bonds between them.

> Lorraine: "It reinforces that what we're doing is a really good thing, that we are important, that we make a difference, and that we're creative."
> Kristen: "Children are the same everywhere. The problems I'm having don't occur only in my classroom. I've received feelings of self confidence and feelings of validation that the things I do are right for kids."
> Carla: "It's nice to be able to talk to the other teachers when I go there and talk to them about situations that have happened in my classroom and see that those situations have happened in their classrooms, too."

Teachers also reported that there were things that they were doing that were just not working—children did not have enough structure or they didn't handle transitions well—and they were able to use the visits to watch—and talk about—how other teachers handled these situations. For example, Kristen reported that her children didn't seem to focus when it came to clean-up time. She was thrilled when she saw that Lorraine (who had struggled with this issue early on) simply went to small groups of children five minutes before and told them that it would soon be time to clean up. When she returned to her own classroom, she transformed this activity by making a sign and walking around the room with it shortly before clean-up time. She excitedly told the group that doing this "really worked!" Lorraine then chimed in to say that, in her experience, the same thing doesn't work all year. She had recently tried a new technique, and she proceeded to share it with the group.

This was also the meeting in which Lorraine presented on map and transportation units that she had done with her children. She began by explaining that she decided to work on maps after doing a home visit and discovering that a four-year old in her classroom had taped maps all over his bedroom. His mother had been downloading maps for him off the Internet. Both were so enthusiastic that Lorraine decided that this would be a good thing to expand on in the classroom. She began by showing us a large sheet of brown paper on which she had drawn the bus route for the members of her class. Because this is a rural area, young Head Start children can be on the bus for up to an hour in each direction. She had given a Polaroid camera to her teaching assistant, who regularly rode the bus with the children, and she had taken photographs of every child in front of his or her house, trailer, or apartment. The next day, the children relived their bus ride on paper, following every bend in the road, and they helped to affix the pictures all along the route.

From this activity grew others: the boy who loved maps brought in maps for each child, and he demonstrated for the class how a map should be folded. At the art table, children planned trips on metro maps, using yellow markers. They made roads in the block area and brought in matchbox cars. They ran their cars through paint to make "tracks." And on and on, through discussions of kinds of roads and how they are represented on maps to a still more elaborate unit on transportation. We all loved it, and Lorraine basked in the glow of appreciation from colleagues and friends who well recognized a "job well done." Jackie then created a curriculum web of all the various activities that had been included. Perhaps the greatest praise of all came from the other teachers who enthusiastically wrote down many of the ideas. Finally, two teachers volunteered to share, at the last meeting of the year, special activities that they also loved to do with children.

The final group meeting in May was thus reserved for teacher presentations. Gone was the anxiety and reluctance that had been palpable early in the year. Rachel presented her "worm farm" and explained how others could make one. She also had handouts for everyone. Suzanne then showed the group a copy of a book she has children make. Throughout the year, they add pictures, and the children then present their books to members of their family at the end-of-year picnic. These two activities served as catalysts for a host of ideas that were generated through group discussion.

In the section that follows, we provide an extended segment of the conversation that revolved around Rachel's "worm farm" as a basis for analyzing how teachers both build on and transform one another's ideas.

Rachel: The reason I wanted to share this with all of you is because I think it's so cool, and it's just a kind of a freebie thing. I have passouts for you. This is a pop bottle, and you just [cut off the top and] put layers of rock, dirt, sand, rocks on the bottom to absorb the water and just layer it up. And then put your earthworms in. We only have three or four in here now because they were really small. We had, the kids and I went out and dug them and it was really hard. The ground is so hard right now.

Doris: You have to pick one of those rainy days when they're all laying on the sidewalk.

Rachel: Exactly. You can see the trails that they make. Some of them you can see, and then they've gone in further. If you turn it around the kids can actually see the worms and how they crawl through it. And then you're supposed to put a layer of leaves on the top of it, and this helps keep the wetness in. If the earthworms are exposed to the sun, they die. (Reads from her notes) "Earth worms are a clean-up crew. They chew up leaves and help clean up. They also help the soil." And I've got some handouts for those, too. I got this little earthworm up in ____ (holds up a rubber/plastic earthworm). Isn't that cute?

Jackie: Where did you get it?

Rachel: Up in _____.

Jackie: At the conference?

Rachel: Mm-hm. There are like five different kinds of worms, and earthworms are segmented worms. And if you cut 'em in half, they still live. They have no ears or eyes, and earthworms are sensitive to direct sunlight. They usually become paralyzed and die. It's estimated that there are several billion worms per acre, in the top five inches of the soil. As they burrow through the soil, earthworms eat seeds, plants, and insect eggs, leaving behind castings that fertilize the soil. Each earthworm has both male and female. We didn't talk about that with the kids. (laughter) Birds, small mammals, and even some humans—we did talk about that—eat worms. Usually the chocolate-covered worms.

Doris: There is a place where you could order them. You should have ordered 'em to see if they would eat them.

Rachel: The kids?

Jackie: Is that on the official nutrition list?

Doris (smiling): I don't know.

Rachel: Doris was gonna come in and try 'em with the kids, right?

Doris: No!

Rachel: Anyway, I have three handouts for everybody. One of them shows you how to make it. I guess that's all I have. (Passes around handouts)

Carla: I can see what's gonna be floatin' around my house this summer.

Rachel: I just thought that was so neat with a pop bottle.

Kristen: That's great because you don't have a lot of materials you have to go out and purchase. We had the worms dying in the sunlight, true life experience at our school. (laughter) They keep digging, you know in the pea stones; they find them really easily in there. And they didn't tell me they wanted to see what happened when they put 'em on the tire. The tire is black and nice and warm, and when I came out they were real hard and crunchy. I was really bummed out. They were bummed. Real life lesson: What not to do with the worms.

Rachel: You don't want to put too much water in there, because it can drown the worms and then they might want to crawl out.

Carol: How often do you water?

Rachel: Actually, I only really keep it for two or three weeks, and I put enough water in there, so I don't have to re-water it.

Jackie: You don't have to put anything in there for them to eat?

Rachel: No, just the soil. Supposedly they chew up the leaves if they want to go up to the top. So you just kind of crunch up some leaves as kind of a mulch on the top.

Jackie: What kinds of things did the kids say?

Rachel: They loved to watch it. They loved to dig them, too.

Carol: Do you keep it in the classroom?

Rachel: Yes, I keep it in the classroom, but making sure that the sunlight doesn't shine on it. I've never had them crawl out.

Carla: I dug up about five inches of sod and dirt and put it in two cans on the shelf. The kids opened up the sod and found a lot of worms in it. There were all kinds of things in the sod.

Jackie: Did you take it from out back there?

Carla: Well, we were landscaping our yard. And we didn't know what else to do with it. I thought the kids would like that. This way the worms lasted the whole week, because they had the ground. (Describes other things the kids found in the sod and dirt, like spiders.)

Rachel: I think the fun time is when you're letting the kids dig 'em themselves, too.

Suzanne: Like our yard with all the gypsy moth larvae. They are everywhere this year.

Rachel: Where are they at?

Carla: Everywhere on the trees.

Rachel: Out in back of the school? There won't be any leaves on those trees.

Carla: We talked about how they were made. They're not from nature but, I believe, they were kind of an experiment. Two different kinds of moths. I said to think a little bit about that.

(People ask what she told the kids to do.)

Carla: Well, I said it's up to you, but the worms will eat the trees to the point where the trees will die. I said, it's up to you. I know that is terrible. I don't like children to squish anything but—it was kind of interesting—they understood. They really did. A lot of kids said, "No that's a spider. We don't want to squish the spider. It's not a gypsy moth."

Jackie: Early environmentalists!

Carla: Yeah.

Rachel: So, what did you do with the gypsy moths?

Carla: They collected them. I think we picked every single moth off every tree. We had sticks like three feet long going up there and getting them off. And they'd fall on your head. We got 'em everywhere. We put 'em in buckets. We'd find like nests of them. One day we walked out, and there was a tree just covered with a whole mound of them. The kids put 'em in a bucket. They have to leave them outside. I told them they could leave them on top of our heaters where they stick out outside. It gets really hot. I told them, just leave them right there. And they're like [indicates dead] by the end of the day. (laughter) Extermination.

Rachel: That would be something you could do: the difference between caterpillars and worms.

As this discussion drew to a close, Suzanne showed the group a book she makes with her children and described related activities. She had affixed little handprints and a poem to the front, and one teacher asked if she would put a copy of the poem in everyone's box. Then a lengthy discussion ensued about handprints, a recipe for painting them, and a recipe for clay that one teacher considered to be better than plaster of Paris. A teacher eagerly asked for the recipe. They also talked about other books like the one Suzanne presented and another kind of book a teacher had made with her children (*Brown Bear, Brown Bear*). The discussion then turned to other projects they have enjoyed with children: growing grass like hair above an egg or cup face and growing marigolds and sunflowers. A discussion of laminated seeds led to Suzanne's description of a laminated sheet she uses that helps children to define things they find swimming in pond water. As teachers inquired about how she does this, Rachel observed: "We'll have to copy that sheet of paper." Before the end of the session, the conversation moved again: to a discussion of how tadpoles turn into frogs.

In Figure 2, we illustrate how the worm farm interchange involves a series of interpretive moves organically related to the central topic.

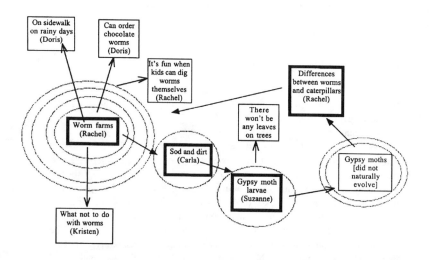

Figure 2.
An example of distributed knowledge in a teaching/learning community: Expansion, inversion, transformation, and contrast.

Knowledge is pieced together through talk, as teachers' questions and additions expand on, invert, and extend the information that Rachel presents.

During this time, several things happen. First, presenting to other teachers provides Rachel the opportunity to deepen her understanding of the worm farm activity (the first bolded rectangle). She has made an example and done additional research, which she provides as handouts. Secondly, the initial topic (making a worm farm) is expanded due to the questions asked by members of the group (here represented by concentric dotted lines). The questions elicit information that is perceived as useful by one or another member (e.g., where she bought a plastic worm, how often to water the bottle, whether the worms require additional food), and this information, in turn, becomes available to everyone.

Thirdly, and importantly illustrating how knowledge and experience are "distributed" across the community, members also build on and transform the information that Rachel provides. Information that expands on Rachel's topic appears in Figure 2 as nonbolded rectangles. Doris points out where worms can easily be found ("on pavement after a rain"), and she also comments that it is possible to order "chocolate worms." Kristen provides a fairly lengthy anecdote about "what not to do with worms." Carla then describes how she got children involved in a similar kind of activity by bringing five inches of sod and dirt into the classroom: "The kids opened up the sod and found worms in it." Suzanne then introduces the topic of "gypsy moth larvae." These new topics are represented as additional bolded rectangles. Both Rachel and Carla further develop the moth larvae topic, especially Carla because of the questions she is asked. This then leads to Rachel's suggestion that links the earlier discussion with the later one: studying the difference between worms and caterpillars.

Our purpose in reproducing the "worm farm" transcript and providing a detailed discussion of it is to underscore a key point. The knowledge construction and dissemination described here works through dynamic interaction, sparked by the free play of ideas. We cannot predict quite what will happen, so it does not work in ways we have been accustomed to appreciate. The logic is neither linear nor causal. What we have instead is something profoundly generative, as knowledge distributed throughout this community is integrated and related through discourse. Members of the group come to see new possibilities as ideas are introduced and discussed. For example, Rachel may not have considered exploring with children the difference between worms and caterpillars, but, after the discussion of moth larvae, she makes this suggestion. The logic is also "situated," grounded in the context in which these teachers work, i.e., a rural area where gypsy moth larvae become a topic of discussion—and a part of the curriculum—because of their presence on the trees in the area.

The teachers, in effect, have breathed into being what Richard Bernstein (1988) has seen as a common factor in new approaches to knowledge: "Each...opens the way to a more historically situated, nonalgorithmic, flexible understanding of human rationality, one which highlights the tacit dimension of human judgment and imagination and is sensitive to the unsuspected contingencies and genuine novelties encountered in particular situations" (p. xi).

Summary and Conclusions

The latter decades of the twentieth century have witnessed a widespread challenge to the use of the natural science paradigm as the only credible means of describing social phenomena. In an effort to reclaim "the hermeneutic dimension of science" (Bernstein, 1988, p. xiv), scholarship has increasingly focused on the transactional character of human experience. Changing theoretical conceptions, as well as the growing acceptance in qualitative research methods in education and other fields, call attention to the dialogic nature of human meaning making.

Head Start came into existence at a time when hopes were high that science and rational planning would inevitably improve the human condition. Johnson's War on Poverty promised to eliminate poverty from the nation and ensure that every child would have a "head start" in life. While the commitment to end poverty waned in the volatile political climate of the ensuing decades, it became incumbent upon policymakers and planners to demonstrate that Head Start was, indeed, having an impact. Consequently, large-scale evaluations (e.g., McKey et al., 1985), as well as small-scale experimental studies were undertaken to confirm that the program was having demonstrable effects. These designs required that certain identifiable aspects of the program be linked to positive outcomes, particularly in terms of child effects. Recent improvement initiatives likewise seem to promise that needs or weaknesses can be identified and remedied through a direct course of action.

Although these efforts have served important purposes, they have also unduly constrained the kinds of initiatives that are possible to those that make general statements about or set general standards for the program and employ a linear, causal logic, with effects nearly always expected to be demonstrated in terms of changes in individual performance. In this chapter, we have described a deliberately contrastive example, but only one of many that might be possible. The example of the Head Start community of practice illustrates the dynamic learning that occurred when a group of teachers had the opportunity to interact with one another over time. Teachers were seen to play an active role in determining their own needs and to use the practical knowledge and experience of other teachers in their community as a resource.

The project described here thus differs in a number of ways from conventional "training" models of staff development. In inservice workshops, knowledge is often seen to reside "in the heads" of individuals and to be transferred from those who know more to those who know less. Observing how teachers construct knowledge together, however, leads to a rather different account of knowledge transmission. People appear to think in conjunction with others—to question, play off, add, invert, transform, and link information. Knowledge can be seen to be distributed throughout the community but also to be jointly and spontaneously constructed through interaction. Indeed, the very process of sharing seems to generate new understandings.

Secondly, teachers are not passive recipients of information. They actively participate in classroom discussions with Jackie and with other teachers; they try out new behaviors and new activities, and are eager participants in group meetings. Thirdly, teachers frequently establish different objectives, and they learn from others precisely because they do things differently, thereby offering provocative alternatives to one's common or current practices. A fourth difference is that, rather than resenting outside evaluations, teachers became often brutal critics of their own teaching, with discussions frequently focused on what wasn't going well or what needed to change. At the same time, however, they were validated by the realization that others faced the same dilemmas that they themselves faced and heartened by the interest and praise of other teachers for those aspects of their practice that were considered exemplary. A fifth, and significant, difference was that the focus of attention was on *practice* rather than on individual performance.

Yet another distinctive feature was the numerous and spontaneous efforts made to suspend asymmetrical relationships, an important factor in distinguishing "associations" from "systems" (Kretzmann and McKnight, 1993). As mentioned earlier, the program had the strong support of the grantee director and education coordinator (now called a child development specialist). The coordinator/liaisons agreed to serve as "teacher assistants"; assistants became lead teachers—and received lead teacher pay—when teachers visited other teachers, and, in the second year of the project, teachers campaigned for the right of the assistants to visit as well. It was decided that they could change places with other assistants, so that they too could benefit from visiting.

Finally, the "logic" of the project was nonalgorithmic, its effects not predictable in a priori hypothesis testing or goal setting and its results unlikely to generalize to other sites in quite the same way. As suggested by the title of this chapter, the community was created by the people involved; as suggested in the "web" and map, what happened was nonlinear, emergent, dynamic, generative. Rather than feeling disheartened by this lack of predictability and control (especially by us), however, we find this to be what makes the work so exciting. There is a strong sense of ownership among the teachers precisely because they can shape the work they engage in to their own interests and needs. During the second year of this project, we have been helping another community of teachers (this time in an urban setting) to launch itself, and, based on what people in that setting wanted to make of it, it has been, from the outset, organized differently than the Labardie community, with those involved currently pursuing a rather different line of inquiry. We feel that this is as it should be.

In undertaking this work, we sought to explore an alternative way of conceptualizing program improvement, and, specifically, staff development, within Head Start. But we also hoped to carve out a space that might, at least in part, be suggestive of Maxine Greene's (1994) lyrical vision of a humane and playful community "at once beautiful and just" (p. 459), a dialogic teaching community "in which reciprocal judgment, practical discourse, and rational persuasion flourish" (Bernstein, 1988, p. 231). We would be remiss, however, if we did not also acknowledge the challenges and pitfalls in attempting to establish such spaces in our modern world. Increasingly, social theorists point to the fact that "rhetoric" can change without changing the underlying attitudes or ways of doing things that surface descriptions imply. Gee, Hull, and Lankshear (1997), for example, provide a startling account of how the corporate vice president at Motorola recently made a case for changing the social relations in the workplace in the interest of better meeting corporate goals. And Popkewitz (1998a) argues the important, if sobering, point that the too simple dichotomies of centralized and decentralized authority, coercion and consent, structure and agency (or "system" and "association") may pivot on alternative forms of "redemptive" discourse that nonetheless serve the same ends. Commenting on the changing role of the teacher, Popkewitz describes the constructivist teacher as remade as an empowered, problem-solving individual capable of responding flexibly to problems that have no clear set of boundaries or singular answers. The teacher is assumed to possess a pragmatic individuality that is tied to the contingencies of situations in which problems arise....This populism textually inscribes research (and the researcher) as promoting the interest of the democratic school and teacher. (Popkewitz, 1998b, p. 13)

The key point is that both teachers and researchers may become complicit in maintaining the status quo, albeit in a new guise.

People find—and make—meaning, however, in local places, and specific classrooms are where education happens. It is where problems arise and are dealt with, and it is also where we, as teachers, ponder who we are and what we are about. We have spoken with many teachers who feel isolated and frustrated in American classrooms, so the Labardie teachers' visits and animated discussions with one another seemed to us to offer a more humane and interesting way to "be" a teacher. Indeed, the excitement at meetings grew to be palpable as ideas spread like wildfire throughout the group. We have also noted, however, that, in the months in which the Labardie teaching community has been forming, the teachers have focused primarily on procedural and curricular issues. Although they vary in the degree of structure and/or control they think is necessary, control issues were a common concern, and methods of control that children would perceive as "fun" (such as Martian ears) were seen as especially useful.

Absent from the discussions thus far has been a deeper questioning of the knowledge that is shared. For example, no one, including ourselves, challenged Carla's decision to encourage the children in her classroom to "exterminate" the gypsy moth larvae. Perhaps more difficult still is discussion of the sort of citizenship training we engage in. How might we be helping to socialize children to do what is expected of them in "fun" ways, just as we ourselves are being reinscribed? These are the hard discussions that begin to tap the concerns that Popkewitz (1998b) highlights. As we learn to learn from one another, these are topics that will inevitably arise, and perhaps, as group members privileged to study social processes, we can contribute to such discussions by putting our own work up to public scrutiny. Jerome Bruner (1986) calls this "going meta," talking, in effect, about the talk.

Ultimately, the creation of a Head Start community of practice is an act of faith, a collective assertion that, to the extent that we can make meaning with others and act as agents in our social milieu, to the extent that we can participate in alternative relational forms, to the extent that we can learn to speak our minds and openly discuss the contradictions and challenges we face, playful and humane communities are possible. It was Wittgenstein who suggested that "the way to solve the problem you see in life is to live in a way that will make what is problematic disappear" and Kearney (1988), more recently, who declared that "to nourish the conviction that things can be changed...is to begin to imagine the world as if it could be otherwise" (p. 371).

NOTES

1   Not all efforts, however, are of this nature. For example, Q-Net, a Head Start training and technical assistance network operating in five midwestern states, has now begun to send program enhancement specialists to local centers, in an effort to help staff with their specific professional development and program planning needs (Fernie, personal communication).

2   Although this approach has dominated research on Head Start, efficacy studies have recently come under criticism for a number of reasons. According to a recent report by the U.S. General Accounting Office (1997), most studies "suffer to some extent from methodological and design weaknesses, such as noncomparability of comparison groups, which call into question the usefulness of their individual finding" (p. 2). In addition, studies were faulted for focusing narrowly on cognitive outcomes for children, and thus ignoring other possible effects of the program.

3   Recent studies have begun to draw on these alternative theoretical perspectives. See, for example, Ames, L., & Ellsworth, J. (1997). *Women reformed, women empowered: Poor mothers and the endangered promise of Head Start*. Philadelphia: Temple University Press; Ceglowski, D. (1994). *Inside a Head Start center*. New York: Teachers College Press; and Ellsworth, J., & Ames, L. (Eds.) (1998). *Critical perspectives on Project Head Start. Re-visioning the hope and challenge*. Albany, NY: SUNY.

4   With the exception of Jackie, the names of all people and places are pseudonyms.

5   The research team has included Mary deVries, Patricia Jessup, Julie Nicholson, Post and Lubeck.

6   We wish to thank Dee Russell for the use of this term.

7   We had decided at the outset that none of us was interested in a "one shot" intervention. In particular, we wanted to support change initiatives that administrators wanted to institutionalize. The plan to have liaisons fill this role was ultimately not implemented in the second year, because so many changes were happening at the same time. Instead, the director hired an experienced substitute to visit half the classrooms each month, while Jackie visited the other half. Over a two-month period, Jackie thus visited all 11

teachers in the project. We expect that the liaisons will serve in this capacity in the future.

8   Only one teacher chose not to participate in the visits, although she was extremely enthusiastic about having Jackie visit her classroom, and she attended all teacher meetings. She was a first-year teacher who simply felt that she should not leave her children, even for a few hours.

The research reported on in this chapter was made possible in part by a grant from the Spencer Foundation. The data presented, the statements made, and the views expressed are solely the responsibility of the authors.

CHAPTER THREE

Critical Pedagogy and the Politics of Play

Shirley A. Kessler
National-Louis University
Mary Hauser
Carroll College

Introduction

The inspiration for this research project was partially derived from the work of Maxine Greene whose ideas we found particularly relevant in one article, "In Search of a Critical Pedagogy" (Greene, 1986). Critical pedagogy has come to mean an approach to curriculum which promotes a decidedly political agenda aimed at critiquing social, political, and economic structures and forms of discourse which have led to the oppression of women and minorities. Greene suggests that we look to our unique past as Americans for possibilities as to what a critical pedagogy for our time might become, rather than look to European philosophical discourses relative to critical theory or to the significant work of Paulo Freire on critical literacy in Brazil. As Greene put it: "Perhaps we might begin by releasing our imaginations and summoning up the traditions of freedom in which most of us were reared. We might try to make audible again the recurrent calls for justice and equality" (p. 440).

Greene reminds us that we have been raised within a tradition of freedom, justice, and equality, and thus, we do know something about these significant topics, even though these ideals are currently far from being realized. Greene suggests we revisit the social visions of educators such as Robert Owen, Colonel Francis Parker, Jane Addams, Susan B. Anthony, W.E.B. DuBois, and others in light of what we now know and believe in our quest for a pedagogy which is emancipatory.

So we asked ourselves, how might concepts such as critical theory and/or critical pedagogy be applied to early childhood education? Upon further reflection, we were able to distinguish at least two important ways in which early childhood education has always differed from elementary and secondary education. One signifying feature of early childhood education is its ties to mothering and child welfare

(Beatty, 1995). A second distinguishing feature of programs for young children is the significance of children's play in the curriculum (Bredekamp & Copple, 1997). We wondered if a theoretical and empirical examination of children's play would illuminate possibilities for a critical pedagogy. Could such a study of children's play help us to envision a uniquely American form of critical pedagogy? Is a critical form of pedagogy "appropriate" in early childhood education, and if so, can play be a vehicle for enhancing a critically oriented approach to curriculum planning? The purpose of this paper is to explore these questions in order to better understand the possibilities for a critical pedagogy inherent in children's play.

In the first part of this paper, we present a brief overview of the politics of the curriculum as well as historical and contemporary views of play in early childhood theory and practice. This section is followed by descriptions of the play of children in several different kinds of early childhood classrooms. In presenting the "stories" of children at play, we focus on issues of power and authority, such as children's ability to challenge received social identities, exercise agency, and resist directives from the teacher and others; as well as issues related to the creation of a classroom culture and community (Willis, 1996). We conclude with a discussion of the possibilities of play for a critical early childhood curriculum and the role of the teacher in fostering play as a vehicle for creating a critical pedagogy.

Politics and the Curriculum

Early childhood educators are not accustomed to viewing the curriculum politically, perhaps because conceptual and empirical research has traditionally focused on children's development (Bloch, 1992) and the application of developmental theory to the early childhood curriculum (Bredekamp & Copple, 1997). However, if we think of politics as that which "pertains to the way in which people join together to accomplish what they could not accomplish alone" (Schubert, 1986, p. 94), the political nature of curriculum deliberation is more obvious. That is, in order to educate its young members, individuals in a particular social group must collaborate to ensure that their children are educated in such a way so as to perpetuate the interests of that particular collective. Obviously, such coming together to focus on the task at hand leads to different perspectives as to how the project should be accomplished. Furthermore, it is natural for individuals to form alliances with those who share their views in an attempt to influence others to see this project as they do, and to exert pressure on others in order to accomplish their agenda which is rationalized as the best way to proceed.

The history of curriculum in the United States has been viewed, in large part, as an account of the political struggles among individuals and groups for dominance in determining the purposes of education, the way in which schools should be funded, how schools should be organized, and the content of the curriculum (Kliebard 1986). Debates surrounding these issues have been heated, contentious, and sometimes visceral. During the past two decades the politics of education, and in particular, the politics of the curriculum have been more widely acknowledged as primary factors in the construction of the formal, enacted, and experienced curriculum. It is now widely held among curriculum theorists that, as Schubert (1986) proclaims, "Curriculum is not a purely rational enterprise in its conception or practical application. It is laden with political and ideological values" (p. 127).

We and many other early childhood educators are openly political in our desire to foster a form of pedagogy aimed at the liberation of human potential and the fostering of democratic communities in the classroom. Schubert (1986) sees this liberation-oriented image of curriculum as "emancipatory," as freeing (the) self from the taken-for-granted ideology of social conventions, beliefs, and modes of operation to enable growth and development. A more critically oriented perspective focuses on the relationship between the school curriculum and specific social and economic forces in our culture which have interacted to produce unequal educational opportunities and results for women, minorities, members of the working classes, and other less advantaged groups. Some critical pedagogies seek to empower students to question the social rules, conventions, and structures that create oppressive educational environments, assuming that conscious awareness of dominating discourses and practices would lead to actions aimed at altering the powerful social and economic structures which are oppressive. While this goal may not be one that early childhood educators would embrace, we believe a heightened awareness of such approaches can lead us to question the social purposes of early childhood education, the content of a curriculum based on "developmentally appropriate practice," and offer unseen possibilities for envisioning a curriculum or educational approach that would realize emancipatory and democratic goals and principles.

A Word About Play

Historically play has been a distinguishing feature in programs for young children. Beginning with Pestalozzi, early childhood practitioners centered their curricula around children and their play. Play continues to be a necessary ingredient in high-quality early childhood programs. The significance of play was recently affirmed by the National Association for the Education of Young Children (NAEYC), the largest professional organization of early childhood educators in the United States, as one of 12 principles of child development that should guide decisions about developmentally appropriate practice. According to the NAEYC (Bredekamp & Copple, 1997), "play is an important vehicle for children's social, emotional, and cognitive development as well as a reflection of their development" (p. 14). Play is thought to support children's language and literacy skills, as well as physical, emotional, and social development. Through play children learn to "express and represent their ideas, thoughts, and feelings, learn to deal with emotions, to interact with others, to resolve conflicts, and to gain a sense of competence. Through play, children also can develop their imaginations and creativity" (p. 14). However, there is no consensus as to the exact nature of play or the ways in which it serves or might serve educational purposes. Classical theories regard play as a means of socializing the young and preparing them for a future in a society where work is separate from play, and where social roles are determined by social structures. Contemporary theories analyze and promote play in terms of psycho-social and intellectual development (Frost & Klein, 1979). Common elements in most definitions are that play includes the active involvement of individuals in activities which are intrinsically motivated, freely chosen, pleasurable, and in some cases, nonliteral (Hughes, 1995).

Despite the historical tradition of play in early childhood education, and the value assigned to it by early childhood educators, there is disagreement as to the purpose and practice of play in school settings. As a case in point, Nancy King (1992) maintains that play, at least according to the way in which children define it (activities that are freely chosen and freely directed), is not allowable in most academic settings because it is not compatible with the goals of education. We believe conflicting perspectives reveal ideological orientations as to the nature of the child, the role of the teacher, and the purpose of schooling, orientations which have not been adequately theorized. This atheoretical perspective perpetuates an unexamined view of play-like activities and their place in the early childhood curriculum. Furthermore, we believe the current practice of examining play in terms of child development represents an individualistic perspective, which fosters a transmission orientation toward curriculum and a conservative political ideology.

For the purpose of this study we looked at social play, that which Garvey considers "engagement in nonliteral behaviors within the context of a social interaction where the successive nonliteral behavior of one child is contingent upon the nonliteral behaviors of a partner" (Hughes, 1995, p. 186). Social play is thought to foster initiative, originality, creativity, and representation (Reynolds & Jones, 1977). Play as a form of representation enables children to construct their knowledge of the world by representing what they know. "It pictures and re-enacts the experiences children have had and can imagine having in the real world" (Reynolds & Jones, 1977, p. 3). Some researchers think that such play, often referred to as "dramatic play" is the developmental precursor to storytelling for four-year olds; dramatic play is story-in-action (Reynolds & Jones, 1977, p. 70). Thus, play has been the subject of much research in early childhood education, but primarily from a developmental perspective. We, however, wanted to view play culturally and sociologically, as a means for transmitting culture and social roles and social norms, as well as a means for creating cultural beliefs and practices and social structures which would promote a critical pedagogy.

Methods of Observation

As feminist educators, we understand learning as a process of making connections that are based on each person's unique set of experiences in the world. In understanding education as a political phenomenon we see part of our responsibility as teacher educators to interrogate the power relationships in education between genders, between teachers and students, and between members of different racial or ethnic groups. Finally in keeping with our personal histories as teachers/researchers/teacher educators, we feel that all of our work must be grounded in the possibility of social transformation that benefits children.

We recognize the political implications of the fact that while neither of us are African American, we are studying play in classrooms of African-American students. While white women researchers in schools of black children may be perceived by some to be inappropriate, researchers who are explicit about their lenses and who clearly articulate their purpose can produce research to be respected in or out of their cultural context (Hauser, 1998). We both have had extensive previous experience working in educational settings in which the majority, if not all, of the children were African-American.

Our observations were in classrooms of three, four, and five year olds. We were observers watching and taking notes—in one case behind a one-way mirror. We attempted to record the events of those play periods defined by teachers as "free play." We observed individually and then shared the field notes of our observations with one another. Using a critical frame of analysis we sought to understand how play events reflected issues of power and authority. As we read over our field notes, we looked for instances of children's play which might be considered conducive to a critical pedagogy for the young child: Instances or situations where children appeared to (a) challenge received social identities; (b) construct and play out interactions related to power and authority in the classroom; (c) exercise agency; (d) resist directives from the teacher and other children; and (e) contribute to the creation of a classroom culture, which includes the development of communal social relations (Willis, 1996). Because our study is currently at the exploratory stage, the examples we present should be interpreted as providing us with the opportunity to raise questions about play in the early childhood classrooms that will refine further research in this area.

Many classroom observations were done in two classrooms at an urban Head Start center. Here children were free to choose an area of the room in which to play each morning after breakfast for a period that lasted approximately one-and-a-half hours. The choices were those one would find in a typical preschool: playing in the art, housekeeping, block, and manipulative center; playing with water; or working on the computer. Children moved freely from center to center; no limits as to the number of children allowed in any area were in force. Sometimes this freedom resulted in children wandering somewhat aimlessly for five or ten minutes or more until they settled on an activity. The two teachers present situated themselves at the art center or the manipulative center, and in nearly all cases facilitated children's involvement in "table activities": drawing pictures, playing shape lotto, making Playdough, etc. Only on rare occasions did a teacher participate in the housekeeping or block building areas. This role was consciously chosen because the teachers did not want to impose their agenda on children's play. Teachers also washed tables and prepared the snack, while they and the children cleaned up. Otherwise the 4 teachers in these 2 classrooms were relatively uninvolved during this lengthy play period.

Challenges to Received Social Identities

Observations related to children's ability to challenge "received social identities" were examined through the lens of gender. Both boys and girls were observed engaging in gender neutral activities, such as painting, working at the computer, playing with Playdough, playing Candyland, and playing with water. However, it seemed to us that boys in the Head Start classrooms played more often with what have been traditionally thought of as "boy" toys and girls with "girl" toys. For example, boys played with blocks to build a fire engine, a super-highway, and a fort; and engaged in various dramas related to the use of guns. When girls were engaged in block play, they often brought into that area items typically supportive of "housekeeping play." For example, one morning we observed Priscilla and Frannie in the block area where they had laid out a large blanket onto which they had set dolls, dishes, and cups from the housekeeping corner. Ken and Frank, with whom they frequently played "run and chase," were at the game table, wearing sunglasses and capes, and playing shape lotto. Priscilla said, "I want to be Ken's queen." She approached the game table, but there wasn't room for her to sit down, so she returned to the block area. "We better stop playing now," she said to Frannie. Frannie answered, "OK" and began to wander off. "Hey," said Priscilla. "Come on and clean up!" Frannie complied. We wondered if Priscilla and Frannie really wanted to play with the blocks or were moving into that area to open up opportunities for communication with Ken and Frank. Whatever the case, their play in the block area seemed to be typical of gendered play in which many girls participate at the preschool level.

It was not clear, however, if boys engaged in more "rough and tumble" play than girls, which typically is the case, but we noticed boys chasing girls more frequently than girls chasing boys. On the other hand, it *was* clear that the girls in both classrooms more often than the boys engaged in what is generally referred to as "housekeeping" play. One example which typifies this type of play occurred one morning when Brenda was in the housekeeping corner playing with a doll. She spent a great deal of time and focused attention caring for this "infant" She put the doll on the changing table and dressed it, and when she had problems fitting the pants on, she found a different outfit in a tote bag and put it on. Soon, another girl approached Brenda and displayed her long "fingernails" (large rubber pegs on the ends of her fingers). Brenda also put pegs on her fingers, dialed a number on the play telephone, and tapped her fingernails on the kitchen counter. We observed Brenda for 45 minutes as she obtained play food from the refrigerator (colored bears), put a pot on the stove, stirred the play food with a fork, and then poured the food from the pot into two cups. She washed the dishes, dusted the counters with a hand broom, stacked the dishes, and dusted the table and highchair. We wondered to what extent gendered play such as this offered opportunities for girls to try new roles and create new identities for themselves.

Power and Authority

As previously mentioned, the teachers at the Head Start center exercised minimal power and authority during the morning play period. In one classroom the teacher was concerned with the noise level and several times admonished Ken and Frank to quiet down. In the other classroom, there appeared to be no attempt to address the noise level. Teachers did intervene, however, when there appeared to be the possibility of danger to any child, and then they spoke clearly and directly to the individual(s) involved. On the other hand, the teachers clearly had the power to determine the beginning and end of the play period, although children frequently resisted conforming to the directive to "clean up and come to the rug."

While the teacher's influence and control appeared weak in this center, due to a conscious decision on their part not to impose their views on children's self-expression and knowledge construction, the children themselves were quite active in their attempts to influence each other and take control of particular situations. Children's behavior related to this category needs to be studied more closely. Their vying for influence seems to form a kind of subtext to the obvious endeavors of children. Earlier, we described an incident where Priscilla ordered Frannie to help clean up the toys in the block area. A few weeks later a similar incident was observed. It occurred at the end of a play period when Teacher Nancy announced, "One more minute until cleanup." Ken said to a boy playing with clay at the same table, "It's time to clean up." He then took off the smock he was wearing, then the cape. He rolled it up and started to walk away. Teacher Nancy said, "You guys have to put all the tools (plastic cookie cutters) in the box." She left and Ken tossed a "tool" in the plastic dish pan in the center of the table. Then to the other boy playing there he said, "I've got to pee." He started to unzip his pants, and left the table. Something fell to the floor. "Pick that up!" he shouted to the other boy. Such attempts to exert influence over others was not uncommon in this classroom. We wondered if the children themselves were filling a kind of void left by the teachers' purposeful relinquishing of authority, and if so, were the children creating the kind of classroom community we believed important to a critical pedagogy? Or was there a natural kind of "power asymmetry" (Gallas, 1997) in these classrooms which, if left unchecked, could lead to a brutal "survival-of-the-fittest" pattern of social interaction.

Exercise of Agency

Free play situations offer children numerous opportunities to choose activities and create learning opportunities for themselves. During one of many observations made in an urban four-year-old kindergarten, we were able to connect the use of classroom materials to children's agency in their construction of knowledge. On this occasion, treasures that the children had collected on a field trip to a farm became the "science center" on a classroom table. One girl, entering the classroom, caressed the large pumpkin that was one of the items on the table. A boy who saw her do this came over to lift the pumpkin and pronounced it "heavy." A second girl arrived at the center and pretended to eat an ear of Indian corn that was in a basket on the table. "Don't eat that!" she was admonished by a classmate standing with her. Undaunted, she called across the room, "Teacher, look!" again pretending to eat the corn. Soon three children came over to the center and took everything out of the basket, named the objects, and stated, "Horses eat corn." While the teacher's objective was probably to give the children the opportunity to construct knowledge about farm objects, the children's use of the materials in a dramatic episode (pretending to eat the corn) and the reference to the relationship between corn and horses, indicated that they were capable of and interested in going beyond that basic knowledge construction activity. Had farm animals been included in the "science center," the children might have engaged in more complex scenarios of dramatic play and created other understandings, which as most teachers realize, are beyond our capacity to predict.

Resistance

Resistance occurred at several levels. Some children resisted cleaning up and listening to stories; occasionally they succeeded. One interesting form of resistance occurred frequently when children rejected the attempts of teachers to engage them in activities in which they had little interest. In some instances, children would comply with the teacher's suggestions briefly, before returning to their original play. In the four-year-old kindergarten a number of examples of the teachers' intrusion into children's play were documented. The teacher, Ms. Mort, was active in incorporating literacy materials and activities into the play environment as a way for children to further make connections using their emerging literacy skills, as well as to help them see the utility of the reading process. One day she brought spaceship books to the block area where children were building a spaceship and pointed out how the pictures could give them ideas about how to build their spaceship. She left the open books in the area for the children to consult, but the books were ignored. Later, when she encouraged another group of children to make signs identifying their block constructions, their minimal participation in the process indicated that they did not see this activity as part of their play. During the 40-minute play period, the children developed a number of themes, and none of them were related to the literacy practices the teacher modeled. The children clearly had an agenda for their play that did not include the teacher's literacy focus.

Developing a Classroom
Culture and Communal Social Relations

This category is perhaps the area where there is a greater role for a critical pedagogy. Despite the relatively short amount of time spent in the Head Start classrooms, we noticed the development of a classroom culture in terms of the creation of symbols and relationships by the children. In one classroom, plastic chips that were a part of a peg board game were always used as "coins." Girls and boys would put these chips in their pockets or purses, even when they were not engaged in a play scenario together. Playing cards also always represented money to boys and girls whether playing with others or alone.

One intriguing use of props occurred in both classrooms at the Head Start center. Children frequently arranged small wooden chairs side by side, sometimes in rows, near the housekeeping corner, and used these chairs to represent what appeared to be church pews. Girls, not boys, would dress up, get their "babies," and sit down on one of the chairs. One day, Samantha and Betty were in the housekeeping corner playing with the stroller and dolls. Two chairs were next to each other in front of the play stove. Samantha got a third chair and struggled to place it next to the other two. She also worked hard to make room for the stroller. When the stage was set, Samantha, Betty, and Bess positioned themselves on these chairs, and just sat, with doll blankets covering their legs.

This play period also fostered the building of friendships, which would seem to be a necessity for the building of communal relations. Where children were expected to be quiet during story time, large group time, or nap time, during free play, children were expected to interact socially. On every occasion when we observed children in one room, Frank and Kenny played together. They played with guns, painted in the art corner, and worked with clay, at the computer, and/or in the block area together. The same was true for Priscilla and Frannie. They always were together.

In the five-year-old kindergarten classroom, we also reported an episode that illustrates children developing communal relations. The teacher had assembled a shelf of math manipulatives to be one of the free play centers that children could choose. Tierra was playing with a set of number/pet cards from this collection that could be arranged in sequence by matching the curves on the edges of the cards. When another girl came by, Tierra asked, "Latoya, do you want to play with me?" Latoya sat down on the floor and was admonished, "Wait till I do my two before you do your three!" They quickly adopted an alternating pattern of participation to complete the sequence. In so doing, this activity became the vehicle for two children to independently establish communal relations of reciprocity.

One very intriguing play scenario was enacted by Ken and Frank one morning. After again wandering around the room with their capes and sunglasses or carrying their "guns," Ken began what teachers refer to as "gun play." (While children were prohibited from bringing guns into this classroom, they succeeded in creating "guns" by putting large Lego blocks together to make a large L-shaped object.) After Ken pretended to shoot Priscilla and Frannie, Lenny, also toting a Lego-gun, joined in and shot at several children who were playing at the water table. They ignored him. Then Ken, Frank, and Lenny squatted behind a square bench-like structure and continued shooting. Next, they brought stuffed animals to their "fort," and Frank used one of the Legos from his gun to create a needle and gave one of the animals a shot. Ken used three Legos from his gun as an oxygen mask and pressed it against one of the stuffed animals, saying, "Breathe! Breathe! Breathe!" Then Frank said, "I got three more over here" (victims), while Ken continued, "Breathe! Breathe! Breathe!" Lenny returned to shoot Ken and Frank, who ignored him and continued to help the victims. Frank announced, "I got one more to go." The two boys worked together saving victims, until Teacher Nancy said, "You boys are too loud!" The boys then left the shooting scene and went to the art area. Teacher Nancy put the stuffed animals in a basket on the table. We were surprised that the aggressive nature of typical gun play evolved into an act of caring and wondered what feelings and ideas these children were expressing? What were Ken and Frank showing us about ways of being together in the world that Teacher Nancy did not see? What might we learn about children's capacity for prosocial behavior that could enlighten us all?

Preliminary Conclusions

These observations have provided a way to represent the meaning of children's play. We observed sociodramatic play that led us to tentatively conclude that it offers few opportunities for children to challenge received social identities. Our observations of the play of girls and boys indicate that children imitate the adults in their lives, and play out themes that often reflect home relationships and adult experiences. If typical play episodes such as those we observed are not redirected by actively involved teachers, who benefits? Stereotypical gender roles can be reinforced in preschools where housekeeping and block corner play if teachers maintain a noninterventionist policy.

On the other hand, free play *does* offer children numerous opportunities to exercise agency, construct and play out interactions related to power and authority in the classroom, as well as resist directives from the teacher and other children. Flaunting school expectations, norms, and rules, can represent a meaningful and even desirable form of resistance because it can be seen as a way of working through, rather than just reproducing dominant discourses and undesirable social dynamics and ways of building a sense of community in the classroom (Grace & Tobin, 1998, p. 179). As we let go of some of our fears about children's behaviors and inclinations, the classroom may become not only a more democratic place, but a more pleasurable one as well (p. 185). Such behaviors have value and importance in the school lives of children. They are sites of energy and powerful affect and can be a rejuvenating and creative force for all involved (p. 186).

Another important role of play in creating a critical pedagogy is its contribution to the creation of a classroom culture which can include the development of communal social relations (Willis, 1996). This layer of the enacted curriculum often goes unnoticed. Children's use of materials as symbols representing meanings held by them, not by adults, is one component of the classroom culture. Children building friendships and enacting creative ways of relating to each other are another component unique to each classroom culture. Children's common ways of resisting authority comprise another. We believe children's play must be studied sociologically in order to discern the ways in which they create a community which is often outside of the teacher's awareness and imagination.

As we re-presented the meaning of children's play, we were keenly aware of the relationship between teacher authority and child autonomy relative to critical pedagogy. At first it seemed like too much authority was detrimental to children's making the most of their free play. Often, teachers unknowingly erase the energy and creativity that children put into their play by refocusing their attention on the teachers' agenda or by ruling out certain aspects of their behavior, as Teacher Kathy did when she admonished Ken and Frank for being too noisy. Upon further reflection, however, it may be the case that encouraging children's autonomy isn't as "liberating" as we think it is. In some situations teacher authority could actually promote a more just and fair community by, for example, mediating the power asymmetry Gallas (1997) describes, which some children bring to their play from life experiences outside of school.

In conclusion, we believe that critical pedagogy does have a role in the early childhood curriculum, especially during children's free play period. However, if the teacher does not demonstrate alternative possibilities for children's sociodramatic play, gender roles could be strengthened, the less assertive children disempowered, and masculine identity affirmed. On the other hand, free play does provide un-imagined possibilities for children to exercise agency, resist expectations of the teacher and others, and create patterns of social interaction which could become a significant aspect of a unique classroom culture. If children are guided by an observant teacher, with the desire to enhance children's development, as well as create *with* children a democratic classroom, there are unforeseen possibilities inherently in children's play for a uniquely American form of critical pedagogy.

Part Two

Young Children's Daily Realities

CHAPTER FOUR

Certifying the Damage: Mainstream Educational
Psychology and the Oppression of Children

Joe L. Kincheloe
The Pennsylvania State University

As class inequality, especially along the lines of race and gender,
continues to expand at the end of the millennium, children, of course,
are the innocent victims caught in the trap of neo-liberal economic
policies and a pervading social unconsciousness. What is particularly
amazing to me is that the very discussion of this growing class
inequality and its impact on children seems somehow out of place in
mainstream educational discourse. Educational leaders frequently tell
me that calls to abolish welfare, exact more severe punishment for
crime, end social programs, and destroy affirmative action have little
to do with questions of childhood education. "Let's keep politics out
of education," they politely ask. My point is exactly the opposite of
such educators—I want to make explicit what everyone wishes would
just go away. My purpose in general and in this chapter in particular is
to expose the tacit political dynamics that exacerbate the class
divisions between children. I am specifically interested in the ways
that mainstream educational psychology often "certifies the damage"
that class politics exacts on contemporary American children.

The term, psychologization, has been used in recent years to
denote the tendency within social, cultural, and educational work to
depoliticize. Embedded in the concept is a moral and ethical
relativism that subverts the attempt to connect teaching with
questions of social justice. In mainstream educational psychology the
insights gained over the past few decades concerning the political and
cultural inscriptions of research seem to have fallen on deaf ears.
Without such an understanding, educational psychologists support a
childhood education that views the poor and nonwhite through the
lenses of dominant Western European, male, upper-middle-class
culture. As cultural actors, such psychologists look only for cognitive
traits with which they are familiar. As a result, only a culturally
specific set of indicators of aptitude is sought. In this way the abilities
of children from cultures different than the psychologists are

dismissed. In a political context, those children who deviate from the socioeconomic and cultural norms of psychology fail to gain the power of psychological and educational validation so needed in an effort to achieve socioeconomic mobility and status in contemporary Western societies.

The discipline of educational psychology and the educational leaders it informs have had difficulty understanding that the poor and the nonwhite children are not stupid. Often children from working class and lower socioeconomic class homes do not ascribe the same importance to the mental functions required by intelligence/achievement tests and academic work that middle- and upper-middle-class students do. In this context the difference between cultural disposition and intellectual ability is lost upon the field of educational psychology. Working class and poor children often see academic work as unreal, as a series of short-term tasks rather than something with a long-term relationship to their lives. Real work, they believe, is something you get paid for after its completion. Without such compensation or long-term justification, these students many times display little interest in school. This lack of motivation is often interpreted by teachers, of course, as inability or lack of intelligence. Poor performance on standardized achievement tests scientifically confirms the "inferiority of the poor students" (Oakes, 1988; Nightingale, 1993; DeYoung, 1993; Woods, 1983).

It happens every day. Educators and psychologists mistake lower socioeconomic class manners, attitudes, and speech for a lack of academic and cognitive ability. Researchers report that many teachers place children in low-ability groups because of their class background (DeYoung, 1993). Their rationale involves the lower socioeconomic class child's social discomfort around students from higher status backgrounds—lower socioeconomic class children should be with their own kind. The standard practices of American schooling are too often based on a constricted view of the human capacity and an uninformed understanding of human diversity. Intelligence in this view is defined operationally as one's performance on an IQ test, not as the unique and creative accomplishments one is capable of in a variety of venues and contexts. The social context and power relations of the culture-at-large and the school culture in particular are central in the attempt to understand the class and cultural dynamics of a child's performance (Block, 1995).

Research on the education of low status groups in other countries provides important insight into the psychological assessment and educational performance of marginalized students in American schools. In Sweden, Finnish people are viewed as inferior—the failure rate for Finnish children in Swedish schools is very high. When Finnish children emigrate to Australia, however, they do well—as well as Swedish immigrants. Koreans do poorly in Japanese schools, where they are viewed as culturally inferior; in American schools, on the other hand, Korean immigrants are very successful (Zweigenhaft & Domhoff, 1991). The examples are numerous, but the results generally follow the same pattern: racial, ethnic, and class groups who are viewed negatively or as inferiors in a nation's dominant culture tend to perform poorly in that nation's schools. Educators, parents, and citizens must attend to the lessons of these findings in their attempt to undermine the class-bias that consumes their children. Such research helps dispose of the arguments that school failure results from the cultural inferiority of the poor or the marginalized. It teaches us that power relations between groups (class, race, ethnic, gender, etc.) must be considered when various children's performance is studied. Without the benefits derived from such understandings brilliant and creative young people from marginalized backgrounds will continue to be relegated to the vast army of the inferior and untalented. Such an injustice is intolerable in America. There is something wrong with a discipline that cannot discern the impact of the social from the psychological, that claims neutrality and objectivity but fails to appreciate its own sociocultural embeddedness, and that consistently rewards the privileged for their privilege and punishes the marginalized for their marginalization.

Developing a Political Awareness of
Child Psychology: Validating Cognitive Difference

How do we induce mainstream educational psychologists and teachers to understand the importance of these political aspects of children's cognition? Within the psychometric web of Cartesian-Newtonian scientific assumptions our arguments are dismissed as empirically unsupported. What exactly does such an accusation mean? A democratic psychology is unsupported in the sense that little experimentation has taken place to determine if sociopolitical awareness actually improves cognition. The way this would be empirically measured would involve controlled observation of a classroom operated by a socially aware teacher and the administration of a research instrument designed to determine if students acquired more "certified data" in this context. Such verification of the "validity" of such teaching would have little to do with our concerns and purposes. In the first place, we do not believe that the measure of our success involves how much unproblematized data children might memorize. Secondly, the types of understandings we seek to generate do not lend themselves to a quantitative measurement that asks "how much." Because of such paradigmatic mismatches, it is hard for critical educators to carry on conversations about the effort to democratize education with many mainstream educational psychologists.

The breakdown of this conversation dramatically affects the character of schooling for children. Mainstream educational psychology's paradigmatic bias operates to "protect" educational administrators and teachers from critical perspectives that would initiate curricular and instructional changes. Firmly in control of governmental and private sources of funding research, grant applications that challenge paradigmatic assumptions about the production of psychological knowledge are summarily rejected. Thus, the public conversation about learning, intelligence, and schooling is edited in a way that often excludes voices that simply raise sociopolitical concerns in the cognitive and educational domain. The way we conceptualize intelligence holds profound implications for the nature of our schools and the characteristics of education.

In a schooling shaped by a sociopolitically contextualized educational psychology, self-reflection would become a priority with teachers and students, as critical educators attend to the impact of school on the shaping of the self. In such a context, learning would be considered an act of meaning-making that subverts the technicist view that thinking involves the mastering of a set of techniques. Education could no longer separate techniques from purpose, reducing teaching and learning to de-skilled acts of rule-following and concern with methodological format. Schools guided by a democratized educational psychology would no longer privilege white male experience as the standard by which all other experiences are measured. Such realizations would point out a guiding concern with social justice and the ways unequal power relations at school destroy the promise of democratic life. Democratic teachers would no longer passively accept the pronouncements of standardized tests and curriculum makers without examining the social contexts in which their children live and the ways those contexts help shape their performance. Lessons would be reconceptualized in light of a critical notion of student understanding. Post-formal educators would ask if their classroom experiences promote the highest level of understanding that is possible.

At its worst, mainstream educational psychology reduces its practitioners to the role of test administrators who help devise academic plans that fit students' abilities. The individualistic assumptions of this work move practitioners to accept unquestioningly the existence of a just society where children, according to their scientifically measured abilities, find an agreeable place and worthwhile function. Thus, the role of the educational psychologist is to adjust the child, regardless of his or her unmeasured (or unmeasurable by existing instruments) abilities, to the society, no matter how unjust the system may be. Thus, the discipline and the practice it supports play an important role in maintaining the power inequities of the status quo. Those children from marginalized racial or class positions are socialized for passivity and acceptance of their scientifically pronounced "lack of ability." Thus, a form of politically passive thinking is cultivated that views good students and teachers as obedient to mainstream educational, psychology-based ways of seeing. In such a context neither students nor teachers are encouraged to construct new cognitive abilities when faced with ambiguity (Martin-Baro, 1994). Piaget labeled this process accommodation, the reshaping of cognitive structures to accommodate unique aspects of what is being perceived in new contexts. In other words, through our knowledge of a variety of comparable contexts we begin to understand their similarities and differences, we learn from our comparison of the different contexts.

Politically conscious teachers push Piaget one more socio-cognitive step to produce a critical emancipatory notion of accommodation. Understanding the socially constructed nature of our comprehension of reality, critical accommodation involves the attempt to disembed ourselves from the pictures of the world that have been painted by power. For example, a teacher's construction of intelligence would typically be molded by a powerful scientific discourse that equated intelligence with scores on intelligence tests. The teacher would critically accommodate the concept as she or he began to examine children who had been labeled by the scientific discourse as unintelligent but upon a second look exhibited characteristics that in an unconventional way seemed sophisticated. The teacher would then critically accommodate (or integrate) this recognition of exception into a definition of intelligence that challenged the dominant discourse. Thus empowered to move beyond the confines of the socially constructed ways of seeking intelligence, the teacher could discover unique forms of intelligence among his or her students—students who under the domination of the scientific discourse of intelligence testing would have been overlooked and relegated to the junk heap of the school.

Even among many critics of educational psychology this political dynamic is missed. Macro-sociopolitical concerns and the impact they exert on human experience in general and learning in particular are not a part of the discourse of the discipline. Until the relationship between extant social structures and power configurations and the questions of educational psychology are addressed, the work of professional practitioners will mystify and oppress more often than it will clarify and liberate. Educational psychology has generally ignored the sociopolitical issues of the day as it pursues its work in "neutral" isolation. The irony of its claims of hands-off objectivity in relation to the sociopolitical realm is not lost on critical teachers who have tracked the discipline's profound impact in this domain. Democratic teachers jump headfirst into the political fray with its overt call to democratize intelligence with an oppositional psychology and a critical pedagogy. Educational psychology is a situated cultural/political practice—whether it wants to be or not—that addresses the ideology of learning. Whenever learning and knowledge are conceived the nature of the conception affects individuals differently: it validates the cognitive processes of some and invalidates others.

So uncomfortable is dominant educational psychology with such pronouncements that many practitioners consider such critical discourse a disfacement of field, a disruption to its orderly proceedings. Thinking construed as a political activity in this context is marked by a hint of scandal or at least a lack of middle/upper-middle class "good taste." Despite such uncomfortable representations critical teachers push their political agenda, confronting the dominant discourse with its erasure of irrationality, emotion, power, paradigms, and morality in the learning process. With this point delineated, such teachers construct the role of a politically conscious educational psychology in terms of its effort to understand the subjective ways learners experience political issues. The focus on this domain delineates a unique and critical role for a reconceptualized educational psychology in macro-transformational efforts. How do political issues play out at the level of consciousness? How is the learning process shaped by issues of power? What is the relationship between school performance and a student's or a teacher's political consciousness and resulting moral sensibility?

Such questions would encourage research involving the subjective experiences of children deemed unintelligent and relegated to lower ability tracks. I frequently visit with students classified as "slow" or "incapable" by educational psychology who can make up creative games that can be played in the confines of an urban neighborhood; who build vehicles out of abandoned car and bicycle parts; who write their own music and choreograph their own dances; who have collected junk from the neighborhood, fixed it up, and sold it at a garage sale; and who have used paint found in the bottom of discarded paint cans to produce sophisticated portraits of themselves and their communities. Critical psychologists and educators recognize the genius of such children early in their school experience. Assuring them of their abilities and engaging them in activities designed to utilize such talents, democratic teachers create situations for these kids that replace their need to employ their talents in illegal, dangerous, and socially damaging activities. The understanding of the politics of cognition that informs such teaching strategies helps democratize intelligence in ways that profoundly change individual lives.

The practical meaning of the effort to contextualize children is easily understood in this example. A central feature of this process involves the study and reappraisal of everyday knowledge that is distributed throughout the society. Indeed, as a discipline educational psychology must explore the previously dismissed margins in order to identify the intelligence and creativity that exist in the lives of the people who reside there. Such talent can be found in everyday conversations, and in fleeting instants of interpersonal indeterminacy only if psychologists are sensitive to its presence and have the disposition to find it in places where their academic cultural capital does not place them in positions of power. To *search* for intelligence where one has previously seen only deficiency is a transformative act that holds radical political consequences. The inability or refusal to recognize such cognitive dynamics is testimony to the dysfunctionality of mainstream educational psychology. This dysfunctional impulse also expresses itself in ways that devalue indigenous knowledge or forms of intelligence that are produced outside of school. Learning in this mainstream configuration is narrowly construed as merely the acquisition of unexamined knowledge that takes place inside the school (Veroff & Goldberger, 1995; Wertsch, Del Rio, & Alvarez, 1995; Schleifer, Con Davis, & Mergler, 1992; Samuels, 1993; Shotter, 1993; Burman, 1994).

Most human activity in the domain of everyday life is surprisingly ingenious, as both children and adults figure out how to survive, how to find their way around their environment, communicate, and negotiate interpersonal relations. Why are these abilities not counted when a child's intelligence is assessed? By any standard such accomplishments require phenomenal cognitive facility. It seems obvious that individuals capable of such complexity in family contexts can learn relatively simple skills taught as basic knowledge in school. For many of those children who do not learn the academic basics, it is safe to conclude that their problem is dispositional rather than cognitive—they fail to grasp any reason to devote the time necessary to master such abilities. When such children come from backgrounds where parents, peers, and relatives have lived stable lives without such understandings, this dispositional dynamic is exacerbated. Mainstream educational psychology's batteries of tests do not address such important processes, thus revealing only a fragment of a description of cognitive ability—a misleading fragment at that.

Critical educators argue that intelligence is not something that manifests itself only on standardized tests and in academic classrooms. If progressive educators and educational psychologists can move their colleagues to study intelligence in ordinary lived situations, they will have initiated an important step in the larger effort to democratize our conception of intelligence. As we begin to gain clearer understandings of the cognitive sophistication of everyday life, we will not only broaden our definition of intelligence but we will be better able as educators to heed Vygotsky's enjoinder to "call out" what our marginalized children already know. In the calling-out process critical teachers would bracket student abilities, bring them to the students' conscious awareness, induce students to think about how to enhance the processes, and engage them in thought experiments and activities designed to facilitate the transfer of the skills into new domains.

Simple examples of this pedagogical process might involve inducing a child who loves baseball and understands the statistics of the game to transfer this ability to academic math; or a child who displays an interpersonal sensitivity to the feelings of others to transfer such a facility to the study of sociology and the critical dynamics involved with an appreciation of the subjective experience of marginalized groups. When educators and psychologists make use of this Vygotskian calling out, the door is opened to a plethora of sociopolitical, cultural, and cognitive understandings that expand the envelope of our educational imagination. The effort to reconceptualize the nature of children's abilities is open-ended and full of exciting possibilities (Weisner, 1987; Perkins, 1995; Horton & Freire, 1990; Hinchey, 1998).

Stepping Outside the Boundaries of
Formalism: Constructing a Postformal Child Psychology

It is in this critique of educational psychology's decon-
textualization of children's abilities that Shirley Steinberg's and my
theory of postformalism emerges (Kincheloe & Steinberg, 1993). In
the name of democratizing intelligence for social justice, we ask what
type of thinking might emerge as individuals operate outside the
boundaries of formalism. Utilizing recent advances in social and
educational theory, we have attempted to construct a sociopolitical
cognitive theory that understands the way our consciousness, our
subjectivity, is shaped by the world around us. Such a perspective
grants us a new conception of what "being smart" might entail. This
postformal view of higher-order thinking induces psychologists and
educators to recognize the politicization of cognition in a manner
that allows them to desocialize themselves and others from
mainstream psychology's and school-based pronouncements of who is
intelligent and who is not. Postformalism is concerned with questions
of justice, democracy, meaning, self-awareness, and the nature and
function of the social context. Such dynamics move postformal
thinkers to a meta-awareness of formalist concerns with "proper"
scientific procedure and the certainty it must produce. In this manner
postformalism grapples with purpose, devoting attention to issues of
human dignity, freedom, power, authority, domination, and social
responsibility.

The point being made here involves the recognition that the
postformal vision is not only about revealing the humanly
constructed nature of all talk about cognition (postformal talk
included), but also about creating new forms of human being and
imagining better ways of life for our children. Reconceptualizing the
abilities of children involves the political struggle to reshape
educational psychology in the service of progressive values. As it
lurks in the shadows of pseudo-objectivity, mainstream educational
psychology denies its political complicity in oppressing the
marginalized. In contrast, postformalism embraces its own politics
and imagines what the world could become. As Gaile Cannella (1999)
puts it, human possibility is enhanced when the tyranny of dominant
ideology, formalist reason, and Cartesian-Newtonian science is
removed. Moving into the conversation from another philosophical
locale, Aostre Johnson (1999) contends that cognitive formalism
undermines the expression of human multidimensionality by
excluding spiritual dimensions of being. Cognitivism, she maintains,
subverts our vision of human possibility by proclaiming the individual

rational mind as the central organizing dynamic in cognition and action.

The new forms of democratic living that postformalism attempts to make possible are indelibly linked to an alternative rationality. Contrary to the claims of some of our critics in mainstream educational psychology, postformalism does not seek to embrace irrationalism or to reject the entire enterprise of empirical research. We borrow the phrase, alternative rationality, from Stanley Aronowitz (1992), whose critique of mainstream science helps shape our vision of postformalism. In this schemata new rationalities employ forms of analysis sensitive to signs and symbols, the power of context in relation to thinking, the role of emotion and feeling in cognitive activity, and the value of the psychoanalytical process as it taps into the recesses of (un)consciousness. The effort to rethink children's abilities extends Aronowitz's powerful alternatives by asking ethical questions of cognition and action. Such inquiries induce educational and cognitive psychologists to study issues of purpose, meaning, and ultimate worth. Do certain forms of thinking undermine the quest for justice? Do certain forms of research cause observers to view problematic ways of seeing as if they involved no issues of power and privilege (Shotter, 1993; Usher & Edwards, 1994; Cannella, 1997; Schleifer, Con Davis, & Mergler, 1992).

Educational psychology has simply never encouraged a serious conversation about the reasons children engage in certain behavior, about the purposes of so-called higher-order thinking, or about the social role of schooling in a democratic society. For the most part the discipline has never considered the implications that Paulo Freire's notion of conscientization holds for the work of practitioners. What happens in the realm of cognition when individuals begin to gain a new consciousness via the process of (a) transforming themselves through changing their reality; (b) grasping an awareness of the mechanisms of oppression; and (c) reclaiming their historical memory in order to gain an awareness of their social construction, their social identity (Freire, 1970)? Such sociocognitive dynamics are necessary features of the effort to rethink child psychology in the larger movement to protect poor children from the ravages of the era. Until such appreciations are a part of the consciousness of educators and psychologists, schools will continue to certify the damage that marginalized children have to endure in the late twentieth century.

CHAPTER FIVE

Take the Money and Run?: Toys, Consumerism, and
Capitalism in Early Childhood Conferences

Glenda MacNaughton
Deakin University
Patrick Hughes
The University of Melbourne

Conference: a meeting for discussion, especially a regular one held by an
association or organization. (Allen, 1990, p. 239)

Each year, tens of thousands of early childhood staff meet to discuss
issues of theory, policy, and practice. Many early childhood staff
regard the regular conferences organized by national early childhood
organizations such as ACEI and NAEYC in the US as a taken-for
granted part of their professional development calendar. Conference
objectives may differ from year to year, from country to country, and
from organization to organization, but the mix of people attracted to
the conferences remains constant. Practitioners abound. They come
to learn about the latest educational research, pick up new ideas for
classroom practice, discuss policies and practices for children, and to
"network." Researchers are fewer in number but always present. They
come to share research, influence practitioners, and to network.
Exhibitors increase in number each year. They come to sell products
and to sell more products.

Conferences offer unique opportunities. To practitioners, they
offer a unique range of professional development opportunities.
Nowhere else offers the same number and diversity of chances to
learn about what's happening and to discuss it with so many
colleagues. To researchers, conferences offer a unique opportunity to
disseminate research. Nowhere else can they find the sheer volume of
practitioners with whom to share their ideas and findings. To
exhibitors, conferences offer unique marketing opportunities.
Nowhere else can they find in one place the sheer volume of
educational consumers to whom they can market their products. For
this reason, competition to gain an exhibition space is enormous. As
more and more manufacturers of "educational" products have

competed for space, the size of the exhibit halls has grown. At some of the larger conferences, such as the NAEYC, it can take hours to walk the length of the exhibit hall, browsing among anything from educational toys and books to jewelry and insurance.

The loose connection between some exhibitors' goods, such as jewelry, and the supposedly educational objectives of early childhood conferences raises political and ethical questions. Should early childhood educators give space, time, and marketing opportunities to manufacturers of goods that have little if any connection to early childhood education? Should exhibition space be reserved exclusively for child-focused, educational materials? Should early childhood educators take an ethical and political stand on what is an educationally appropriate product?

In their turn, these questions raise another one: What differentiates educational and noneducational materials? In this chapter, we explore this question by examining the political, economic, and social issues involved in defining a toy as "educational."

Seeking the "Educational" in Toys

At one level there is an obvious and simple answer to the question, "What is an educational toy?" An educational toy is one that educates. It helps a child to learn and/or it teaches a child something. However, this answer doesn't take us very far because children learn something from all toys. For instance, war toys are rarely considered educational, yet children certainly learn about war and aggression through playing with them (Dodd, 1992). Indeed, many people are aware that such learning happens, and they see this as highly problematic (Holmes, 1991; Dodd, 1992). Similarly, *Barbie* toys are rarely regarded as educational, yet children learn many things from playing with *Barbie*, including how to be traditionally gendered (Hughes & MacNaughton, 1998). So, if we define a toy as "educational" because it enables and encourages children to learn something, then the distinction between educational and noneducational toys becomes very difficult to sustain.

Another way to judge whether a toy is educational is to look at the toy manufacturers' aim in producing it. Many writers on the toy industry do this by differentiating "educational" toys from what they describe as "promotional" toys, for reasons which will become apparent below.

Promotional Versus Educational Toys

Many contemporary toys have been developed not as independent novelties but as elements of a web of commercial and organizational relationships. These relationships are very complex, but for ease of analysis we can say that the web consists of three concentric strands.

1. At the center is the toy itself, such as a *Care Bear*, a *Transformer*, a *Barbie*. Many of these toys are called "promotional" toys because their main function is to promote other toys in their product line as well as other products associated with the product line. For instance, Mattel's *Barbie* doll promotes *Barbie* accessories, *Barbie* books and magazines, and *Barbie* brand name clothes, bedding, and make-up.

2. The second strand of the web consists of commodities related with the toy, such as animated television programs, movies, T-shirts, magazines, and books. The companies that produce these products aren't, obviously, toy manufacturers—they are animation companies, television production companies, publishers, etc., but they are likely to have been involved from the beginning in the toy's design and development.

3. The final "outer" strands of the web consist of the various commodities that are associated with the toy and/or with its related commodities and that are produced by still other companies under license. These last commodities are anything that has a picture, a logo, or some other representation of the toy and/or of its television programs, movies, etc.

That explanation—complex enough in itself—is but a simplified version of the commercial and organizational interrelationships that characterize the development, manufacture, and sale of contemporary toys. In reality, a contemporary toy emerges onto the market as but one element of a whole panoply of commodities, each of which promotes all the others. So close are the interrelationships between these products that it can be hard to describe the toy as the "primary" product, the related merchandise as "secondary" products and the merchandise produced under license as "tertiary" products. Instead, no product is regarded as primary because the toys, the related television programs, and the licensed products featuring the logo promote each other. It doesn't matter which element of that web of interrelated commodities a child encounters first, because each one will lead the child to all of the others.

In a further degree of complexity, the trend within the industry is away from individual, stand-alone toys and toward "product lines," i.e., groups of toys representing characters in an animated television series, such as *Transformers*. When you give a child a Transformer, you aren't giving her/him a complete toy, as you would if you gave a doll, a toy train, etc. Instead, you are giving only part of a product line—an incomplete toy, as it were. Unless you can afford to give the whole set of *Transformers*, your gift will always be incomplete encouraging the child to complete her/his collection of the toys that make-up that product line. In this way, like it or not, giving a child a *Transformer* or a *Barbie* encourages her/him to be acquisitive and to be an avid consumer of as many as possible of the network of interlinked products (Farrell, 1997).

An increasingly common element of the networks of commercial relationships for promotional toys is the animated television series (e.g., *Teenage Mutant Ninja Turtles, Transformers, Smurfs*) and/or the feature film that is subsequently released on home video (e.g., *The Lion King, Pocahontas*). Although the children's home-video market was established in the early 1980s, there have been only minor variations in its structure. Disney products and movies dominate recent sales charts, although cross-promotions with restaurants, television programs, and product tie-ins are increasing in importance. Videos have always been marketed to a wide range of ages, but video distributors are increasingly segmenting the market, with the result that home videos are now heavily marketed to preschool children. Disney, Sony, and Warner each has a specific preschool home video division (McCormick, 1995).

Animation is the preferred format for many television series and movies because it combines several benefits (Pecora, 1998, p. 161). Firstly, the animated feature itself generates revenue. Secondly, animated characters are far easier than human (or humanoid!) characters to replicate as toys—just glance at the barely recognizable toy replicas from *Star Trek*! The third benefit of animation is that the simplistic drawings are easy to dub for an international market. Finally, within the tightly structured storylines, animation gives greater creative possibilities such as timelessness and geographical anonymity—qualities which also, of course, make it easier to market animated features (and the associated toys) across barriers of time, space, and cultures.

These interrelationships between the toy, leisure, and entertainment industries benefit the companies involved in three ways:

they bring stability to the industries; they extend the life of a particular toy; and they spread the economic risks associated with new products. Firstly, the relationships bring an element of stability to the industries because each toy no longer has to stand or fall on its own merits. Instead, its sales are supported by, and linked with, sales of other products in its product line, and the product line is itself supported by, and linked with, that web of economic and organizational interrelationships.

The second benefit is that those interrelationships extend the life of a particular toy, as is clearly illustrated by the career of the *Care Bears*. The *Care Bears* were introduced in 1983 as toys, media stars, and licensed products (twenty-five licensees). They were developed jointly by two companies: Those People from Cleveland (the licensing division of American-Greetings, the card company) and Marketing and Design Service, a division of the General Mills toy group. The release of the toys was accompanied by a network television special, followed by a mini-series and two movies, plus the release of a *Care Bears* branded cold-care product (diversification indeed!). A third *Care Bears* movie in 1986 was accompanied by department store tie-ins and "personal" appearances by the *Care Bears* at daycare centers, hospitals, parades, and on radio. In 1992, *Care Bears* were available on television and home video, and licenses were granted to 40 new licensees; and in 1994, *Care Bears* started appearing on Disney's cable television channel. An 11-year career, then, covering as many as three new generations of child consumers.

Thirdly, those commercial and organizational interrelationships spread the economic investment and the risks associated with new products between toy manufacturer, television station/network, program production company, and the firms which "buy" the audiences created by the programs. A major means of avoiding those economic risks is to license other companies to produce products featuring the characters or the logo associated with the toy. This spreads the economic risk far beyond the toy and entertainment industries, encompassing clothing companies, crockery manufacturers, luggage-makers, and food-packagers. The *Star Wars* trilogy of movies proved a watershed in this practice. Prior to *Star Wars*, movies rarely offered merchandizing or licensing deals, but such was the success of the merchandising around the trilogy that such ideas are now an integral part of film financing. For example, the *Batman* movies have generated an enormous range of merchandising, including bedding, clothing, watches, cosmetics, beach towels, videos, and breakfast cereals. Similarly, *Home Alone 2* generated more than 50 licensed products, which between them generated $400–$500 million beyond ticket sales.

By 1986, the Toy Manufacturers of America estimated that close to half of the toy industry's sales were of licensed products (cited in Carlsson-Paige & Levin, 1990, p. 72). In a specific instance of this growth, the Children's Television Workshop (CTW), makers of *Sesame Street*, has seen revenue from licensing rise from $3m in 1975 to $30.76m in 1993 (Pecora, 1998; p. 106). More recently, Disney and Mattel signed an exclusive agreement in 1996 in which Mattel has first option on all Disney characters worldwide for 3 years (Levin, 1996). Mattel is one of the largest licensees of Disney characters, benefiting from the continual exposure of those characters on video and film, audio, software, and books, as well as at Disney's various theme parks. Each of those outlets promotes Mattel's licensed products without Mattel having to spend a dollar. Mattel is also a licensee of the more than 400 products associated with the Nickelodeon children's cable channel.

A few firms have enjoyed not just those three types of benefit from the commercial and organizational interrelationships, but also an ever-increasing share of the market. In the past decade, the toy market has become dominated by a handful of toy firms, many of them multinational enterprises. In 1980, three firms shared 20% of the toy market: Hasbro, Mattel, and Coleco. (Coleco would release the *Cabbage Patch* dolls in 1985.) By 1986, the market consisted of 700 firms, but 45% of it was shared between those same three firms, plus Kenner Parker Toys and Fisher-Price; and by 1990, the ten largest firms controlled 60% of the toy market (Pecora, 1998).

Those complex economic and organizational relationships surrounding and supporting the launch of new toys have also brought increasing power to a handful of toy retailers. These companies have not generally been included in the consortia that launch new toys, but they nonetheless influence what toys are produced because they determine which toys are available at any one time. Pecora (1998, p. 60) has gone so far as to suggest that those corporate interrelationships have instigated what she calls a "material culture" of children's play that is driven by whatever characters are currently available at Toys"R"Us, rather than by the child's creative imagination. She illustrates this view with a hypothetical scenario:

> After going to see *The Lion King* with a grown-up, a child as young as 3 is primed to pop a tape of the award-winning theme song, *Circle of Life*, performed by adult musician Elton John, into the Fisher-Price cassette player and follow along with the *Adventures of Simba* storybook (while

wearing Lion King pajamas and hugging a Lion King doll). That child is
also an audience for the videocassette. (Pecora, 1998, p. 124)

In such circumstances, an early childhood organization or
conference that associates itself with promotional toys risks
becoming just another marketing site for the toy industry—albeit a
highly specialized one. At the least, it risks a public perception that it
has become subsumed to the economic imperatives that drive the toy
industry. Either way, it is implicated in the industry's subordination of
"play" and "education" to consumption; it is, therefore, also implicated in the increasing power of the handful of multinational firms
that dominate the toy, leisure, and entertainment industries.

In particular, early childhood organizations that consort with the
toy industry risk being seen as contributing to the creation of the
child as a consumer. In her study of Toys"R"Us, Seiter (1992, p. 234)
found that the firm has driven many independently owned stores out
of business by offering slim profit margins on the most popular toys
and that many department stores ceased selling toys in the 1970s
because they were unable to compete with the prices of Toys "R" Us.
The company wields a powerful influence on toy manufacturers as
well as retailers. Buying for each of the U.S. stores is centralized in
New Jersey, so buyers for Toys"R"Us have enormous commercial
clout, enabling them to make or break each new mass-market toy. By
the 1980s, as a result of those commercial and organizational
relationships and the dominance of retailers such as Toys"R"Us, pre-
literate children were making their own choice of brand-name
merchandise, based on easily recognizable icons such as Ronald
McDonald, encouraged by tie-ins, product merchandising, and media
characters.

> Sneakers were no longer bought because of cost or quality, but it was the
> novelty of a readily identifiable symbol such as the Little Mermaid that
> made them saleable. Images of the Little Mermaid on a pair of shoes
> transforms a pair of ordinary sneakers to LITTLE MERMAID SNEAKERS,
> a possession to be envied and discussed over milk and cookies at day care.
> Conversely, the pair of Little Mermaid sneakers leads to a recognition of the
> Little Mermaid video, television program, motion picture or story book.
> (Pecora, 1998, pp. 20, 23. Original emphasis.)

Creativity and the Educational Toy

Those social criticisms of promotional toys sit alongside an
educational criticism that they banish creative play in favor of play

that is predetermined by the design of the promotional toy itself. The argument here is that promotional toys are identified so closely with the storylines of the animated features with which they are associated that they fail to stimulate children's creativity. Proponents of this view often contrast the "closed" nature of these contemporary toys with more "open" traditional toys, which leave children with more room to decide just what the toy is, what it could do and, therefore, how they might play with it. For example:

> Toys demand less imagination when the generic teddy bear is replaced by a Lion King who comes with a history by Disney. Although stories are still about good versus evil, the tenor change when cartoon characters bring quick fixes to problems that are solved in 30 minutes, with time for commercials. (Pecora, 1998, p. 153)

In a similar vein, Carlsson-Paige and Levin (1990, p. 57) argued that children can use (play with) open-ended and less-structured toys and play materials in many different ways, encouraging them to be creative. They contrasted such open-ended toys with contemporary highly realistic, single-purpose toys (e.g., Rambo's action gun), which effectively "tell" children how to use them, thus preventing children from playing creatively. The authors apply these general ideas to the specific instance of war toys.

> In the past, children determined the content of their war play. They made guns out of whatever materials they could find and they invented pretend enemies using their imaginations. In doing so, they were in charge of their war play and the ideas they formed from it (and) they used their play in the service of their development. With the pressures that influence war play today, this often is no longer the case. (Carlsson-Paige & Levin, 1990, p. 16)

These two lines of criticism of promotional toys suggest a clear distinction between educational and promotional toys. Educational toys are "open," promote children's creativity and do not aim to promote the consumption of other products. However, several recent developments in the toy industry have undermined this distinction almost before it has been made. First, in the late 1980s, toy companies recognized that the critics of promotional toys constituted a niche market of affluent, educated parents willing to spend lots of money on "quality" toys for their children. The result of this recognition was the emergence of toy marketing that has a strong educational emphasis, together with the establishment of "upmarket" toy stores that posed alternatives to Toys "R" Us and featured names like the Early Learning Center, Imaginareum, and Creative Kids (Seiter, 1992, p. 238).

Second, the toy industry increasingly presents all toys as educational in order to increase the attractiveness of a new commodity. An example of this marketing strategy is a new, promotional, brand-named, Winnie the Pooh CD:

> Developed in conjunction with education specialists, Disney Interactive's new CD-ROM, *Ready To Read With Pooh*, helps children ages 3 through 6 to develop the skills they need to start reading. In this delightful adventure...play one of many fun learning games...nine fun activities that teach and reinforce essential pre-reading skills...children are rewarded with fun items. (anon, 1997, p. 1)

Third, the toy industry is actively developing educational product lines that build profit and a strong consumer base in just the same way as promotional toys. For example, most educational toy retailers include Lego in their catalogue. An early childhood center that purchases Lego often purchases just a part of the Lego product line. Few centers can afford the complete product line, which includes portable playtables, DACTA playmats, specialty sets, community vehicles, community people, DACTA wheels, etc. The 1996 J. L. Hammett Co. Early Learning Catalog included over 30 different add-ons to the basic Lego set. There are also multicultural product lines, consisting of multicultural materials for dramatic play, dramatic play furniture and utensils, dramatic play costumes, and multicultural dolls. Suppliers of educational toys also offer products that are derived from commercial relationships between companies, just like promotional toys. For example, children's books such as *The Paper Bag Princess* and *Mike Mulligan and His Steam Shovel* are now available as home videos.

Elitism and the Educational Toy

While the toy industry increasingly blurs the distinction between educational and promotional toys, there is increasing concern that the distinction between the two types of toys is elitist. The distinction between educational or creative toys and promotional toys resembles the distinction between high culture and popular culture. Indeed, the two distinctions are often drawn by the same people. Supporters of high culture expound the spiritual and moral merits of classical music, ballet, theatre, and literature while dismissing forms of popular culture such as television soap operas, popular music, and sport as merely entertainment. Similarly, supporters of educational toys expound their developmental merits while dismissing promotional toys such as *Power Rangers* and *Barbie* as "merely" entertainment—and commercialized entertainment at that!

Thus, a lot of the criticisms (of promotional toys) by parent and consumer groups doesn't concern the problem of children wanting toys that their parents can't afford, but the fact that children want toys of which their parents don't approve. Seiter (1992, p. 236) complains that consumer protection groups such as Action for Children's Television rarely make explicit the class values embodied in their criticisms. She reinforces this by arguing that:

> (O)ften the differences between promotional and quality toys have more to do with aesthetics and the taste codes associated with different classes than they do with any observable differences in how creative children can be with the toys. (Seiter, 1992, p. 249)

The distinction between educational and promotional toys may seem a helpful starting point from which to decide which toys should be exhibited at early childhood conferences. However, can early childhood professionals afford to snub promotional toys? These toys and the companies associated with them are steadily increasing their dominance of the toy industry through the complex organizational and commercial arrangements we have discussed. If the industry trends that we have identified continue, then early childhood professionals who just dismiss promotional toys as worthless will find themselves increasingly marginalized in any debate about toys, play, and education in early childhood. Such a dismissive stance will increasingly be seen as elitist and, thus, irrelevant. Perhaps early childhood professionals should seek to educate children using what the children themselves want to play with, rather than with what they think children *should* play with. Cupit (1996, p. 5) encapsulated this approach when he said, referring to the problems associated with young children's exposure to the media: "A media-fed imagination needs to expand from that basis. The input should not be ignored but used."

Similarly, perhaps early childhood professionals should consider identifying what young children actually receive from promotional toys in terms of creative stimulation and, as Cupit suggested, "expand from that basis. The input should not be ignored but used." After all, there is no point in presenting educational toys as somehow outside of the toy industry—they are, in fact, just a particular sector of it. Nor is there any point in trying to pretend that this sector is in some way better or more noble than the rest of the industry. As Seiter (1992, p. 248) put it:

> I wish to challenge...the notion that total resistance is possible when, in fact, we are usually talking about participation in an *alternative* market. That alternative is more elite and its advertising and its retailing practices more "refined" in that they continually lay claim to higher aspirations. But it is a market none the less. (Original emphasis.)

Is "educational toy" just another way of saying "middle-class toy"? If we dismiss promotional toys are we being classist? Are we teaching children that social status depends on having access to particular sorts of toys? Young children can, and do, notice the "more concrete manifestations and implications of social class" (Ramsey, 1995). They do learn that clothing, housing and possessions show social status. Is there a risk that by dismissing promotional toys we are teaching children that toys also show social status?

Conferences and Toys and the Privatization of Professional Development Space

Alongside the concerns about what children learn from toys is a growing criticism of the toy industry's role in privatizing public life. This criticism is not directed solely at the toy industry but at the retail sector as a whole, and it concerns the way in that urban space that was formerly public, has been privatized by being incorporated into a shopping mall. As the number of covered markets, shopping centers, shopping villages, plazas, piazzas and precincts increases, the amount and number of public spaces declines. The result is that opportunities for public life also decrease. For example, while a group of young people has every right to "hang out" in the town square, if that town square is converted into the Town Square Shopping Mall, they can only hang out under the gaze and sufferance of the private security guards employed by the mall's owners.

Not only is public space being privatized and subordinated to shopping, public time is changing in the same way. An increasing portion of people's leisure time—what we might call "public time"—is spent shopping. This has particular implications for young children when happiness is equated with a trip to McDonald's or to Toys"R"Us. Seiter (1992, p. 236) showed how Toys"R"Us stores have become new apparently public spaces in which public time is intimately associated with shopping for toys:

> Toys"R"Us is one of the best public arenas outside of church or the mall for parents to show off their new babies....For many, Toys"R"Us is a place where children can be brought to kill time, to play on indoor equipment when the weather is too bad to go to the park. It is an experience in which parent and child are at once "in public" and yet more anonymous than they would be at a neighborhood store or playground. Parents and children come "just to look" as a form of entertainment in itself.

We are living, then, in circumstances where "the shopping mall is the playground and the video is the storyteller" (Pecora, 1998, p. 153). The significance of these broad sociological processes for the early childhood world is that they represent a commodification of space and time. In other words, these processes transform public spaces into marketing sites for the toy, leisure, and entertainment industries; and they transform public time into consumption time—to the benefit of those same industries. Thus, an early childhood organization contemplating an association with the toy industry needs to recognize that by doing so it will—perhaps unwittingly—support and reinforce these processes of commodification and their influence on the lives of young children.

More specifically, an early childhood organization who invites the toy industry to its conference and creates a large space for the marketing and selling of toys is commodifying conference space and time. It transforms professional space (a meeting to discuss common professional concerns and current research) into a marketing site for the toy industry, and it transforms professional time into consumption time. When this happens, who are the winners and who are the losers?

Conclusion

While the distinction between toys as entertainment and toys as education becomes increasingly blurred, one thing remains clear. *All* contemporary toys are produced and promoted *primarily* in pursuit of economic objectives rather than educational ones because they are major elements of the leisure, entertainment, and communications industries. In a stark contrast to Carlsson-Paige's and Levin's view that toys are gifts given to express love, Pecora (1998, p. 3) suggests that "toys, no longer presents or surprises, have become staples in a consumer market." Consequently, any assessment of toys' educational significance and their role in play cannot ignore their economic significance.

Toys' economic characteristics pose ethical dilemmas for people in early childhood education who wish to create exhibition space for toy companies and/or who wish to accept sponsorship, advertising, or any other form of revenue from toy companies. Some people see no problems in involving the toy industry in the world of early childhood education and in early childhood conferences because they regard toys as simply elements of play, education or ideally both. For example, Swiniarsky (1991, pp. 161, 163) suggested that toys are "uni-versals" and "natural," rather than associated with *specific* cultural, social, economic, and political circumstances; and that *children* define a toy as an expression of the spontaneity of childhood.

> Toys and play are universals in childhood and as such offer a bonding that serves as a natural basis for a global education curriculum...Children's demands for toys are usually uncomplicated...Children...can turn rocks, beans and cornhusks into imaginative toys...In any analysis of play and toys, adults must not be to nostalgic and stylize play by dissecting from it the spontaneity of childhood.

Despite this idealized, universal view of toys, Swiniarsky admits elsewhere (1991, p. 162) that few "store-bought toys" number among the possessions of the Third World's children, except in the homes of affluent families. The distinction here between "third world" and "first world" countries undermines Swiniarsky's claims to "universality."

Similarly, despite their critical perspective on war toys, Carlsson-Paige & Levin (1990, p. 69) present toys as independent of specific cultural, social, economic, and political circumstances. Perhaps unwittingly, they discuss toys in terms that are so general as to be almost universal.

> Starting at birth, relatives and friends often give children gifts on special occasions to express love. Children quickly learn to associate the acquisition of objects, especially toys, with a sense of being loved and with a general feeling of well-being.

Such statements present toys as if capitalism doesn't exist or as if it has no relevance to, or impact upon, either the production and distribution of toys, or children's play with them, or practitioners' decisions to purchase them. From such a perspective, an early childhood organization faces no major problems if it chooses to associate itself with or give space to any toy manufacturer—"educational" or otherwise. However, the structure and operations of the contemporary toy industry have very little to do with spontaneous childhood or universal values, and contemporary toys are designed not to express love between donor and recipient but to encourage children and early childhood practitioners to become avid consumers. The primary goal of the multinational companies that dominate the industry is to minimize the commercial risks associated with the launch of a new product, and they do so by creating complex commercial and organizational relationships between themselves and other multinationals in the entertainment and leisure industries.

The structural and economic analysis of the toy industry that we have presented poses three questions:

1. To what extent is the industry's influence on child development benign or malevolent?
2. Can an association between an early childhood organization and the toy industry be as simple and unproblematic as it appears to people (e.g., Swiniarski) who see childhood as spontaneous, natural, and universal?
3. How can early childhood organizations (e.g., NAEYC) decide whether to accept support from, and involvement by, a toy company in their conferences, given the inextricable link between profit and commercialism in the toy industry?

Rather than automatically distinguishing between "educational" and "promotional" toys, we need to examine the extent to which dominant notions of education and quality are associated with a specific class base and how those dominant notions relate to the learning that happens around promotional toys and their associated products. These issues must be debated if we are to find a reasonable ethical and political answer to the question of which toys, if any, should have space in our conference halls when we meet to confer about research in our field.

CHAPTER SIX

Are Disney Movies Good for Your Kids?

Henry A. Giroux
The Pennsylvania State University

Although it appears to be a commonplace assumption, the idea that culture provides the basis for persuasive forms of learning for children was impressed upon me with an abrupt urgency during the past few years. As a single father of three, eight-year-old boys, I found myself somewhat reluctantly being introduced to the world of Hollywood animation films, in particular those produced by Disney. Before becoming an observer of this form of children's culture, I accepted the largely unquestioned assumptions that animated films stimulate imagination and fantasy, reproduce an aura of innocence, and, in general, are good for kids. In other words, such films appeared to be vehicles of amusement, a highly regarded and sought-after source of fun and joy for children. However, within a very short period of time, it became clear to me that the relevance of such films exceeded the boundaries of entertainment.

Needless to say, the significance of animated films operate on many registers, but one of the most persuasive is the role they play as the new "teaching machines," as producers of culture. I soon found out that for my children, and I suspect for many others, these films appear to inspire at least as much cultural authority and legitimacy for teaching specific roles, values, and ideals as do the more traditional sites of learning such as the public schools, religious institutions, and the family.

The significance of animated films as a site of learning is heightened by the widespread recognition that schools and other public sites are increasingly beset by a crisis of vision, meaning, and motivation. The mass media, especially the world of Hollywood films, on the contrary, constructs a dreamlike world of childhood innocence where kids increasingly find a place to situate themselves in their emotional lives. Unlike the often hard-nosed, joyless reality of schooling, children's films provide a high-tech visual space where adventure and pleasure meet in a fantasy world of possibilities and a commercial sphere of consumerism and commodification.

The educational relevance of animated films became especially clear to me as my kids experienced the vast entertainment and teaching machine embodied by Disney. Increasingly, as I watched a number of Disney films first in the movie theater and later on video, I became aware of how necessary it was to move beyond treating these films as transparent entertainment in order to question the messages behind them.

But at the same time, I recognized that any attempt to take up Disney films critically rubbed against the grain of American popular opinion. After all, "the happiest place on earth" has traditionally gained its popularity in part through a self-proclaimed image of trademark innocence that has protected it from the interrogating gaze of critics. Of course, there is more at work here than a public-relations department intent on protecting Disney's claim to fabled goodness and uncompromising reverence. There is also the reality of a powerful economic and political power that staunchly protects its mythical status as a purveyor of American innocence and moral virtue.[1] Quick to mobilize its monolith of legal institutions, public-relations spokespersons, and professional cultural critics to safeguard the borders of its "magic kingdom," Disney has aggressively prosecuted violations of its copyright laws, exercised control over who has access to the Disney archives, and has attempted to influence the uses of material researched in the archives. In its zeal to protect its image and extend its profits, Disney has gone so far as to take legal action against a small-time day care center that used Disney cartoon characters in its advertising. In this instance, Disney, as a self-proclaimed defender of family values, compromised its Dan Quayle philosophy for an aggressive endorsement of property rights. Similarly, Disney has a harsh reputation for applying pressure on authors critical of the Disney ideology and enterprise. But the power of Disney's mythological status comes from other sources as well.

Disney's image as an icon of American culture is consistently reinforced through the penetration of the Disney empire into every aspect of social life. Children experience Disney's cultural influence through a maze of representations and products found in home videos, shopping malls, classroom instructional films, box offices, popular television programs, and family restaurants. Through advertising, displays, and use of public visual space, Disney inserts itself into a network of commodities that lends itself to the construction of the world of enchantment as a closed and total category. Disney goes to great lengths to boost its civic image. Defining itself as a vehicle for education and civic responsibility, Disney sponsors "Teacher of the Year Awards," provides scholarships to students, and, more recently, offers financial aid, internships, and educational programs to disadvantaged urban youth through its ice-skating program called Goals. In what can be seen as an extraordinary venture, Disney plans to construct in the next few years a prototype school that one of its brochures proclaims will "serve as a model for education into the next century." The school will be part of a 5,000-acre residential develop-ment called Celebration, which, according to Disney executives, will be designed after "the main streets of small-town America and reminiscent of Norman Rockwell images."[2]

What is interesting here is that Disney no longer simply provides the fantasies through which childhood innocence and adventure are produced, experienced, and affirmed. Disney now produces prototypes for model schools, families, identities, communities, and the way the future is to be understood through a particular construction of the past. From the seedy urban haunts of New York City to the spatial monuments of consumption shaping Florida, Disney takes full advantage of refiguring the social and cultural landscape while spreading the ideology of its Imagineers. For instance, not only is Disney taking over large properties on West 42nd Street in New York City in order to produce a musical a year, it has also begun building Celebration, which is designed to accommodate 20,000 citizens. According to Disney, this is a "typical American small town... designed to become an international prototype for communities."[3] What Disney leaves out of its upbeat promotional literature is the rather tenuous notion of democracy that informs its view of municipal government, since the model of Celebration is "premised upon citizens not having control over the people who plan for them and administer the policies of the city."[4] But Disney does more than provide prototypes for upscale communities; it also makes a claim on the future through its nostalgic view of the past and its construction of public memory as a metonym for the magical kingdom.

French theorist Jean Baudrillard has captured the scope and power of Disney's influence by arguing that Disneyland is more "real" than fantasy because it now provides the image on which America constructs itself. For example, Houston models its airport monorail after the one at Disneyland. Towns throughout America appropriate a piece of nostalgia by imitating the Victorian architecture of Disneyland's Main Street USA. It seems that the real policymakers are not those that reside in Washington, D.C., but those in California calling themselves the Disney Imagineers. The boundaries between entertainment, education, and commercialization collapse through the sheer omnipotence of Disney's reach into diverse spheres of everyday life. The scope of the Disney empire reveals both shrewd business practices as well as a sharp eye for providing dreams and products through forms of popular culture in which kids are willing to materially and emotionally invest.

Popular audiences tend to reject any link between ideology and the prolific entertainment world of Disney. And yet Disney's pretense to innocence appears to some critics as little more than a promotional mask that covers over its aggressive marketing techniques and influence in educating children to the virtues of becoming active consumers. Eric Smoodin, editor of *Disney Discourser*, a book critical of Disney's role in American culture, argues that "Disney constructs- childhood so as to make it entirely compatible with consumerism."[5] Even more disturbing is the widespread belief that Disney's trademark innocence renders it unaccountable for the diverse ways in which it shapes the sense of reality it provides for children as they take up particular and often sanitized notions of identity, culture, and history in the seemingly apolitical cultural universe of "the Magic Kingdom." For example, Jon Wiener, professor of history at the University of California at Irvine, argues that "Disneyland's version of Main Street America harks back to an image of small towns characterized by cheerful commerce, with barbershop quartets and ice cream sundaes and glorious parades." For Wiener this view not only fictionalizes and trivializes the history of real Main Streets at the turn of the century, it also represents an appropriation of the past to legitimate a present that portrays a world "without tenements or poverty or urban class...conflict...It's a native white Protestant dream of a world without blacks or immigrants."[6]

I want to venture into the contradictory world of Disney through an analysis of its more recent animated films. These films, all produced since 1989, are important because they have received enormous praise and have achieved blockbuster status. For many children they represent their first introduction into the world of Disney. Moreover, the success and popularity of these films, rivaling many adult features, do not engender the critical analyses often rendered on adult films. In short, popular audiences are more willing to suspend critical judgment about such children's films. Animated fantasy and entertainment appear to collapse into each other and as such fall outside of the world of values, meaning, and knowledge often associated with more pronounced educational forms such as docu-mentaries, art films, or even wide-circulation adult films. Given the influence that the Disney ideology has on children, it is imperative for parents, teachers, and other adults to understand how such films attract the attention and shape the values of the children that view and buy them.

Below I argue that it is important to address Disney's animated films without either condemning Disney as an ideological reactionary deceptively promoting a conservative worldview under the guise of entertainment, or simply celebrating Disney as the Hollywood version of *Mr. Rogers' Neighborhood,* doing nothing more than providing sources of joy and happiness to children all over the world. In part, Disney does both. But the role that Disney plays in shaping individual identities and controlling the fields of social meaning through which children negotiate the world is far too complex to be reduced to either position. Disney inscribes itself in a commanding way upon the lives of children and powerfully shapes the way America's cultural landscape is imagined. Disney's commanding cultural authority is too powerful and far-reaching to simply be the object of reverence. What Disney deserves is respectful criticism, and one measure of such respect is to insert Disney's scripted view of childhood and society within a critical dialogue regarding the meanings it produces, the roles it legitimates, and the narratives it uses to define American life.

The question of whether Disney's animated films are good *for* kids has no easy answers, but at the same time it necessitates examining such films outside the traditional register of fun and entertainment. Disney's most recent films, which include *The Little Mermaid, Aladdin, Beauty and the Beast, and The Lion King,* provide ample opportunity to address how Disney constructs a culture of joy and innocence *for* children out of the intersection of entertainment, democracy, pleasure, and consumerism. All of these films have been high-profile releases catering to massive audiences. Moreover, their commercial success is not limited to box-office profits. Successfully connecting the rituals of consumption and moviegoing, Disney's animated films provide a "marketplace of culture," a launching pad for an endless number of products and merchandise that include videocassettes, soundtracks, children's clothing, furniture, stuffed toys, and new rides at the theme parks.[7]

On a more positive note, the wide distribution and popular appeal of these films provide diverse audiences and viewers the opportunity to challenge those assumptions that allow people to suspend judgment regarding Disney's accountability for defining appropriate childhood entertainment. Critically analyzing how Disney films work to construct meanings, induce pleasures, and reproduce ideologically loaded *fantasies* is *not meant as* an exercise in disparagement. On the contrary, as a $4.7 billion company, Disney's corporate and cultural influence is so enormous and far-reaching that it should go neither unchecked nor unmediated.

Disney's recent films embody structuring principles and themes that have become the trademark of Disney animation. As sites of entertainment, Disney's films work because they put children and adults alike in touch with joy and adventure. They present themselves as places to experience pleasure, even when we have to buy it. Hollywood glitz, colorful animation, and show-stopping musical scores combined with old-fashioned cheer create a celluloid zone of aesthetic and emotional comfort for children and adults alike. The rousing calypso number "Under the Sea" in *The Little Mermaid,* and "Be Our Guest," the Busby Berkeley-inspired musical sequence in *Beauty and the Beast,* are indicative of the musical talent at work in Disney's animated films. The four films draw upon the amazing talents of songwriters Howard Ashman and Alan Menken, and the result is a series of musical feasts that provide the emotional glue of the animation experience.

Fantasy abounds as Disney's animated films produce a host of exotic and stereotypical villains, heroes, and heroines. Whereas Ursula, the large, oozing, black-and-purple squid in *The Little Mermaid,* gushes with evil and irony, heroine-mermaid Ariel appears as a cross between a typical rebellious teenager and a fashion model from Southern California. Disney's representations of both evil and good women appear to have been fashioned in the editorial office of *Vogue.* The wolflike monster in *Beauty and the Beast* evokes a rare combination of terror and gentleness, whereas Scar, the suave and scheming feline, adds a contemporary touch to the meaning of evil and betrayal.

The array of animated objects and animals in these films is of the highest artistic standards. For example, the Beast's enchanted castle in *Beauty and the Beast* becomes magical as household objects are transformed into dancing teacups, a talking teapot, and dancing silverware. Such characters are part of larger narratives: freedom, rites of passage, intolerance, choices, the injustice of male chauvinism, and the mobilization of passion and desire are just some of the many themes explored in these animated films. But enchantment is not without its price if it seduces its audience into suspending critical judgment on the messages produced by such films. Even though these messages can be read through a variety of interpretations and are sometimes contradictory, there are a number of assumptions that structure these films that represent the hidden face of Disney.

One of the most controversial messages that weave in and out of Disney's animated films concerns the portrayal of girls and women.

In both *The Little Mermaid* and *The Lion King* female characters are constructed within narrowly defined gender roles. All of the women in these films are ultimately subordinate to men and define their sense of power and desire almost exclusively in terms of dominant male narratives. For instance, mermaid Ariel, modeled after a slightly anorexic Barbie Doll, at first glance appears to be engaged in a struggle against parental control, motivated by the desire to explore the human world and willing to take a risk in defining the subject and object of her desires. But in the end the struggle to gain independence from her father, Triton, and the sense of desperate striving that motivates her, dissolves when Ariel makes a Mephisphelean pact with Ursula: Ariel trades her voice to gain a pair of legs so that she can pursue handsome Prince Eric. Although children might be delighted by Ariel's teenage rebelliousness, they are positioned to believe in the end that desire, choice, and empowerment are closely linked to catching and loving handsome men. In *The Little Mermaid* Ariel becomes a metaphor for the traditional housewife-in-the-making narrative. When Ursula tells Ariel that taking away her voice is not so bad because men don't like women who talk, the message is dramatized when the Prince attempts to bestow the kiss of true love on Ariel even though she has never spoken to him. Within this rigidly defined narrative, womanhood offers Ariel the reward of marrying the right man and renouncing her former life under the sea—a telling cultural model for the nature of female choice and decision making in Disney's worldview. It is difficult to see how a film such as this does more than reinforce negative stereotypes about women and girls. Unfortunately, this type of stereotyping is reproduced, to varying degrees, in all of Disney's animated films.

In *Aladdin* the issue of agency and power is centered strictly on the role of the young street tramp, Aladdin. Jasmine, the princess with whom he falls in love, is simply an object of his immediate desire as well as a stepping-stone to social mobility. Jasmine's life is almost completely defined by men, and in the end her happiness is ensured by Aladdin, who finally is given permission to marry her.

The gender theme becomes a bit more complicated in *Beauty and the Beast*. Belle, the heroine of the film, is portrayed as an independent woman stuck in a provincial village in eighteenth-century France. Seen as odd because she always has her nose in a book, she is pursued by Gaston, a vain, macho male typical of Hollywood films during the 1980s. To Belle's credit she rejects him, but in the end she gives her love to the Beast, who holds her captive in the hopes she will fall in love with him and break the evil spell that was cast upon him while a young man. Belle not only falls in love with the

Beast, she "civilizes" him by instructing him to eat properly, control his temper, and dance. Belle becomes a model of etiquette and style as she turns this narcissistic, muscle-bound tyrant into a model of the "new" man, one who is sensitive, caring, and loving. Some critics have labeled Belle a Disney feminist because she rejects and verifies Gaston, the ultimate macho man. Less obviously, *Beauty and the Beast* can also be read as a rejection of hypermasculinity and a struggle between the macho sensibilities of Gaston and the reformed sexist, the Beast. In this reading Belle is less the focus of the film than prop or "mechanism for solving the Beast's dilemma."[8]

Whatever subversive qualities Belle personifies in the film, they seem to dissolve when focused on humbling male vanity. In the end, Belle simply becomes another woman whose life is valued for solving a man's problems.

The issue of female subordination returns with a vengeance in *The Lion King*. All of the rulers of the kingdom are men, reinforcing the assumption that independence and leadership are tied to patriarchal entitlement and high social standing. The dependency that the beloved Mufasa engenders from the women of Pride Rock is unaltered after his death when the evil Scar assumes control of the kingdom. Lacking any sense of outrage, resistance, or independence, the women felines hang around to do his bidding. Given Disney's purported obsession with family values, especially as a consumer unit, it is curious as to why there are no mothers in these films. The mermaid has a domineering father, Jasmine's father is outwitted by his aides, and Belle has an airhead for a father. So much for strong mothers and resisting women.

Jack Zipes, professor of German at the University of Minnesota and a leading expert on fairy tales, claims that Disney's animated films celebrate a masculine type of power. More importantly, he believes that they reproduce "a type of gender stereotyping...that have an adverse effect on children in contrast to what parents think....Parents think they're essentially harmless—and they're not harmless."[9] Disney films are seen by enormous numbers of children in the United States and abroad. As far as the issue of gender is concerned, Disney's view of the relationship between female agency and empowerment is not merely nostalgic—it borders on being overtly reactionary.

Racial stereotyping is another major issue that surfaces in many of the recent Disney animated films. But the legacy of racism does not begin with the films produced since 1989; on the contrary, a long history of racism associated with Disney's work can be traced back to denigrating images of people of color in films such as *Song of the*

South, released in 1946, and *The Jungle Book,* which appeared in 1967.[10] Moreover, racist representations of Native Americans as violent "redskins" were featured in Frontierland in the 1950s. In addition, the main restaurant in Frontierland featured the real-life figure of a former slave, Aunt Jemima, who would sign autographs for the tourists outside of her "Pancake House." Eventually the exhibits and the Native Americans running them were eliminated by Disney executives because the "Indian" canoe guides wanted to unionize. They were displaced by robotic dancing bears. Complaints from civil rights groups got rid of the degrading Aunt Jemima spectacle.[11]

The most controversial example of racist stereotyping facing the Disney publicity machine occurred with the release of *Aladdin* in 1989, although such stereotyping reappeared in 1994 with the release of *The Lion King. Aladdin* represents a particularly important example because it was a high-profile release, the winner of two Academy Awards, and one of the most successful Disney films ever produced. Playing to massive audiences of children, the film's opening song, "Arabian Nights," begins its depiction of Arab culture with a decidedly racist tone. The song states: "Oh I come from a land/From a faraway place/Where the caravan camels roam. Where they cut off your ear/If they don't like your face. It's barbaric, but hey, it's home." In this characterization, a politics of identity and place associated with Arab culture magnifies popular stereotypes already primed by the media through its portrayal of the Gulf War. Such racist representations are further reproduced in a host of supporting characters who are portrayed as grotesque, violent, and cruel. Yousef Salem, a former spokesperson for the South Bay Islamic Association, characterized the film this way: "All of the bad guys have beards and large, bulbous noses, sinister eyes and heavy accents, and they're wielding swords constantly. Aladdin doesn't have a big nose; he has a small nose. He doesn't have a beard or a turban. He doesn't have an accent. What makes him nice is they've given him this American character....I have a daughter who says she's ashamed to call herself an Arab, and it's because of things like this.''[12]

Jack Shaheen, a professor of broadcast journalism at Southern Illinois University in Edwardsville, with radio personality Casey Kasem, mobilized a public-relations campaign protesting the anti-Arab themes in *Aladdin.* At first the Disney executives ignored the protest but, due to the rising tide of public outrage, agreed to change one line of the stanza in the subsequent videocassette and worldwide film release; it is worth noting that Disney did change the lyrics on its popular CD release of *Aladdin.*[13] It is also worth noting that Disney executives were not unaware of the racist implications of the lyrics when they were first proposed. Howard Ashman, who wrote the title song, submitted an alternative set of lyrics when he delivered the original verse. The alternative set of lyrics, "Where it's flat and immense/And the heat is intense" eventually replaced the original verse, "Where they cut off your ear/If they don't like your face." Although the new lyrics appeared in the videocassette release of *Aladdin,* many Arab groups were disappointed because the verse "It's barbaric, but hey, it's home" was not altered. More importantly, the mispronunciation of Arab names in the film, the racial coding of accents, and the use of nonsensical scrawl as a substitute for an actual written Arabic language were not removed.

Racism is also a powerful but subtle structuring principle in Disney's more recent animated film, *Pocahontas.* In the Disney rendition of colonial history, Pocahontas is converted into a brown, Barbie-like supermodel with an hourglass figure whose relationship with Aryan hunk John Smith transforms a historical act of colonial barbarism into a sentimental romance. In this romantic allegory, the rapacious and exploitative narrative of colonialism is rewritten as a multicultural love affair in which issues of human conflict, suffering, and exploitation are conveniently erased. Captain John Smith, whose historical reputation was founded on his unrelenting, murderous pursuit of "Indians," is mystified in Disney's *Pocahontas.* Rather than being portrayed accurately—as part of a colonial legacy that resulted in the genocide of millions of Native Americans—Disney turns Smith into a morally uplifted white male who ends up being Mr. Right for an ill-fated, brown-skinned version of Calvin Klein model Kate Moss. Although Disney's rendition of Pocahontas as a strong-willed woman may seem too politically correct for conservatives, the film is, in actuality, a deeply racist and sexist portrayal of Native Americans.

It is worth noting that racism in Disney's animated films does not simply appear in negative imagery or through historical misrepresentation; racist ideology also appears in racially coded language and accents. For example, *Aladdin* portrays the "bad" Arabs with thick, foreign accents, whereas the Anglicized Jasmine and Aladdin speak in standard, Americanized English. A hint of the unconscious racism that informs this depiction is provided by Peter Schneider, president of feature animation at Disney, who points out that Aladdin was modeled after Tom Cruise.[14] Racially coded language is also evident in *The Lion King,* where all of the members of the royal family speak with posh British accents while Shenzi and Banzai, the despicable hyena storm troopers, speak through the voices of Whoopi Goldberg and Cheech Marin in racially coded accents that take on the nuances of the discourse of a decidedly urban, black, and Latino youth. The use of racially coded language is not new in Disney's films and can be found in an early version of *The Three Little Pigs, Song of the South,* and *The Jungle Book.*[15] *What is* astonishing is that these films produce a host of representations and codes in which children are taught that cultural differences that do not bear the imprint of white, middle-class ethnicity are deviant, inferior, ignorant, and a threat to be overcome. There is nothing innocent in what kids learn about race as portrayed in the "magical world" of Disney. The race card has always been central to Disney's view of cultural and national identity, and yet the issue of race only seems to warrant public discussion when it appears allegedly in the discourse of civil rights to benefit black people either through affirmative action or in the outcry over the recent O. J. Simpson verdict. The fact of the matter is that when the race card is used to denigrate African Americans and other people of color, the issue of race as an act of racism seems to disappear from public discourse.

Another central feature common to all of Disney's recent animated films is the celebration of deeply antidemocratic social relations. Nature and the animal kingdom provide the mechanism for presenting and legitimating social hierarchy, royalty, and structural inequality as part of the natural order. The seemingly benign presentation of celluloid dramas in which men rule, strict discipline is imposed through social hierarchies, and leadership is a function of one's social status suggests a yearning for a return to a more rigidly stratified society, one modeled after the British monarchy of the eighteenth and nineteenth centuries. For children, the messages offered in Disney's animated films suggest that social problems such as the history of racism, the genocide of Native Americans, the prevailing sexism, and the crisis of democratic public life are simply willed through the laws of nature; clearly, this is a dangerous lesson for powerlessness and is a highly conservative view of the social order and relations of the contemporary world.

Does this mean that Disney's children's films should be ignored or censored? I think a number of lessons are to be learned from recognizing the deeply ideological messages behind Disney's view of the world. First, it is crucial that the realm of popular culture that Disney increasingly uses to teach values and sell goods be taken seriously as a site of learning, especially for children. This means, at the very least, that it must be incorporated into schools as a serious object of social knowledge and critical analysis. Second, parents, community groups, educators, and other concerned individuals must be attentive to the messages in these films in order to both criticize them when necessary and, more importantly, to reclaim them for more productive ends. The roles assigned to women and people of color, along with ideas concerning a rigid view of family values, history, and national identity, need to be challenged and transformed. That is, such images and their claim to public memory need to be rewritten as part of the script of empowerment rather than be simply dismissed because they thrive to undermine human agency and democratic possibilities.

Third, Disney's all-encompassing reach into the spheres of economics, consumption, and culture suggests that we analyze Disney within a range of relations of power. Eric Smoodin argues rightly that the American public needs to gain a new sense of Disney's importance because of the manner in which Disney's work in film and television is connected to other projects in urban planning, ecological politics, product merchandising, United States domestic and global policy formation, technological innovation, and constructions of national character.''[16] This suggests undertaking new analyses of Disney that connect rather than separate the various social and cultural formations in which the company actively engages. Clearly, such a dialectical position not only provides a more theoretically accurate understanding of Disney's power, it also contributes to forms of analysis that rupture the notion that Disney is primarily about the pedagogy of entertainment. Equally important, research about Disney must be at once historical, relational, and multifaceted.[17] Moreover, this type of study is perfectly suited for cultural studies, which can employ an interdisciplinary approach to such an undertaking, one that makes the popular the object of serious analysis, makes the pedagogical a defining principle of such work, and inserts the political into the center of the project.[18]

Fourth, if Disney's films are to be viewed as more than narratives of fantasy and escape, as sites of reclamation and imagination that affirm rather than deny the long-standing relationship between entertainment and pedagogy, cultural workers and educators need to insert the political and pedagogical back into the discourse of entertainment. In part this suggests analyzing how entertainment can be rendered as a subject to work on rather than as something to be passively consumed. This suggests a pedagogical approach to popular culture that engages how a politics of the popular works to mobilize desire, stimulate imagination, and produce forms of identification that can become objects of dialogue and critical investigation. At one level, this suggests addressing the utopian possibilities in which children often find representations of their hopes and dreams. At another level, cultural workers need to combine a politics of representation with a discourse of political economy in order to understand how Disney films work within a broad network of production and distribution as teaching machines within and across different public cultures and social formations. Within this type of discourse, the messages, forms of emotional investment, and ideologies produced by Disney can be traced through the various circuits of power that both legitimate and insert "the culture of the Magic Kingdom" into multiple and overlapping public spheres.

Moreover, films such as these need to be analyzed not only for what they say but also for how they are used and taken up by adult audiences and groups of children within diverse national and international contexts. That is, cultural workers need to study these films intertextually and from a transnational perspective. Disney does not represent a cultural monolith ignorant of different contexts; on the contrary, its power in part rests with its ability to address different contexts and to be read differently by transnational formations and audiences. Disney engenders what Inderpal Grewa and Caren Kaplan have called "scattered hegemonies."[19] It is precisely by addressing how these hegemonies operate in particular spaces of power, specific localities, and differentiated transnational locations that progressives will be able to understand more fully the specific agendas and politics at work as Disney is both constructed for, and read by, different audiences.

Fifth, pedagogically it is imperative that parents, educators, and cultural workers be attentive to how these Disney films and visual media are used and understood differently by diverse groups of kids. Not only does this provide the opportunity for parents and others to talk to children about popular culture, it also creates the basis for better understanding of how young people identify with these films, what issues need to be addressed, and how such discussions would open up a language of pleasure and criticism rather than simply shut such a conversation down. This suggests that we develop new forms of literacy, new ways of critically understanding and reading the electronically produced visual media. Teaching and learning the culture of the book is no longer the staple of what it means to be literate. Children learn from exposure to popular cultural forms, and these provide a new cultural register to what it means to be literate. This means that educators and cultural workers need to do more than recognize the need to take seriously the production of popular art forms in the schools; it also means there can be no cultural pedagogy without cultural practices that both explore the possibilities of different popular forms and bring out students' talents. The point here is that students should not merely analyze the representations of electronically mediated, popular culture—they must also be able to master the skills and technology to produce it. This means making films, videos, music, and other forms of cultural production. Needless to say, this suggests giving students more power over the conditions for the production of knowledge, but a cultural pedagogy also involves the struggle for more resources for schools and other sites of learning.

Finally, I believe that since the power and influence of Disney is so pervasive in American society, parents, educators, and others need to find ways to make Disney accountable for what it produces. The recent defeat of the proposed theme park in Virginia suggests that Disney can be challenged and held accountable for the so-called "Disneyfication" of American culture. Although it is indisputable that Disney provides both children and adults with the pleasure of being entertained, Disney's public responsibility does not end there. Rather than being viewed as a commercial public sphere innocently distributing pleasure to young people, the Disney empire must be seen as a pedagogical and policymaking enterprise actively engaged in the cultural landscaping of national identity and the "schooling" of the minds of young children. This is not to suggest that there is something sinister behind what Disney does as much as it points to the need to address the role of fantasy, desire, and innocence in securing particular ideological interests, legitimating specific social relations, and making a distinct claim on the meaning of public memory. Disney needs to be held accountable not only at the box office; but also in political and ethical terms. And if such accountability is to be impressed upon the "magic kingdom," then parents, cultural workers, and others will have to challenge and disrupt the images, representations, and values offered by Disney's teaching machine. The stakes are too high to ignore such a challenge and struggle, even if it means reading Disney's animated films critically.

NOTES

1   The reality of the Disney Company as a powerful economic and political empire can be seen in the record of its profits and its ever expanding corporate cultural reach. For instance, the Disney Company in 1994 took in nearly $5 billion at the box office, $3.5 billion from Disney theme parks, and almost $2 billion from Disney products. In addition, in the summer of 1995 the Walt Disney Company made the biggest deal of the American media industry by investing $19 billion to acquire Capital Cities/ABC. See, for example, Bruce Hovovitz, "Company Has Cradle-to-Grave Sway," USA *Today* (September 7, 1995), p. B1. On the specific properties involved in the merger between

Disney and Capital Cities/ABC, see Jack Thomas, "For Viewers, Changes Not Expected to Be Big Deal," *Boston Globe* (August 1, 1995), pp. 33, 45, especially the chart on page 45.

2   Cited in Mark Walsh, "Disney Holds Up School as Model for Next Century," *Education Week* 13(39) (June 22,1994): 1.

3˙   Cited in Tom Vanderbilt, "Mickey Goes to Town(s)," *Nau'on* 261 (6) (August 28/September 4, 1995): 197.

4   Ibid., p. 199.

5   Eric Smoodin, "How to Read Walt Disney," in Smoodin, ed., *Disney Discourse: Producing the Magic Kingdom* (New York: Routledge, 1994), p. 18.

6   Jon Wiener, "Tall Tales and True," *Nanon* (January 31, 1994), p. 134.

7   The term "marketplace of culture" comes from Richard de Cordova, "The Mickey in Macy's Window: Childhood Consumerism and Disney Animation," in Eric Smoodin, ed., *Disney Discourse: Producing the Magic Kingdom* (New York: Routledge, 1994), p. 209.

8   Susan Jefford develops this reading of *Beauty and the Beast in* Susan Jefford, *Hard Bodies: Hollywood Masculinity in the Reagan Era* (New Brunswick, NJ: Rutgers University Press, 1994), p. 150.

9   Cited in June Casagrande, "The Disney Agenda," *CreanZJe Loafing* (March 17–23, 1994), pp. 6–7.

10   Upon its release in 1946, *Song of the South* was condemned by the NAACP for its racist representations.

11   These racist episodes are highlighted in Wiener, "Tall Tales and True," pp. 133–135.

12   Yousef Salem, cited in Richard Scheinin, "Angry Over 'Aladdin,'" *Washington Post* (January 10, 1993), p. G5.

13   Howard Green, a Disney spokesperson, dismissed the charges of racism as irrelevant, claiming that such criticisms were coming from a small minority and that "most people were happy with the film." *Washington Post* (January 10, 1993).

14   Cited in Rene Graham, "Can Disney Do It Again?" *Boston Globe* (June 11, 1995), p. 57.

15   See Susan Miller and Greg Rode, who do a rhetorical analysis of *The Jungle Book* and *Song of the South* in their chapter, "The Movie You See, the Movie

You Don't: How Disney Does That Old Time Derision," in Elizabeth Bell, Lynda Haas, and Laura Sells, eds., *From Mouse to Mermaid* (Bloomington: Indiana University Press, 1995)

16   Smoodin, "How to Read Walt Disney," p. 5.

17   Such work is already beginning to appear. For example, see the special issue of *South Atlantic Quarterly* 92(1) (Winter 1993), edited by Susan Willis, which takes as its theme "The World According to Disney." Also, see Smoodin, *Disney Discourse;* and Bell, Haas, and Sells, *From Mouse to Mermaid.*

18   For an example of such an analysis, see Stanley Aronowitz, *Roll Over Beethoven* (Middletown, CT: Wesleyan University Press, 1993); Henry A. Giroux, *Disturbing Pleasures: Learning Popular Culture* (New York: Routledge, 1994).

19   Inderpal Grewal and Caren Kaplan, "Introduction: Transnational Feminist Practices and Questions of Postmodernity," in Inderpal Grewal and Caren Kaplan, eds., *Scattered Hegemonies* (Minneapolis: University of Minnesota Press, 1994).

Part Three

Critical Multiculturalism in the Early
Childhood Education Curriculum

CHAPTER SEVEN

"At Risk" or "At Promise"? From Deficit Constructions
of the "Other Childhood" to Possibilities for Authentic
Alliances with Children and Families

Beth Blue Swadener
Kent State University

The meaning of experience is perhaps the most crucial site of political struggle over meaning. (Chris Weedon, 1987)

More attention must be paid to the linkages between those who suffer and those who care, so that caring becomes a committed advocacy, so that a concrete praxis may emerge. (Valerie Polakow, 1993)

In this chapter, I draw from my work in comparative child and family social policy, critical feminist analysis, and unlearning oppression/alliance building to frame a number of issues that relate to the dynamics of social exclusion in the United States. I also draw briefly from some of my research in sub-Saharan Africa, particularly my work with street children and their mothers in Nairobi, Kenya. I raise several questions derived from an applied semiotic analysis of ways in which the "other" is constructed in dominant education and policy discourses, as well as in popular constructions of those who inhabit the "margins" of contemporary society and are systematically excluded from many of its benefits. Throughout the chapter I will be making reference to, and deconstructing, the rhetoric of "children and families at risk," the currently popular language for describing those who are *socially excluded* or at risk of failure in various systems or contexts, including education, future employment, and access to "the good life," or middle-class opportunities. I will attempt to frame these issues in nested contexts (Lubeck, 1987) within which children and families operate, including cultural and linguistic, community, school, national, and political.

When I began a critical analysis of the evolution or "etiology" of the risk rhetoric ten years ago, I found over 2,500 articles, conference papers, and monographs that used this label and assumed its validity. In the U.S., the terminology had shifted from "culturally deprived and deficient" (used widely in the 1960s and 1970s) and "disadvantaged" (used in the 1980s) to the currently popular label "at risk" (Swadener, 1990, 1995). Questions I grappled with then, and which are still relevant today, include the following: Is "at risk" merely a cultural deprivation/deficit model retooled for the 1990s? In what ways is the discourse of risk preventing an *authentic dialogue* in which voices of the "real" stakeholders—parents, children, and communities—could be heard? In what ways are our "common sense" assumptions about children and families labeled "at risk" racist, sexist, class, and ablest? How can "success stories" (Soto, 1993), culturally sensitive pedagogy, family literacy, and community empowerment interrupt the hegemony of the risk rhetoric and ideology—and get needed programs funded? Most recently I have been concerned with the *criminalization* of children, highlighted recently in the arrest on felonious assault charge of a 38-pound five-year-old kindergartener in our local school district. When did young children become criminals? How does this relate to the ever-expanding prison industrial complex, as Angela Davis calls it?

Since 1989, a growing number of state and national education reports in the U.S. have continued to address the "at risk" theme; perhaps the most publicized was the report titled *A Nation at Risk*. Countless local and state committees, task forces, and reports have made recommendations for addressing this "crisis" in American education and have received wide media attention and growing public and private funding (Swadener, 1990). In the 1990s, many states passed laws defining and mandating programs for "at risk" children and families. In short, the term "at risk" has become a buzzword, and is often added to the title of proposals in order to increase the likelihood of funding. I have argued that there is a clear ideology underlying the use—indeed the overuse—of the medical metaphor "at risk," and suggest that we reconceptualize *all children* as "at promise" for success, versus "at risk" for failure. The problem of locating pathology in young victims of oppression (and their families) is, in my opinion, the most objectionable tenet of the "at risk" rhetoric.

Concurrent to my reading and critique of this literature, I have had literally hundreds of conversations with parents—African American, Latino/Latina, Native or indigenous American, Kenyan and South African, many of whom are single parents living below the poverty line. These conversations have focused on their children, their childrearing challenges, ways in which teachers responded to their children, and their vision for the future, including aspirations and goals for their children. At some point in many of these conversations, the issue of having their child—or their entire family—labeled "at risk" came up. To a person, they found this label highly problematic and felt that it stigmatized both themselves and their children. I believe that my passion for this critique is anchored in their concerns and active resistance to that social construction of their lives and the future potential of their children.

In the following sections of the chapter, I use two U.S. public policy issues, welfare reform or devolution and public school funding, to further unpack the rhetoric of risk and its relationship to ideological and political debates concerning private versus public constructions of the family and the "savage inequalities" or "savage distributions" of school funding and related dynamics of race and class-based stratification.

Public versus Private Constructions of Children, Families, and Poverty

In the U.S., poverty is generally seen as a private affair versus a public responsibility (Polakow, 1993, p. 46). In her book *The Tyranny of Kindness*, Theresa Funiciello (1993) uses the following quote from ancient Greece (Thuicydides): "There will be justice in Athens only when the uninjured parties are as indignant as the injured parties" (p. xiii). Self-interrogation of power and privilege is virtually absent from public policy discourse regarding poverty and educational marginalization or exclusion in the United States. The prevalent ideology surrounding poverty espouses that the poor are "deficient" in some way. This "flawed character" view is the basic tenet of recent "underclass" theory (Reed, 1992). Or, as Ayre (1996) put it, in describing French popular attitudes about parents in prison, "the roots of taboos run deep, particularly when imagination triumphs over reality and stereotypes flourish" (p. 62).

Blaming the victim is one way of locating pathology and deficiencies within the individual and/or family, and has had the devastating effect of being accepted as common sense (Reed, 1992) and a pervasive stereotype of those at the margins of dominant culture. In reality, the vast majority of impoverished people are law abiding, resourceful, and willing to work (Sidel, 1992). The U.S. literature since the late 1970s (Pearce, 1978) has documented that greater social and economic forces are at fault for much of the poverty in the U.S. As a result of these forces, those most likely to find themselves poor are women and children (Children's Defense Fund, 1994; Goldberg & Kremen, 1990; Polakow, 1993; Sidel, 1992), a phenomenon often referred to as the "feminization of poverty."

The language of deficiency, whether applied to parenting, academic potential, preparation for success in school and work, or health-related factors, is pervasive in public policy discourses concerning young children and their families. In calling for an "at promise" view of *all* children and families, we (Swadener & Niles, 1991; Swadener & Lubeck, 1995) have not intended to play a semantic substitution game of trading the "at-risk" label for an "at promise" one. Rather, we would encourage everyone working with children and families to look for and build upon the promise in all children and to concentrate valuable energies and resources on building on these strengths while addressing the many structural and environmental factors that have been argued to place many children "at risk." I share the view with many colleagues that early childhood and the broader field of education should move beyond the persistent tendency to pathologize the poor (Polakow, 1993) and to construct children in poverty and their mothers as an urban, or rural, "other." Such othering is inconsistent with a more inclusive feminist perspective, which has an explicit political project of naming exclusions and oppressions and addressing these inequities while advocating for and with families.

Instrumental Individualism versus
Existential Collectivism in Public Policy

Unlike the majority of industrialized nations, particularly in Europe, child and family social policy questions in the United States have *not* been universal, existential questions such as "What are the rights of *all* children and families, and how can the state respect and support these human rights?" They have been particularized and pragmatic (e.g., "How can we get low income women to stop having so many children?" or "How can we get mothers on public assistance into the labor force?").

Several of us (e.g., Grubb & Lazerson, 1982; Polakow, 1993; Swadener, 1995; Wrigley, 1991) have argued that the U.S. childcare and early education "system" has always been highly stratified or caste-like. In the past, day nurseries, which were a form of welfare that existed as little more than custodial care facilities, served poor working mothers while nursery schools existed for middle-class children. The largest public preschool program in the U.S., Head Start, serves predominantly children and families of low income and has lower standards of education for its teachers than most private, middle-class childcare and preschool programs. Such programs become stigmatized or socially excluded from the mainstream of the early childhood education profession and function in a largely class-based de facto *apartheid* of early childhood programs in the U.S. (For a more in-depth analysis of the history of stratification in early childhood programs and policies, see Swadener, 1995.)

The inherent contradictions in many of the attempts to remedy the social inequities affecting young children and their families in the United States is reflected in this quote from *Broken Promises* (Grubb & Lazerson, 1982):

> Each time children are found in need, humanitarian and benevolent activists propose government programs to overcome the deficiencies of family life. Yet we invest reluctantly in those programs, clinging to a desperate wish that parents would adequately fulfill their private responsibilities and resenting their children for requiring public attention and for making demands on our private incomes. The result is that public programs are the "cheapest possible care"....We end up with a corrupted notion of public responsibility in which the benevolent assumptions of *parens patriae* are subordinated to private responsibility. (p. 51)

Single Mothers and the Dismantled U.S. Welfare State

In her history of single mothers and welfare in the U.S., titled *Pitied But Not Entitled,* Linda Gordon (1994) describes the hostility with which most people refer to "welfare." Ironically, this hostility is, in her description, "remarkably democratic" and "hated by the prosperous and the poor, by the women who receive it and by those who feel they are paying for it" (p. 2). As frequently discussed in both scholarly and popular literature, the welfare system stigmatizes, humiliates, and undercompensates its recipients. Funiciello (1993), Gordon (1994), Polakow (1993), and Sidel (1992) document ways in which low income mothers suffer invasions of their privacy, inferior childcare, and many road blocks to self-sufficiency and a living wage (including sufficient health and childcare). Such accounts convey the perspectives of women and children directly influenced by welfare policy and call for transformative policy changes to be made.

These verbal assaults on single mothers in poverty reached a peak during the 1995 U.S. Congressional debate of legislation aimed at dismantling a part of the Social Security Act, in place since 1935, which had guaranteed federal (national) aid to all poor mothers and their dependent children. During debate of the "Personal Responsibility Act," as it was ironically titled, poor mothers were vilified by Republican lawmakers as "breeding mules," as "alligators," and as "monkeys" (Polakow, 1997, p. 246). The Chairman of the House Ways and Means Committee stated, in reference to restricting benefits to welfare mothers, "it may be like hitting a mule with a two by four but you've got to get their attention" (DeParle, 1994). When the bill reached the Senate, a senior senator demanded, "We've got to get a provision that denies more and more cash benefits to women who have more and more babies while on welfare" (Toner, 1995).

Valerie Polakow, from whose recent work I draw heavily in this section, examines the circumstances of the growing numbers of women living below the poverty line, and asks:

> Who are these "mules" and breeding females exploiting taxpayers' money and benefiting from what House Speaker Newt Gingrich bemoaned as "the tragedy of American Compassion?" They are the women who do not fit the patriarchal "family values" frame of the traditional male-headed household. They are the women who choose to separate or divorce; the women whose standard of living drops dramatically when their male partners fail to support their children; the women who choose to have solo pregnancies; the women who are poor and who are unable to exercise reproductive choice due to Medicaid restrictions on abortions; the women who lack education and training and earn only minimum wage; the women in the pink collar ghetto who work part-time and receive no benefits; the women whose low wage earnings can neither pay childcare costs nor support a family; the women and teen girls who are molested and raped; the women who are forced to flee domestic violence with their children—in short all these women now constitute our post-modern categorization of "feminized poverty." (p. 247)

The anti-welfare and "underclass" discourses that have so brutally targeted single mothers have also promoted a continuing perception of poverty as a private and behavioral affair, leading to a proliferation of "racialized and sexualized fictions about *them* so that the causes of family poverty are seen as rooted in failed and fallen women, failed mothers, failed children, and a failed work ethic, but not a failed and diminishing public economy, nor the histories of class, race and gender discrimination, not the actual consequence of failed public policies (Polakow, 1997, p. 247).

If, instead of blaming the victim, the choice is made to look toward economic and societal forces and dynamics, one is compelled to ask who benefits from this growth in poverty—particularly among women and children in the U.S. (Swadener, 1995). Cook and Fine's (1995) case study of twelve African American mothers ("Motherwit") reveals:

> how deeply caught these women are between institutions which stand as evidence of their "inadequacies" as parents, and children who carry all the conflicting messages of racism and classism inside the U.S. underclass. These narratives...suggest that radically different policies are needed to

replace the current contradictory, usually punishing ones that affect them today and threaten to affect them tomorrow (p. 212).

Ironically, just a year after this was published (in a book I co-edited on Children and Families "At Promise"), welfare "reform" legislation was signed into law, dismantling the national program in favor of block grants and greater state (decentralized) control, and making the deepest cuts in federal entitlement programs in over 50 years. Among those most targeted by this year-old legislation were *legal immigrants,* who can no longer obtain health and welfare benefits, including those assisting families with children with disabilities. Other limitations included a "two years and you're out" policy in which benefits were limited to two years, job training was required, and states were given far greater control of programs affecting low income families. Of many concerns regarding this legislation, the persistent trilemma of health care, childcare, and employable skills/livable wages were all issues that the majority of lawmakers—from a safe, privileged distance—failed to acknowledge in their rush to put most entitlement programs into block grants and therefore limit benefits (Swadener & Jagielo, 1997). More recently, further immigration legislation, more aptly described as "anti-immigration" policy, has required that legal immigrants who wish to bring relatives to live with them in the United States must earn a minimum of $26,000 and have a documented sponsor willing *to repay the government* should services such as food stamps or Medicaid be used.

This protracted political shift in the U.S. to the Right is often referred to as a "new federalism" or "devolution" of more centralized, national entitlement programs and social policies, and is not without paralléls in Europe and former communist and socialist nations. Yet, the "U.S. now stands alone among democratic industrialized nations in failing to provide family support policies for children and families. We have no universal health care, no national subsidized childcare system, no paid maternity or parental leave, no child and family allowances, no entitlement to subsidized housing, and now—with welfare 'reform,' no entitlement to public assistance for all children in poverty" (Polakow, 1997, p. 246). A further irony, from an advocacy perspective, is that with deeper cutbacks have come further regulations and requirements on families living in poverty; greater regulation of the lives of people in poverty, often creating new hardships (e.g., forcing families to use marginal childcare or simply leave children alone or forcing single mothers to travel long distances to where required work is available, etc.). Indeed, the current state of welfare "deform," as some welfare rights activists have named it, brings to mind Foucault's observation *that "need is also a political instrument, meticulously prepared, calculated and used"* (1979). Recently, I have found it particularly interesting and troubling to consider the multiple meanings of the large sums of money being spent to document the impact of welfare devolution. One national set of studies, focusing on four cities, has a budget of $15 million over a three-year period. It is not difficult to imagine creative ways in which the foundations who funded this study might have invested the same sum of money in microenterprise loans, education funds, and other forms of direct access to persons eligible for public assistance.

Popular (state) models of welfare reform, which are now being widely replicated across other states, have included programs such as BrideFare (requiring mothers receiving public assistance to marry the father of their child(ren), WorkFare (requiring volunteer or paid work or work training to continue receiving benefits), and DriveFare (youth in families receiving welfare lose their drivers license for school truancy). All of these programs make the receipt of already limited benefits contingent upon meeting state-imposed regulatory demands within a climate that frequently does not provide the scaffolding or basic supports for such "sink or swim" requirements of self-sufficiency or independence. The notion that people who are already excluded from the mainstream of American life must be highly monitored and regulated again echoes Foucaultian themes of surveillance, as well as the very "American" notion of pulling up oneself by the bootstraps. This popular bootstraps metaphor builds upon the myth of meritocracy (McIntosh, 1988), which assumes a level playing field of equal opportunities and denies the existence of oppression, particularly racism, classism, sexism, and linguisism. I turn now to the contrasting case of European social policy and a brief overview of recent sociopolitical and ideological changes in several European states.

Savage Inequalities (Savage Distributions) in U.S. Public Education

Shifting the focus to school-age children and public education, much has been written in recent years on the dramatic economic inequities—or savage inequalities (Kozol, 1991)—of public school funding in the U.S. Public education is funded, in most states, almost exclusively by property taxes. Thus, school resources reflect the property values and income levels of their local community. Briefly stated, poor communities—particularly central city and rural—typically have poor schools, and middle class to wealthy communities, often in the suburbs or settings with a healthy economy, have far greater resources for education. The range of annual per pupil expenditures for students can range from as low as $4,000 per student in a poor district to over $15,000 per pupil in a wealthy one. (This includes personnel and overhead costs, such as buildings and materials.)

Several states, including my state of Ohio, have been the target of lawsuits in recent years, based on the assertion that the current funding systems are unconstitutional in that they violate children's civil rights to equal education and are discriminatory by class and race. Similar to the earlier civil rights movement, the school funding equity battle is gaining momentum with more and more states under federal court order (including Ohio, as recently as 1996) to change their funding formulas in ways that more equitably distribute the state's overall wealth and remove some of the vast disparities between school districts.

In several of his books (e.g., *Savage Inequalities: Children in America's Schools* and *Amazing Grace*), Jonathan Kozol has provided a dramatic exposé of the economic disparities that exist between schools for white middle-to-upper-class children and schools for low-income and working class children. Kozol provides a shocking journalistic account of the "present day reality in public education" in the U.S., and asks his readers to reflect on the setbacks to education caused by the Reagan-Bush conservative agenda in the form of (a) rigidly segregated schools and (b) gross disparities in educational funding. The strength of his recent books is found in Kozol's clear and impassioned analysis of the role of the government and those responsible for funding formulas for local districts in the cause and maintenance of the "savage inequalities" in public education. As he states (1991):

> Unless we have the wealth to pay for private education, we are compelled by law to go to public school—and public school is our [local] district. Thus, the state, by requiring attendance but refusing to require equity, effectively requires inequality. Compulsory inequity, perpetuated by state law, too frequently condemns our children to unequal lives (p. 56).

Throughout his books, Kozol points to racism as a connecting theme running through the deliberate and shameful neglect of children in urban public schools. Kozol also outlines the historical legal challenges led by parents and community leaders (as discussed above) against inequitable state funding formulas (Arnold & Swadener, 1993), and formulates a clear indictment of the structural and political forces that foster the "separate and unequal" public schools in neighboring communities.

Yet, even books such as Kozol's, which have proved helpful in raising public awareness and winning battles in the school funding equity "war," have also played into the discourse of risk, with its implicit racism, classism, and sexism. A colleague with whom I do unlearning oppression workshops (Mary Smith Arnold) and I have been particularly concerned about ways in which such accounts of the urban "other" are framed in the dominant discourse or "masterscript" of risk and poverty. Implicit in accounts such as these, for example, is the perceived lack of agency, promise, resiliency, resistance, and full lives of those living in poverty—often children and families of color. A view of children and families "at promise" requires a critical examination of the dominant culture and popular media's "common sense" about "ghetto" schools, the urban "underclass," and "high risk" children. Accounts such as this also work within the tradition of the social meliorists, who evoke image of pity in their advocacy for social reform and change. Using pathos as an appeal can be problematic on several grounds, including the tendency for the targets of pity to also become targets of contempt, further exclusion or isolation, blame and attribution (Arnold & Swadener, 1993, p. 262). Perhaps a better question to be asking, in the face of resistance to more equitable school funding is, "Is privilege at risk?"

We would argue that without a more thorough interrogation of privilege, including the school and larger life experiences of the children in suburban and other middle-class schools, the savage inequalities described so vividly by Kozol and others will not change. What is at stake for these more privileged children who are often the victims of white flight from cities into the "green grass" of the American suburbs? As advocates for children and families we applaud the basic honesty, critical arguments, and mission of Kozol's message, even as we understand it as a partial truth. While the stark picture of education for the dispossessed is captured in sharp contrasts and cold truths about material deprivation and disrepair in public schools experienced primarily by African American and other children of color, such accounts leave us with the question, "What of the white children who have so much green grass?" Implicit in this question is a deep concern for the children of privilege who are force-fed harmful assumptions—and myths—about their history, power, unexamined privilege, and world (Arnold & Swadener, 1993).

Whether we refer to the "savage inequalities" of publicly funded education or the "savage distributions" of resources and opportunities within the larger society (Polakow & Swadener, 1993), stratification, as reflected in both family and educational policy, persists in the U.S. To quote African American poet Audre Lorde (in a 1984 quote that uses the metaphor of the slave master):

> For the master's tools will never dismantle the master's house. They may allow us temporarily to beat him at his own game, but they will never enable us to bring about change (p. 112).

While equitable funding is necessary for improved schools, restructuring the educational system is *not sufficient* for creating culturally relevant, nonsexist, liberatory education. Stated another way, a subtext of accounts such as Kozol's is often that, given equal funding, the children in poor schools will approximate the children in middle-class (white) schools, which are assumed to be best and are left uninterrogated. Forced assimilation is still the master's tool—particularly if dominant culture students are not educated multiculturally. Those of us who advocate on behalf of children and fight for parity in resources must not forget the insidious and multifaceted nature of oppression (Arnold & Swadener, 1993, p. 269). The elimination of persistent racist and classist educational policies, procedures, and practices requires measures that go beyond fiscal concerns and force us to honestly examine human, existential themes of both ourselves and those for whom we would advocate.

I am also concerned that our attempts to solve problems of social exclusion or inequalities in educational opportunity lock us into false dichotomies, including oppressor/oppressed, donor/recipient, and benefactor/beneficiary roles, which function to preclude authentic collaborator or reciprocal ally relationships. Perhaps one of the most powerful questions we can be asking throughout this conference and in our work with socially excluded children and families is, "How can we better *listen to,* rather than talk about or speak for, those who are at the margins of the culture of power?" This is a similar question to those asked by feminists and poststructuralists (e.g., Ellsworth, 1989; Greene, 1986; Lather, 1991; Polakow, 1993), including "How can educators—and parents—gain control of their discourses and practices, instead of being controlled and manipulated by them?"

Building Alliances with Parents
and Strengthening Home-School Relations

"No one has ever asked me what I think. They'll tell me what I should do. Lots of that. I'm feeling good—I'm getting a lot off my chest!"

This quote came at the end of an interview that a white urban primary teacher and researcher (Kay Dunlap) had with an African American mother whose son was in a special reading program for low income children. These interviews were part of a research project that looked at emergent literacy and the role of home-school cultural continuities, discontinuities, and communication patterns, building on the work of researchers such as Heath (1989), Dyson (1990), Taylor and Dorsey-Gaines (1988), and Delpit (1988, 1993), all of whom deal with the language and culture of power and teachers' ability and willingness to make those roles explicit so that all children have access to acquiring "cultural capital." The research focused on family literacy and strengthening two-way communication between home and school for families who had been socially excluded in dominant culture schools. Their research has also examined how some family routines support school-like behaviors and others do not. The parent quoted above addressed the sociocultural relationship between literacy in families, particularly as connected to power relations (Swadener, Dunlap, & Nespeca, 1995):

As an African American parent, my biggest fear is that the teacher might not be genuinely able to code-switch. Can the teacher, from the child's point of view, code-switch to really communicate? Can the teacher use code-switching when she needs to? (p. 274)

These concerns are similar to Delpit's (1988) perspective on the rules for participating in power: "The codes or rules I'm speaking of relate to linguistic forms, communicative strategies, and presentation of self; that is, ways of talking, ways of writing, ways of dressing, and ways of interacting" (p. 283). Parents in our study agreed with Lisa Delpit that some African American (and other children from nondominant cultures) may need to be explicitly taught to code-switch, and teachers need to become more sensitive to the kinds of instruction that are relevant and appropriate to particular children or settings. Gloria Ladson-Billings (1992) studied teachers who were particularly successful, from both community and school perspectives, with African American students and suggests that bicultural code-switching and a *relational* approach to working with students helps create *culturally relevant pedagogy and culturally inclusive classrooms.*

Turning to implications for parent involvement and communication, another theme was the need to match parent involvement to various time, talent, and energy frameworks. The following quote from a parent illustrates this point (Swadener, Dunlap, & Nespeca, 1995):

> When teachers get resistance from a parent I wonder sometimes if it's because a parent thinks, "You don't expect much cause I'm a single mother." It's the missionary zeal thing, "you poor-pitiful-people-golly-gee-whiz." Sometimes people who are different will look at an organization and will say, "It's up to us to integrate, but it's just too much. I don't have the energy to integrate an organization that is already functioning well without me." The PTAs (parent teacher associations) of the world can help by saying, "It's OK for you to get involved. You don't have to work at integrating it. Just come in." (p. 275)

This quote supports much of the recent U.S. literature on the importance of authentic relationships between home and school and the need for authentic partnerships that integrate parents and the home culture into the school's instructional plan. In her ethnographic account of Mexican families in the United States, Delgado-Gaitan (1990) asserted the critical function of parent empowerment for language-minority families and children:

> The challenge for educators to prepare minority students for successful participation in the school system is dependent on the ability of schools to incorporate the parents and the culture of the home as an integral part of the school instruction plan. The concept of literacy and empowerment...challenges the stereotypes often attributed to Mexican families in the United States, particularly in regard to their participation in schools. (p. 1)

Similarly, in a book titled *Growing Up Literate: Learning from Inner City Families*, Taylor and Dorsey-Gaines (1988) emphasize a participatory and democratic vision of family-school partnerships. Using similar arguments as my critique of the construct "children and families at risk," they encourage educators to challenge mainstream assumptions about poverty, gender, and race as predictors of family literacy, as well as school, success, and failure, and forge genuine relationships with families of different backgrounds than their own:

> Sex, race, economic status, and setting cannot be used as significant correlates of literacy. The myths and stereotypes that create images of specific groups (families who are poor, inner-city families, teenage mothers

and their children) have no relevance when we stop counting and start observing and working with people. (pp. 201–202).

This is not, of course, to deny that the most appropriate manner of teaching children or working with families may differ across socioeconomic levels or ethnically diverse groups. It is, rather, to emphasize the importance of looking beyond stereotypes, middle class, and privileged assumptions, and to ask parents what they think about the education of their children. I conclude this section with a brief example of how well this can work in a school that is rich in cultural and religious diversity.

As part of an Institute for Education that is Multicultural, a team of colleagues and I worked for several years with urban public schools undergoing school-wide reform and emphasized a better understanding of the communities they serve and more equitable and effective academic preparation of the students. These reforms have included portfolio assessment of children's progress, part of which is starting each school year with a parent-teacher-student conference in which parents are asked, "What are your goals for your child this year?" This sounds like a simple question, but it is one that is rarely asked of parents in U.S. schools—particularly low income parents and parents of color. Another change has been the "de-tracking" of the curriculum away from ability groups, which tended to have far more white, middle- and upper-middle-class students enrolled in the advanced or honors courses, and encourage a more culturally inclusive curriculum for *all* learners.

The results were evident within the first two years of this "experiment," using both qualitative and quantitative assessments; parent involvement was greatly increased, as were student achievement test scores at the end of the school year. This work is not easy and results are not immediate; many white teachers continue to resist these reforms and have recently succeeded in undermining some of the school-based reforms. Yet, we know that genuine interest in families' goals for their children, combined with follow-through based on their recommendations, can go a long way in building alliances with families to improve education for socially excluded students. Convincing teachers who already feel overburdened with their complex roles in urban schools that this is work well worth doing remains a challenge.

Preparing Teachers for Culturally
Inclusive Pedagogy and Parent Partnerships

In a course I teach on "Home, School, Community Relations," we anchor many of our readings, discussions, and community experiences in the question, "How can I be a more powerful ally with families of children I teach?" We begin with an activity I call "Parent Perspectives," which uses quotes from parents who differ by culture, language, gender, sexual orientation, family structure, religion, income, etc., and encourage students to say how they might feel if they were that parent. Examples of quotes include the following Single mother: "I feel my son's behavior at school is always blamed on the fact that I am a single parent." Native American parent: "I couldn't believe when my daughter brought home a paper 'Indian headdress,' just when she was learning what it means to earn an eagle feather." Puerto Rican mother: "My children are discouraged from speaking Spanish at school and are embarrassed by my accent—I am afraid they are going to lose much of their culture in this school."

This activity is followed by a three-hour "Unlearning Oppression" workshop, in which students are exposed to a multicultural alliance model and its assumptions through experiential activities and discussion. The major *assumptions* of our model include: (a) racism and other forms of oppression are pervasive and hurt everybody; (b) oppression is not our fault—we came into the world naturally loving, zestful, and curious, but racism and other forms of oppression are our responsibility (and should be since oppression hurts everyone); (c) it is not our differences that keep us apart, it is our attitudes about difference that separate us; (d) we all stand in the shoes of both victim (target) and agent (victim) of oppression; (e) racism and other forms of oppression are learned and can be unlearned, and it is never too early to start or too late to begin (Arnold & Swadener, 1993).

Other activities include completing a family tree and oral history interview (to put them in touch with their own cultural and family heritage), interviewing a single parent, developing a monthly budget to support a family living in poverty, including visiting various social service agencies, volunteering in a community-based setting (often a homeless shelter), and developing resources for communicating with, and involving parents in, their early childhood setting in the future. We constantly revisit the question of how we can be stronger allies, including participating in active listening activities, interrogating our own power and privilege, and continuing the challenging work of unlearning oppression. Guest speakers include many parents and professionals working in programs that actively involve parents.

I mention these specific examples from my teaching, because they relate to the question of how we can encourage teachers and future teachers to transcend some of the deficit-based constructions of children in difficult circumstances to see the promise in all children they teach. Other classes I teach involve field placements in culturally diverse, low income schools in which we use the expressive arts and social (cultural) studies to involve children. The combination of respect for children's families, ability to listen to both children and their parents, and the use of learning projects that actively involve and empower children can go far in helping future teachers find "promise" even in the most desolate "inner city" landscapes because they engage as allies with young, excited learners.

Children in Difficult Circumstances: Experiences with Street Children in Kenya

Before concluding this chapter I would like to say a few words regarding my experiences working with children in what UNICEF calls "extremely difficult circumstances." During the years 1994–1995 I lived in Nairobi, Kenya, while I carried out a Fulbright-sponsored collaborative study on impacts of rapid social and economic change on childrearing. During this time I volunteered with street children and later with some of their mothers. I started an arts program literally on the street (at the site of an informal feeding and tutoring program staffed entirely by volunteers) and helped found an arts apprenticeship group home for four of the older boys who showed great promise in the arts. Later, I helped some of the mothers organize a self-help and income-generating group and have continued to support these projects since my return home, including organizing exhibits of the children's art and fundraising for the mothers group. As others (e.g., Aptekar, 1994, 1996; Kilbride & Kilbride, 1990; Munyakho, 1992; Muraya, 1993) have documented, street children show remarkable resilience, problem-solving skills, and frequently develop a "peer culture" of survival and mutual support which their precarious existence demands. And, as you are aware, street children are not unique to the so-called third world—in fact, in sub-Saharan Africa they are a very recent phenomenon.

These are young people, ranging in age from 5 to 17, who could certainly be labeled "children at extreme risk," as they have been shot and killed, arrested and placed in terrible conditions in remand homes, have frequently experienced abuse, actively use drugs (primarily sniffing glue), and have high rates of HIV/AIDS. Yet, one has only to spend time tutoring them, seeing their work in the expressive arts, and informally observing daily life, to be struck, not in a romanticized or missionary zeal way, but in a very real, existential way, by these marginalized children's passion for life, their resilience, and—indeed—their promise or human potential. Taking an existential view and showing affection, offering a hand, a lap, a story, or just a warm handshake were vital connections for both the children and for me. Getting out-of-school children back into school or enrolled in vocational programs was a major agenda of our volunteer organization, but I found that the arts program and the use of dance, drama, song, and visual arts (drawing, painting, and wood carving) were powerful antidotes to life of and on the streets. I use this brief example to underscore my intent that we view *all children as children "at promise,"* however privileged or difficult their circumstances may be.

It is also critical for readers to understand that this deconstruction of the discourse of risk is not merely emantic, nor is it a panacea for the increasingly difficult circumstances of children, as documented powerfully in reports such as *The State of the World's Children* each year by UNICEF, in Bernard van Leer reports (e.g., Ayre, 1996), and many other publications with which you are familiar. Those of us who fight for educational equity must not lose sight of the multiple forces that converge in a brutal assault against children, particularly poor children and children of nondominant culture backgrounds, as they seek the mandated knowledge, differentially packaged, in our schools. Advocacy for and with children and families is extremely urgent in these times and stronger alliances between educators and families—particularly families who are socially excluded—offer promise for a more inclusive and equitable future. We must find the will and the character to view all children through the lens of promise.

I conclude with the words of an eight-year-old Mexican-American writer, who many would describe as "at risk." She has been empowered as a writer through participation in a bilingual family literacy program and "recreates the event of her birth in universal and mythological symbols, emphasizing the central role of her family" (Quintero & Rummel, 1995):

On the day I was born the earth shook and the angels wept.
On the day I was born the sky turned green, the clouds turned orange.
On the day I was born, they discovered Atlantis.
And books overflowed my house.
On the day I was born the earth was clean and there was peace.
On the day I was born my family scampered in to see me.
On the day I was born the sun fell in love with the moon.

In making a strong case for reconstructing our views and the language used to talk about children at the margins of our various societies and educational institutions, we must not forget to listen to the voices of children and to honestly interrogate our own biases, or we will never be able to hear their pride or see their promise.

I would like to acknowledge the significant influence of the activist scholarship of Professor Valerie Polakow on this chapter and on my work. Her contributions are evident throughout the chapter, particularly those sections addressing welfare devolution and its impact on single mothers and their children.

Note: This chapter is based on a paper presented at "Human Dignity and Social Exclusion: Educational Policies in Europe" Conference, Athens, October 2–4, 1997, sponsored by the Council of Europe and the "Nikos Poulantzas" Society.

CHAPTER EIGHT

Native American Perspectives: Connected to One
Another and to the Greater Universe

Nila M. Rinehart
Blue Sage Community Partners

An imaginary Tlingit blanket, red and black with abalone shell buttons formed in the shape of her mother's bear clan; her friends; a remembered piece of a Tlingit song, "ya ha oo way, ya ha oo way, ya haa oo way, ya ha oo way...and she makes proud dance and song for herself and her friends at recess. She is 6 and in kindergarten, and she is Tlingit.

To grow to their fullest potential, Native American children need strong and loving families and communities who care for their needs. Equally important, tribal children need a careful balance of teachings about their traditions, tribal values, and languages. Tribal children need to experience and recognize that their center of strength and identity comes from feeling and understanding the sacred meanings behind their tribal practices. While learning to understand their tribal heritage, Native American children are also gifted learners of academic skills. Tribal children need an academic learning environment that nurtures their natural curiosity and their path to knowing. This balanced preparation of Native American children fully enables them to participate in their place in Native American communities as well as in the larger world community. Practice and preparation in their cultural traditions together with a strong academic preparation helps them to understand and participate in their rightful place in our universe.

The National Association for the Education of Young Children's position statement on linguistic and cultural diversity emphasizes that for optimal development and learning for all children to occur, educators and society must accept the legitimacy of children's home language and value the child's home culture. The position statement recognizes that the language and culture of the home is what children have learned and used since birth. The child's foundation of home language and culture is used to establish meaningful relationships and the experiences they have had are used to form their knowledge and their learning. Parents and educators must operationalize this statement by investing energy and resources into making it happen.

Understanding the influence of culture and language on a child's development seems very complex, yet children understand this profound premise. Tribal children understand the significance of their cultural practices and struggle to make meaning for themselves. They intuitively know and understand the sacredness of tribal custom.

He stands in a buckskin colored canvas tipi, his hands cupped very slightly before him, his eyes are full and reverent as he waits to accept the cedar smoke blessing offered to him by his grandfather. No one tells him this is what he must do, yet he intuitively knows and understands the sacredness and significance of this moment. He is 5 and he is Taos Pueblo. And now he is 13 and this same young man says when he feels alone and scared that all he has to think about are the mountains behind his grandfather's house because he knows from time immemorial, it is the place where his grandmothers and grandfathers went to pray. He knows that this place is where he can gather courage.

From a very early age, some could argue before birth, many tribal children are taught about their connection to the world. They are taught to honor the reverence of tribal practices and they are taught to think of themselves as connected to one another and to the greater universe. This interconnectedness is essential for tribal children's social and emotional development, and it is the centerpiece for the development of the self. Language, culture, and the home environment tell children who they are and how to construct their learning. It is from these incredible eyes that tribal children see and interpret their world.

Historical Pain

Just as many minorities in the United States have suffered great discrimination in the educational system, the historical record for educating tribal children has been a devastating account. Whole generations of Native American children, uprooted from their home environments, were moved into boarding schools, and targeted for assimilation into the dominant society's traditions, values, and languages. While some children were stolen from loving families and communities, others were willingly sent by their families and communities to learn and bring back new knowledge to help Native communities gain back what was being lost. These children and families paid a great price for a nation's unwillingness to accept diversity and flat-out greed for the rich lands and natural resources held by Indian nations. These simple words on pages do this whole period of Native American life injustice because this period brought so much pain and suffering to many Native children, families, communities, and nations.

In deliberate defiance of this vehement effort to annihilate Native cultures and languages, Native American people are ever persistent to keep instilling in their children the important and time immemorial values that make them tribal children. Educators working with Native American children, families, communities, and nations will need to learn how to better prepare their teaching practices and learning environments because recognition of tribal cultures and languages will continue to get stronger and Native people are going to become more persistent and forward in demanding change. Albert Kookesh, Alaska state representative and respected Tlingit tribal leader made this remark concerning the Alaska Native subsistence issue in a 1998 Native issues forum sponsored by the Central Council of the Tlingit and Haida Indian Tribes of Alaska.

> We've tried to work with the Senate and House leadership, to try and bring a good closure to the subsistence issue, to uphold the indigenous rights of Alaska Native people to hunt, fish, and subsist as we have always done, but it appears as if the closure will not be beneficial to Alaska Natives or to the State as a whole. I keep telling my fellow policy-makers that they better get along with and work things out with today's Native, because we're nicer and willing to work things out so that there is a win-win ending. I tell them this, my friends, because tomorrow's Native will be smarter, more educated, better grounded in their culture, more experienced, and less willing to be nice and wait for others to make decisions for them. Tomorrow's Natives will be lawyers, politicians, teachers, scientists, and engineers, and all of them will be leaders and will be connected to the Native cause.

We will have to come to terms with the challenge of preparing ourselves to better serve Indian children and families because the patience for tolerance is being lost.

Constructing the Native American Learning Environment

Given what we know about Native children and the values placed on culture and language, how do educators construct the learning environment to help Native children use these strengths to succeed?

Culturally appropriate learning environment. The need for Native children to understand their own culture, language, and connection to the tribal community is no different than the need all children have to acquire a sense of belonging. For Native children this means that it is important that they be consistently exposed to their culture, language, and history throughout their learning years. This process must begin in the earliest years, beginning first with the family and community. Then, continuity is established when this special learning is reinforced and continued through early education programs, and later in elementary and secondary schools.

Politics of language and culture. Teaching or integrating Native culture and languages in schools is a politically and emotionally sensitive issue in most Native American communities. There has been so much loss and psychological trauma associated with this issue that many people are angry, concerned, and are cautious about new initiatives. These attitudes especially exist toward schools because they are the primary vehicles for socialization and, therefore, assimilation. Native parents and families care about their children's success and work at providing the best for them. Because of this inherent need to protect and to ensure that their children can fully participate in the outside world, many parents have been socialized to believe that teaching English first is the best goal for their children even when it risks the loss of the home language. Overt and covert discrimination is very real and very much alive. When an Indian child learns to be grounded in tribal traditions and languages, their speech patterns are different and they think and interact in a different way. It is this difference that is often shunned by those with ignorant attitudes and knowledge. Lastly, many Indian communities refuse to let the schools become a place where language and culture are taught, because culture and language are the responsibility of the family. There are many, many solid reasons why educators should not integrate the language and culture of Native children into the school setting. However, there are many more reasons why responsible educators should. A beginning approach is to engage Native people and to begin talking about a plan to support Native children to succeed and to learn about how best to integrate their language and culture in the schools.

How Native children learn. There have been many debates across the nation about how Native American children learn. Some educators assert that Indian children have particular learning styles that are more characterized as right-brained. Some learning styles often seen in Indian children include a greater capacity for artistic expression and symbolism; conceptualizing from a holistic framework, whole to part, rather than from fragments and pieces. Right-brained dominant strengths include musical, visual/spatial, and intuitive characteristics. As with any theory, we should be cautioned that concentration on these learning styles must not diminish the individuality of Native children because they are all very unique. This information is another piece among many to consider when planning a developmentally appropriate learning environment for Native children. Planning deliberate classroom environments that are developmentally appropriate, individualized, and rich with carefully planned experiential activities is essential for young Native children.

Outcomes for Native children. Before a teacher can facilitate learning, the teacher must know what learning objectives and outcomes are expected. For many years schools and teachers developed their own outcomes. These outcomes were based on the teacher and school's culture and values. In order to facilitate learning for Native children, teachers and schools need to know what a successful Native child will be like once the child has gone through the educational system. What skills will he/she possess, what things will he/she be able to do in life, what things will he/she have experienced? Only the parents, extended family, communities, and nations into which Native children are born can answer these questions. In early education programs, Head Start has taken the lead in determining educational outcomes by instituting locally developed plans. These plans are used as a tool to document, for the community and program, the kinds of skills, abilities, hopes, and dreams parents and families have for their children, and what kind of commitment the Head Start program will have to fulfill the need. Teachers and schools can only expect participation and support from families and communities if the family and community's priorities become the teacher and school's priorities.

Many Native communities are documenting their tribal values so that families, schools, and communities can facilitate learning in a way that respects and activates important values that help children succeed. In this way, the community begins to voice the things that make Native children unique.

Teacher and school administrator hire. Teachers and school administrators should reflect the population of children and families. It is important for children to see that their school includes caring adults from their own families and communities. Equally important, parents and families need to be reassured that their children are learning in a way that is familiar to them and that someone understands their family's history, values, and languages. Too many times, schools use lack of qualified culturally diverse teachers as an excuse to not hire teachers and administrators that reflect their communities. If unwillingness continues to be a problem then the community must take action by whatever means is necessary to change the climate so that schools hire appropriate staff.

Family and community partnerships. Native parents and community leaders must be involved in decision making in early education programs. Head Start again leads the way by assuring that programs enhance and utilize family and community partnerships so that there is community involvement in policy making. Empowering families means working in partnership with them to jointly make the best decisions possible for the well-being of Native children.

Tests and assessments. Now more than ever, early childhood education programs and educational systems must prove their effectiveness. Accountability is often measured by standardized achievement tests that are not designed to measure true child outcomes. These tests can be harmful to children if they are interpreted and used in the wrong way. For example, standardized tests were normed according to Caucasian middle-class children, and these tests measure values and learning priorities from those perspectives. In addition to biased tests, too often teaching to the test becomes an acceptable practice. Lastly, news of poor test scores among Native children seriously undermines the dignity of Native children, their families, communities, and nations. Educators must be careful about how standardized tests and assessments are delivered and used.

Anti-biased environment. There is so much in our society that gives Native American children a bad view of themselves. Hollywood films, storybooks, posters, and television shows tell people who Native Americans are or should be. Because of the tremendous power of stereotypes in mass media and from inappropriate distinctions made by native neighbors, educators must actively provide an anti-biased environment where inappropriate things are challenged, always. When we let biased comments slide or choose not to address inaccurate information or beliefs, we silently approve and accept untruths.

Self-reflection. In order to teach children, especially children from different cultural and linguistic backgrounds, teachers must know themselves. We all come from different places in life. Our experiences are different, and these experiences have an enormous impact on our belief systems and in the way we process information. Our beliefs are our own and may not be shared by people with different experiences. No belief system is the true or right one because all perspectives are different and are important. As teachers, it's important to know where our belief systems come from so we don't inappropriately force ours on others who have important perspectives that help us to learn and think in new ways.

Research and development. When working with Native American children and families, it's critically important to use research as a tool to help better practice. However, there have been few studies that focus specifically on Native American children. We are such a small percentage of the population that we are often left out. When studies are brought about, we are forced to make comparisons across tribal groups, which can be very problematic. For example, although there are many similarities among American Indian and Alaska Native tribal groups, we are also very different. Native American and Alaska Native people speak different languages, some of them are written, but most are not. Our tribal histories are different. We live in small rural communities and large urban ones. We live in close-knit tribal communities, but many of us do not. Our social systems are structured differently as are our governments. Lastly, there are always differences, even among families that are affected by demographics, socioeconomic status, and many other variables. All of these issues make research and the interpretation of research extremely difficult.

Finances. Although educators know and understand the importance of, and interdependence of, children's home culture and language with learning, little financial resources are provided to support language and cultural knowledge and the connection between tribal traditional concepts and Western thought in children's learning. Meanwhile, schools and communities watch as Native American children continue to score in the lowest percentiles on standard achievement tests and begin to drop out of schools before they are ready. These "failures" tell a much different story to parents and communities who know their children as exceptional and gifted children. Native American children that have been immersed in traditional practices are taught according to tribal values and have many kinds of intelligences; they come to schools as perfect children. We must stop our practice of blaming Indian children and families for our own failures to provide appropriate learning systems. Our wealthy nation has to find the means to support all children and their families by providing adequate resources for home language and culture to be a significant part of schools.

What would it look like if it were done right? If I had it my way, Native children would be attending community-based early care and education programs or would be learning in their own homes. Native children would be learning with and among Native teachers and administrators. They would predominately speak their Native language until they were proficient, and when they were developmentally ready, they would learn English. They would learn English well because they would have had a firm foundation and competence in their home language. They would practice and participate in their tribal ceremonies and family and community activities only when they are developmentally capable of doing so.

They would feel like they belonged. Their parents and grandparents, aunts and uncles, cousins and neighbors, would care for them. Every adult would be invested in every child's upbringing. The tribal community as well as the broader world would put children first and care for their basic needs as well as provide the extra essentials for developing happy and healthy children. These promises would be kept by action and not by empty words.

These young children would attend well-provisioned and safe, aesthetically beautiful early care and education programs that were specifically designed for their tribal community. The curriculum would incorporate everyday life in a way a young child understands. The curriculum would be individualized for the community, it would be experiential, and it would help develop their physical, cognitive, social, emotional, environmentalism, spiritual, and artistic skills. The learning environment and significant adults would nourish the child's individual and communal spirit. The children would be read to in their home language as well as in English.

These Native children would have the best-trained teachers and administrators. These experts would know and understand what these particular children need in order to grow to their inherent abilities, and they would use every resource to ensure that the children received what they needed. The whole early care and education environment would be based on the individual child and community's strengths and assets.

Young children would move into a primary school environment that complemented and continued to grow from the primary value that Native children are incredibly gifted children. Exceptional teaching practices, and family and community involvement would continue in the primary school setting. Children would continue to excel and learn and grow to their best abilities.

These methods are not impossible goals. Tribal nations must realize the essential gift that children bring to our futures. We must learn to nourish every child by providing every essential that children need to grow and thrive in our world. The broader community must understand that there is not one right and true way and that many perspectives are desirable and are necessary for survival and growth. We must all realize that the only thing stopping us from providing young Indian children with the essential things they need to grow and learn so they can assume their rightful place in our world is ourselves.

CHAPTER NINE

Redefining Child Care and Early Education in a Diverse
Society: Dialogue and Reflection

Hedy Nai-Lin Chang
Amy Muckelroy
Dora Pulido-Tobiassen
Carol Dowell
California Tomorrow

You don't ever "finish" with culture and diversity issues. They continue
to surface in human relationships. It's forever. Part of the problem is that we
don't have good ways in childcare programs to sustain ongoing
exploration of any issues. (Marcy Whitebook, Founder of the National
Center for the Early Childhood Workforce)

There has to be some way of looking at what it means to say that diversity
is a high priority. What does that really mean? Is it a question about human
value? Are you thinking about setting up a situation in the classroom
where you believe every person in the classroom is trying to be as good as
they can possibly be or achieve whatever is available for them in terms of
their own human potential? As a first step you would have to do a lot of
talking about what you mean. (Mary Cardenas, Cabrillo Community
College)

Trust and communication develop over time, so there has to be a
commitment made in terms of time and money to offering ongoing
opportunities to build that trust and communication...I don't know that
people can successfully jump over a horrendous value conflict or cultural
conflict if they haven't invested any energy prior to that in communication
and trust. People need to have time to learn about each other, as well as to
go over what the program is going to be. (Melinda Sprague, Reducing
Exceptional Stress and Trauma Project)

Open and ongoing dialogue about race, language, and culture—as they
relate to the children in care, their families, and the practices of
caregivers—is crucial for programs to effectively and positively address diversity issues.

Implicit in all of this work is the need for continual, thoughtful
dialogue and personal reflection. California Tomorrow, in its own
experience as an organization committed to equity, as well as in its

work with other educational and community institutions, has learned that a habit of open communication about race, culture, and language is the foundation for any successful effort to address diversity. No strategy or policy can be fully effective without this foundation.

Becoming aware of our own identity as individuals, our own beliefs, values, and philosophy, is key to addressing issues when they arise with children in the care setting. So, too, is understanding that the views and values of other providers or families may be different based on their life experiences. Examining and discussing our own biases is critical in a program—each person's own biases, where they came from, how to become more aware of them, and how to prevent perpetuating bias in the classroom. Eleanor Clement Glass of the San Francisco Foundation said:

> What are the harmful things you bring and how does the harm manifest itself? It is also important for people to understand that they have been hurt themselves by biases and to share, on the emotional level, how it plays out in human interaction. I think people need to get back to their own feelings of hurt in order to start understanding others' hurt. Everybody has experienced that.

The most important and accessible resources for discussions on issues of diversity are the adults connected to a program. There is a wealth of knowledge and experience among the teachers and parents waiting to be tapped into. Sometimes we don't even realize that we have a particular opinion or viewpoint until we come into contact with someone who sees the world differently. We may have a gut reaction but aren't able to explain it until we have had the practice of telling it to someone else. People who recognize how their beliefs are grounded in their background are less inclined to judge others negatively. Rather, they will weigh the information to see if their own approach may be enhanced, or consider whether they may be doing something wrong. Fully exploring different cultural styles of caregiving can also help people understand that not all practices can or should be universally applied.

Dialogue about diversity is important in any setting, whether or not the children and staff are very diverse. A homogeneous or ethnic-specific center has just as much need to examine and clarify program philosophies, practices, and policies regarding race, language, and culture, and how bias and prejudice are to be addressed with children and among staff. Such dialogue may not be considered as pressing when most staff and families are from the same racial, cultural, or linguistic group and everyone seems to be alike. People may have a more difficult time, for example, articulating how culture influences their lives and how they care for children when there is no apparent contrasting culture in the environment. However, through sharing and discussion, a staff which appears to be all of the same background will learn that there are variations within the group. National origin, religious beliefs, economic class, gender, sexual orientation, as well as race, culture, and language will vary even among people who appear to be the same.

It is also just as important to create vehicles for dialogue whether the childcare setting is large or small. For example, family childcare providers, who typically work alone or with one or two staff members, can greatly benefit from utilizing networks and associations to engage with other providers in discussions about diversity issues.

Programs should strive to create an atmosphere where diversity is discussed routinely, and where ongoing reaming by all of the adults—caregivers and parents—is fostered. In the ideal atmosphere, people are encouraged to ream, to trust and support one another, to feel that it is safe to make mistakes while working to understand diversity issues, and to make it a habit to notice and discuss matters as they arise. A few of the programs visited by California Tomorrow had achieved atmospheres of open communication, and many other programs were working toward this goal. Providers and trainers offered a variety of thoughts on the value of dialogue and how to sustain it.

The Benefits of Creating an
Atmosphere of Open and Ongoing Dialogue

Several teachers at Live Oak Migrant Head Start, a program of primarily Mexican and Punjabi staff and families, talked about their efforts to create openness among their staff to sharing experiences and reaming about one another. Teacher Carmen Arredondo described how one of the Punjabi teachers brought her wedding sari to share with her colleagues. The dress inspired a conversation among staff about wedding traditions in their countries and the symbolism of the colors used in different rituals. At Live Oak, this type of dialogue took place informally during staff meetings and also more extensively during the planning of curriculum themes around culture. Carmen talked about the conditions necessary for this type of comfortable exchange:

> Most importantly, we respect each other, so we are able to exchange
> information. We see a lot of similarities among the two cultures, despite the

differences. We feel comfortable asking each other questions. We really appreciate one another. We are also role modeling for the children and parents.

Another teacher, Balwinder Singh, continued to describe the open and supportive atmosphere among the teachers at Live Oak: "One person will say, This is what we do in our culture. Do you do the same thing?" Then we share it with other staff or parents. It is easy."

Opening up to coworkers is not always an easy thing to do. But it can be made less difficult if trust is created so that each person in the group will genuinely try to learn from others, forgive mistakes, and not misuse what others say. One trainer said that too often fear prevents innovation:

> People are so afraid of making mistakes...because of not wanting to hurt someone or offend someone or appear to be racist, or appear to not know or not to do it right. When you get to application, you have to be willing to make some mistakes. You have to be willing to try it.

Eric Peterson, one of the codirectors at Step One School, a center committed to an anti-bias philosophy, talked about how important it has been to foster an atmosphere where people realize that it is acceptable to take risks when talking to each other and asking questions: "Through our mistakes—that's where the learning is happening."

Janis Keyser, an instructor at Cabrillo College, noted that in the most fruitful dialogue, people listen carefully and trust that they will also be heard:

> Listening is not just a tool we can use to get information which can help us come up with common solutions. It is also a statement to the speakers that who they are as people is important to us. It is a way of bonding. It is a way of valuing people's experiences.

One of the primary benefits of dialogue in a program is the development of deeper understandings of the complexities of race, culture, ethnicity, bias, home language, and other concepts. Through this kind of dialogue, we can also sometimes best learn more about ourselves. For example, Eleanor Clement Glass talked about how difficult it can be to identify and articulate how culture affects our own lives. We are "swimming around" in our cultures, she said, so that it is sometimes hard to see what is cultural about the way we behave and what we believe. To help sort through this, she said: "It's best to juxtapose your culture with other cultures, and to discuss the various points of view and then where those points of view came from."

Eleanor stressed the importance of talking about the nuances and variety of experiences within a racial, cultural, or linguistic group as well:

> All African Americans are not alike and all are not going to have the same experience. Culture is not monolithic. When people have the opportunity to talk about it, that helps to break up the monolithic perceptions they have about other cultures, and to begin to understand it when they do have a monolithic perception about a culture and where it came from.

Carmen Arredondo at Live Oak told us that reflecting on the individual experiences of the teachers in the program has heightened her understanding of the cultural differences in childcare:

> We have children whose parents were born and raised in the States and children whose parents were raised in Mexico. Even though we are all Latinos we understand that we care for our children differently.

Ardella Dailey, adjunct faculty with Pacific Oaks College and an administrator with the Alameda Unified School District, said that personal reflection and dialogue have helped her sort through her questions about different childrearing values:

> There are parenting styles which are authoritarian, versus permissive, versus empowering. How I really accept and respect a culture that doesn't have my values and approach it is difficult. I know I impose more than I should—but then, I don't know, because there are things I can't go along with. And it is possible that they are about a cultural difference and not about right or wrong. I've found that to be my most difficult personal struggle. I find that if you are not dialoguing it internally, let alone externally with other people, then you don't address it at all or you reactively address it without careful thought.

If people feel included and respected, open communication and dialogue about diversity will enhance the sense of community and trust within a program. Building this sense of a team has wide-reaching benefits. Specifically regarding diversity issues, providers cannot only grow to rely upon others within the program, but become open to reaching out to extended networks for information and support. Mary Cardenas at Cabrillo Community College addressed this issue:

> If we don't have the answer, especially if it is not something particular to our own background and experiences, there are ways to call on the expertise of one another and not to sit and stew in isolation.

In a program that incorporates vehicles for communication about diversity, problems have a better chance of being prevented or defused before becoming destructive. Melinda Sprague talked about the need to have this foundation in place:

> If a crisis occurs, you already have the tools to handle it. If you don't do that stuff on an ongoing basis and you have a big problem come up, that's when people go underground and you have parking lot conversations where nothing gets resolved.

Finally, the most fundamental reason to engage in ongoing communication is the benefit it can bring to the children in care. Teachers who are comfortable talking about these issues will be more prepared to proactively respond to incidents in the classroom and to answer questions from children about race, culture, language, bias, and differences. Teachers will be better able to use such incidents as teaching moments, rather than be silent or silence the children. Julie Olsen Edwards of Cabrillo Community College said she "tries to get people to move through the walls of silence."

> The key is breaking the silence. What is ineffective with children is whatever people won't talk about. If the grown-ups are so immobilized, there is no way children will work their way through it. The worst things children carry are secrets. Nothing is more damaging, putting up huge blocks to their thinking and rigidity to their souls. The key thing is an atmosphere where the issues of bias, fear and differences are part of the conversation.

Building Personal Foundations for Dialogue

Among individuals that California Tomorrow interviewed who have closely focused on diversity in their work, several attributed their ability to think and talk critically about diversity to their own strong sense of cultural and racial identity. The process of understanding cultural and racial identity is different for every individual. Programs striving for effective communication can encourage individuals to think about and share what the process has been like for them. This can contribute to a sense of community and help individuals think about the sources of their beliefs and values.

Janet Gonzalez-Mena, who teaches at Napa Valley College and has written extensively about cross-cultural issues in childrearing, shared how important it was for her to come to terms with her identity as a white European American woman:

I realized early on who I had to focus on. One of the steps I had to take was to accept myself and my culture, to discover I had a culture. About the time I discovered that, I didn't like it very much. I thought maybe I could be somebody else. I do remember the day it hit me that I am who I am, and it is really okay. That was an exciting time for me and I've been working on reaming more about my culture and its roots since then.

Intesar Shareef, an instructor at Contra Costa Community College, found that being involved in the Nation of Islam contributed to her pride in, and connection to, others of her race and culture:

I spent seven years of my life in the Nation of Islam, in a Black separatist organization. So I was very steeped in an experience that elevated the Black experience. I saw Black people in positions of authority—uncompromisingly…People from communities that have been historically targeted, marginalized or oppressed need to be strengthened in their minority status. They have to connect in that marginal status to see their own strength and then to emerge from it. I don't think it has to last forever. As a matter of fact, from my own experience, I don't think it does.

Individuals will have experiences throughout their lives that contribute to their understandings and emotions about race, language, and culture. Childcare programs alone cannot be responsible for ensuring that teachers understand these issues, but they can provide a valuable service to adults and children as a safe and supportive place to begin the exploration.

There are several specific strategies we identified that programs can use to ensure ongoing and productive dialogue. Above all, adults in the program need to be encouraged to engage in discussion and exploration about race, culture, and language, and to work from a framework that diversity in our society is a valuable asset. What follows is a description of strategies for helping to create ongoing dialogue and reflection:

1. Create activities to engage people in discussions.
2. Develop facilitation skills.
3. Create the time and opportunity for dialogue.
4. Include diverse perspectives in discussions.

The challenges associated with dialogue are often daunting, including the fear of saying something that will make things worse, and the lack of quality time, facilitation, and other resources for childcare providers to discuss many important topics. Because the challenges are interrelated and apply to most strategies, we discuss them together at the end of this chapter, in a small departure from the format of previous principles.

PROMISING STRATEGIES

Strategy 1

Create activities to engage people in discussions.

"What is your earliest memory of noticing someone was different than you?" "What childhood messages did you get about differences and how you should view people who are different than you?" Sharing stories at an adult level or reviewing differences that exist among the staff in an open climate does a lot to alert people to how they need to think about these issues for kids. People get a heightened awareness of how young they were and how sharp the images still are for them. (Margie Carter, Author and Trainer)

There are a variety of strategies groups can use to spark self-reflection and discussions about diversity. A structured activity can help take the awkwardness *out* of broaching these subjects, open up new ways of thinking, or provide avenues for sharing information or lessons. Here are a few tools to direct and enhance the discussion, whether in a single program or across programs.

Sharing Life Stories

Sharing life stories, values, and beliefs is important for many reasons. It can help to create a safe and trusting environment. It can help in identifying ways in which the program can use the resources and expertise represented among the staff. And it can help individuals to clarify how race, language, and culture are interrelated in their own lives and caregiving styles.

The *Anti-Bias Curriculum* strategies described in our Principle on Race give an example of how dialogue can be inspired through the sharing of life experiences. California Tomorrow has used "journey maps" to encourage personal sharing. Participants draw a map, or some representation using pictures and words, of their personal journey that shaped their views on race, language, and culture. They then share their map with others, describing why they took certain roads. We used this technique at a retreat with a group of teachers and directors of centers whom we had visited for this research.

Participants were asked to share their maps with someone they thought would have an interesting point of view or who they wanted to know more. One of the pairs was two African-American women, one the director of a program with a multicultural philosophy, and the other the director of a program with an African American focus. Earlier in the day, the two had a debate about the merits of their respective approaches. After they had a chance to talk about their journey maps with each other, they shared their conclusion with the larger group: "We are much more alike than we are different." The process led them to appreciate how their individual strategies were leading toward the same ultimate goal.

Trainer Margie Carter, who directed a program with a diverse staff, told us some of the ways she tried to encourage and facilitate dialogue about differences, bias, and practice.

> We devoted time in every weekly staff meeting to try to recognize and hear and listen to the different life experiences and the reasons we approach things differently. Some of these discussions are described in the "Honoring Diversity" chapter in the book Alike and Different. We started with simple, concrete things like, "What did you do in your family when someone had a cold?" which built up trust, interest and curiosity in each other. When we got to the more heated issues of race, and of lesbian and gay staff members, people had already developed a sense of trust and respect and were willing to look at things in new ways, to look at their own racism and homophobia. But it took this very strong commitment to look at this, talk about this, also to learn to get the conflict on the table and not be afraid. Then we looked at the implications of what we were discussing. Things would come up and we would recognize the inconsistency between what we said we believed in and what our actual policy or practice was. It was center-wide heightened awareness and focus of growth for all of us. Seeing each other as really valuable resources, we rarely brought in an outside person. We created the climate internally to recognize the expertise among each other. It was not without its anchor in tears, but we felt okay about that.

Videos

There are a variety of videos on the market that address diversity in the early childhood care setting. One is *Essential Connections: Ten Keys to Culturally Sensitive Child Care* by the Program for Infant/Toddler Caregivers at Far West Laboratory for Educational Research and Development. *Ten Keys,* said Eleanor Clement Glass, "is the very first thing I've seen that illustrates how to begin those negotiations, to identify areas and raise them" among a group of providers. Dialogue can be sparked regarding how the issues raised in the video are affecting a program. In the Early Childhood Training

Diversity Video Series coordinated by Janet Gonzalez Mena for Magna Systems, Inc., a group of providers and professional development trainers of diverse backgrounds explores diverse childrearing practices through role play and discussion. According to Laura Mason Zeisler, a multicultural and anti-bias trainer, "the videos give viewers a lens through which to view their own practices and to consider other ways of addressing the many issues related to an anti-bias approach."

There are also videos available that focus on issues of race, language, and culture, not specifically in early childhood education, but still very useful for program staff who wish to begin to identify their own biases. The video *The Color of Fear,* produced by Stir Fry Productions, can also inspire thought-provoking dialogue. Both of these videos are used in structured workshops where skilled facilitators lead the groups in discussions about the issues raised.

Reading Materials

Julie Olsen Edwards assigns her students at Cabrillo College to read novels about the experiences of people of color growing up in America. Novels are a wonderful way to gain insights into cultures other than one's own and raise questions in readers' minds that can lead to a rich discussion. Manuel Garcia, the director at Plaza Community Center in East Los Angeles, regularly asked staff to read interesting and provocative articles that they discuss at staff meetings. Staff members also bring in articles they think would be of interest to their peers, and they take turns presenting and facilitating the discussion. Case studies, research, children's stories, magazine articles, and other types of reading materials can also stimulate rich dialogue.

Anecdotes From the Classroom

Every day, providers "live" stories and observe examples of ways in which culture, race, language, and bias emerge in the early care setting. If time is taken to focus on some of those anecdotes and to analyze their implications for the program, everyone can ream.

Role Play

Step One School sometimes uses role playing to help teachers gain the skills to address bias in the classroom. Sue Britson, the co-director at Step One School, talked about how role play can increase teachers' willingness to implement the curriculum while strengthening their skills. For example, when a child or adult says something inappropriate or prejudiced, Britson says, "It is easy to pretend it did not happen, to ignore it, to [fail to] deal with it—or even see it." Teachers are asked to bring examples of any incidents like this from their classrooms to the staff meetings. Staff may first get into small groups to discuss the incident, and the ways in which the teacher might have responded. Then some of the teachers role play the incident, acting out some of the suggested strategies generated by the small group discussions.

Question of the Week

An innovation for bringing awareness of diversity issues to the forefront on an everyday basis is to post a question of the week, or a short scenario in the staff room or somewhere staff can read it. Margie Carter uses this strategy to provoke discussion and offer staff new resources, with the understanding that they will commit to doing the work of exploring the questions.

Strategy 2

Provide Appropriate Facilitation.

Activities such as those listed above are helpful for creating opportunities to share, ream, reflect, and analyze race, language, and culture in people's lives and work. Often, however, it is also important for groups to pay attention to how to facilitate the discussions that can be sparked through these types of activities. Dialogue about equity and diversity can be intense and raise conflict. If participants have a bad experience participating in a discussion around diversity, they may not learn from the interaction and may resist future attempts to create a dialogue.

A variety of strategies can be used to ensure that a conversation is appropriately facilitated.

Adopt Group Practices that Facilitate Dialogue

Groups can adopt certain practices that increase the capacity of a group to engage in a productive dialogue with mutual respect. For example, it is often helpful if a group develops a set of ground rules by which everyone agrees to abide. Ground rules clearly state agreements between participants about how to conduct a meeting or event. Ground rules can be very helpful in creating an atmosphere where everyone's voice can be heard and positive dialogue can occur. Confidentiality, for example, is an important condition for dialogue about sensitive issues. When written down for everyone to see, ground rules become a record of the group's values about how to discuss issues. Such a record is a useful reminder for staff or parents who have been with a program for a while and a helpful orientation for new people.

At Step One School, staff have developed ground rules for meetings, which include "Use respectful terms," "No one speaks twice on a topic until everyone has had input," and "Try to keep your statements reflecting personal respect and sensitivity." Codirector Eric Peterson explains that the ground rules were developed through trial and error. As the program grew more experienced in talking about anti-bias and diversity issues, they began to develop the ground rules. They periodically revisit the list to see whether the group is abiding by the ground rules and whether there is a need to add or make changes to the list.

Another approach is to create opportunities for the group to assess what works and how an event could be improved. Ardella Dailey observes:

> We need to let people know it is a process [and that it won't always go right]. I have found teachers who even reflect with children. "How did the day go?" "What do you think we could have done differently?" and "Why did it work for you—or didn't it?" And, three-year-olds can tell you very clearly. Reflection is essential whether it is with children or adults because it opens you up for a diversity of style.

Time for debriefing and reflection is important because it allows a group to hear and draw upon the diverse perspectives of participants. It also creates a forum for people to express and address concerns and misunderstandings so that issues do not fester in the background. Groups can create these opportunities in a variety of ways. They can, for example, leave five minutes at the end of the meeting to review how it went. Evaluation forms can also be used as a mechanism for feedback, especially if there is an opportunity for the group to hear about the results and how concerns will be addressed.

Identify and Designate a Facilitator

Groups should identify people who are willing and able to take on the responsibility of facilitating a conversation or meeting to ensure that the discussion is productive. Typical facilitator tasks include making sure that everyone has an opportunity to express their opinion, creating and following an agenda, making sure the ground rules are understood and honored, helping the group to identify areas of consensus and recognize disagreements, and defusing tense situations. Sometimes, responsibility for facilitation is designated to one person. It can also be shared, provided the designated facilitators have time to plan how they work together.

Clearly designating to the group which person will facilitate is important. Individuals who take on this role often need time to plan how they will manage a meeting. Clarity of the facilitator's role is also important for group dynamics, to help ensure he or she has the authority to guide the process. Otherwise, participants may misinterpret attempts to facilitate as dominating or controlling. People also appreciate having someone to whom it is acceptable to direct comments about the process or the agenda. Facilitators need to let the group know whether and how they themselves will partake in the dialogue.

Facilitating can be difficult. Several directors we interviewed said that they wanted *to* have more staff discussions around issues about diversity, but they were not confident about their facilitation skills, particularly for when situations became emotionally loaded. While facilitation is usually easier for people with strong intuitive and interpersonal skills, the ability to facilitate can be developed through both observation and practice. Groups should think about ways to develop the facilitation and intergroup skills of staff and directors. People can:

1. Attend workshops about facilitation and running effective meetings.
2. Learn by observing and discussing the techniques and strategies used by facilitators running meetings and conferences.
3. Team new staff with experienced facilitators and encourage the experienced staff to share their techniques and thinking.

As a start, it is a good idea to practice facilitating conversations in low-pressure situations. Some organizations, for example, encourage staff to practice facilitation by rotating responsibility for running their staff meetings.

There are times when the director or a staff person should not be the facilitator. It is important for everyone to participate in sensitive conversations, but this is difficult if you are also responsible for guiding the discussion. In some cases, staff or directors should not facilitate because they have a vested interest in the outcome of a conversation. Neutrality of the facilitator helps ensure that all participants feel comfortable expressing their views.

For such cases, programs should identify an appropriate outside facilitator. Paid consultants can be useful. If a program has limited resources, a trusted colleague at another program may be able to facilitate negotiation of a low fee or trade of services. However, outside facilitators should always be selected carefully. Programs should observe prospective facilitators in action or at least obtain references from other groups. Programs should also take some time to reflect on the characteristics they most value in a facilitator. Sometimes the top priority is effectiveness at negotiating issues, other times it is matching interpersonal styles with the staff and director. Particularly if the topic for dialogue is loaded, programs should spend time identifying a consultant with whom everyone feels comfortable.

One of the techniques used in diversity training is to break adults into discussion groups by racial or cultural groups, or by people of color and whites. These exercises can be very fulfilling and thought provoking, allowing participants the chance to reflect on common strengths, personal and professional experiences as members of the group, and individual issues. But experienced facilitation should definitely be sought for exercises such as these. A skilled facilitator needs to be able to both explain to groups the purpose of the exercise, as well as be cognizant that some people may feel uncomfortable in the process. A facilitator should also be prepared to guide participants through difficult emotions or points of disagreement that may arise.

Strategy 3

*Create the Time and Opportunities
for Reflection and Discussion to Take Place.*

> Everything we are talking about requires time and training. Both these things require money. What we are asking child care workers to do is the hardest work that can be done. To ask them on the kind of pay they get, without the training, and with the time pressures they are up against is utterly unrealistic. We have to change these things. Things take time and time has to be made available. Child care workers are in the primary place to

make a difference in family life. (Julie Olsen Edwards)

Talking and learning take time. There are two kinds of opportunities that programs need to maximize for talking and learning about diversity, both of which involve time: "everyday" opportunities and "dedicated time." Both are critical, and dialogue about race, language, and culture must become second nature to the routines of the center.

"Everyday" opportunities are those times during which staff already get together to discuss work-related issues. In most programs, communication takes place daily about the activities and accomplishments of the children. However, this routine exchange does not necessarily delve into individual cultural expectations and assumptions about childrearing or program policies about second language acquisition or bilingualism, among other questions. Each of the following can be an "everyday" opportunity to discuss some aspect of diversity.

1. A standing item in staff meetings focusing on some aspect of diversity.
2. Team/classroom planning meetings.
3. Staff retreats.
4. Staff development workshops/in-service training.
5. Intake and orientation.
6. Everyday in the classroom.
7. Staff evaluations.

Once programs develop a supportive environment and a habit of discussing diversity, staff awareness will grow about the interrelatedness of race, language, culture, and bias—in hiring, enrollment, parent relationships, curriculum, environment, and practice. Thus, opportunities to address diversity issues will arise regularly in meetings and less formal conversations, lessening the need for staff to wait for "separate" or "special" meetings to get to important diversity issues.

Nonetheless, "dedicated time" to focus on diversity issues is still also important—time away from the children, during a professional development session or retreat. Both everyday and dedicated opportunities for dialogue require a work culture that prizes time for adults to spend together for coprofessional development and learning. Childcare workers have not often been afforded this kind of work culture.

Strategy 4

Include Diverse Perspectives in Process.

> Once a program opens itself up to dialogue with the parents, there is almost
> like a loop that develops between the school and the home. The school
> environment becomes sort of a laboratory for teachers to work on ideas they
> can share with parents. The parents also become resources that the teachers
> utilize. There isn't this sort of estranged relationship between the two. That
> cooperation seems to be the greatest asset toward children developing
> healthily. That would be the case anyway, but it's especially true when
> you have parents and teachers who are from different cultural backgrounds.
> (Intesar Shareef, Contra Costa College)

All dialogue, planning, and reaming about race, language, and
culture are enhanced by the inclusion of diverse perspectives. While it
may be the ultimate responsibility of the administration of a program
to make final decisions regarding policy and philosophy, it is still
important for staff and often parents to be a part of the process.
Assistant teachers, teachers, head teachers, and directors all have
important perspectives to offer. If the program has a board of
directors, they, too, should be included in these discussions. The staff
who work directly with the children, and who actually implement the
philosophy and guidelines on a daily basis, must understand and feel
committed to the approach of the program.

Step One School is committed to including parents in the process
of learning about and implementing the *Anti-Bias Curriculum.* The
program organized parents into caucuses that met periodically,
separate from the staff and administration. During those caucus
meetings, parents were able to freely express themselves and to come
to a common understanding of the issues facing parents in that group.
They were also able to strategize about possible solutions. When they
participated in a whole group discussion, the caucus leaders were able
to clearly articulate the needs and concerns of those parents in a
constructive way.

It may be a challenge to include the voices of parents with
different language backgrounds who do not speak English, even if
there are staff who speak their languages. Running a meaningful
discussion in two or more languages is not easy, but it can be done well
if the participants decide it is important and develop strategies to
make it work. This means using effective translators and making sure
to fully translate not only what is said by providers, but what is said by
parents for all to hear.

The more people included in any discussion around race, language, and culture, the more perspectives, fears, hopes, expectations, and experiences will be revealed for incorporation in the work of the program. Tension may arise regarding who to include in discussions about diversity, in analysis of current practices, or in decision-making processes. Each program will have to decide the extent to which parents will be included. It is important to allow for some process by which, at a minimum, parents can give input, because of the important perspectives they can bring.

True, this will open more potential for disagreements and sometimes for misunderstandings and conflict. But this should not deter programs from trying to include the voices of many different stakeholders. The benefits to the quality of care to children outweigh the inconveniences and challenges. There are ways to work through conflict and misunderstandings, such as the use of facilitation techniques and tools.

Challenges to Dialogue

Dialogue about race, language, and culture is usually missing in early childhood education settings—among childcare providers, between providers and parents, and among faculty in college early childhood education departments. Yet, our interviews revealed that people in the field are hungry for dialogue. Caregivers want to give the best care possible to children, but at times they are at a loss as to what cultural, racial, and linguistic differences really mean in terms of caregiving, and what to do regarding differences once they are understood. They want to feel that they can ask coworkers, parents, or community members for advice on how to work with children or families from a particular racial, cultural, or linguistic background. They yearn for opportunities to compare strategies and approaches with colleagues. They value the moments when they can engage in reflection about themselves and their programs. But, we heard repeated again and again that people rarely have the time or opportunity for these exchanges.

Challenge: Overcoming Fear and Hesitation
About Talking About Race, Language, and Culture

Talking about diversity means treading into difficult terrain, causing many to hesitate or remain silent. Carol Brunson Phillips offered the following observation:

> We need to help caregivers be at ease in talking cross-culturally about things that they do not know or understand. The dialogue that could help teachers to be better teachers never happens because the teachers are afraid or don't know how to get the dialogue going. It is the questions we don't ask because we don't want to feel stupid or incompetent or be perceived as racist or ethnocentric...People could learn a lot from each other if they know how to talk to each other. Instead they talk about how to make Playdough or what songs to sing.

People's fears of being misunderstood or of inadvertently offending another person are not unfounded. The field of early care and education is not isolated from the larger social and political dynamics of society. Issues of race, language, and culture have always been loaded, and this is a time of backlash. The current moves to abolish affirmative action, to deny immigrants access to education and social services, and to prevent people from speaking their non-English family languages are polarizing communities. The public debate is far from friendly. People find themselves in situations where even well-intentioned comments, observations, or even questions about race, language, or culture may be perceived by another person as offensive or attacking.

People hesitate to talk about race, culture, and language also because the issues are so very personal; some simply do not feel comfortable discussing them in the workplace. Sue Britson, one of the codirectors at Step One School, realized this when her staff first started working to implement anti-bias principles in their program. There were people who did not want to come to work and be required to share their "childhood stories," and who did not see the direct connection between reflecting on one's background and one's work in the classroom:

> We realized we had to be careful. There is always this tension between personal and professional because we work so much with the heart and the head when working with kids. It takes conscious communication about what is our role as educators, what is going beyond our role, how far do we take things and how much do we have to delve into ourselves?

The discussions can be hard and emotional. Sometimes confrontation will arise. Confrontation does not always fit into some people's vision of a professional culture where, "if you can't say something nice, then you shouldn't say anything at all." Louise Derman-Sparks observed:

> People want to believe in the structure in which they participate. But, if you are going to face racism, you have to come up against the fact that our

society does a lot of hurtful things to people. And that we perpetuate that, even if we don't want to...There are enormous resistance and defenses against facing it. It happens both to white people and people of color. Because what people of color also are facing is some of the internalized oppression that they've bought into. Here is where you get the explosions of emotions—great sadness, pain and anger. How can you think that the institutions you were raised to believe were benign and caring are, in fact, so screwed up without a strong emotional reaction?

Unless people are prepared with skills to face a certain amount of tension and emotion, dialogue is not likely to occur. People who feel uncomfortable or unskilled when dealing with conflict shut down, and those who may want to express a contrary viewpoint feel silenced. De Anza Community College instructor Christina Lopez-Morgan believes:

The real way to change is in the context of relationships that you care about, because those relationships provide the incentives for change. It involves taking the time to understand another person's perspective. Blowing up is part of the process. You need to be able to hang out with your discomfort. It is an essential part of change. If you don't, diversity will only be dealt with at a superficial level.

Coming to an understanding and agreement across cultures—or just between individuals—can be time and energy consuming. Carol Brunson Phillips encourages people to trust in each other's ability to communicate:

I think that if the group is committed to using the conflict situation as an arena to resolve, grow and transform everybody, they can do it. I have a lot of faith in people, even without an expert there to shepherd them through the process. Although expertise in that area is very helpful, I think the answer is among the people at work. The answer is not in any book that I know about. That is why I concentrate on the process, encouraging people to develop an atmosphere at the work site where these issues can be discussed when they come up—naturally—and where there is a commitment to work through them to some resolution, if not solution.

There are some techniques that can reduce people's fears of speaking out. Lorrie Guerrero, a teacher at a Head Start Program in Santa Clara, said that one of her most powerful professional experiences was a week-long session devoted exclusively to African American culture, history, and experience. The consultants emphasized that participants should feel free to ask questions. To reduce fears that people may have been feeling, they placed a box in the room in which participants could drop in any questions they had but were always afraid to ask. They committed to trying to answer them as best they could by the end of the week. This session was then followed later in the year by a week on Latino families and culture.

Challenge: Avoiding Tokenism

Multicultural Issues in Child Care by Janet Gonzalez-Mena speaks to some of the toughest issues around staff diversity and how it is easy for the one person representing a culture to become the "token opinion." This should be avoided by reaching out to find multiple perspectives by people of the same background. A program can draw upon parents, staff at other programs, and even friends and family to add additional points of view to the discussion.

Mary Cardenas suggested a strategy of interviewing parents to diversify the perspectives offered:

> You could do parent interviews so the folks from the staff could find out what parents believe about how children develop and what values parents have for their children—what their goals and wishes are—so there is not just one person who is supposed to represent what every Hispanic believes about children. Each teacher might have an assignment to gather information to bring back to a staff meeting.

Challenge: Extremely Limited Resources

The early childhood field is severely underfunded. All licensed childcare programs have a battery of training activities they must provide to their staff within these limited resources. In many programs, a major reason dialogue does not occur is that resources are not available to set aside additional time for groups to engage in these discussions. Providers receive low wages and many are paid on an hourly basis. Often, meeting time is not compensated, and so the amount of time teachers are able to dedicate to meetings is very limited. Often, centers try to squeeze in meetings during children's nap times, but this is usually not sufficient, particularly if a group intends to address a difficult subject or one that requires the attention of all. Some programs rely heavily upon part-time staff, and schedules are such that there is no time during the day when all of the staff can be present for a meeting.

Given these constraints, very few programs can take advantage of the other types of opportunities for dialogue, such as holding staff retreats or hiring outside trainers or facilitators. Several directors said that even if they could hire a facilitator, they would not know how to find one who would have expertise in these issues.

However, as described above, several programs also found ways to foster an ongoing dialogue using time in staff meetings, encouraging teams to discuss issues in their planning meetings, or posting a question of the week.

Challenge: Staff Turnover

A symptom of the low funding of the childcare field is very high turnover as a whole among teachers. When there is high turnover in a program, even if the program is committed to issues of diversity, there is a need to repeatedly establish a level of trust as the composition of the group changes. Also, when the members of the staff change frequently, people are at different levels of familiarity with the issues. As new teachers arrive into a group that has been discussing diversity in some depth for a time, there is a need to bring that person "up to speed," while at the same time continuing to address difficult issues of diversity.

Louise Derman Sparks believes that the key to overcoming the challenge that turnover creates is to have in place an atmosphere that encourages communication:

> I think that if you've created a culture that allows, encourages and supports this kind of cross-cultural communication, it shouldn't be from scratch [when new staff are hired]. But that is theoretical. You'd have some of the old people sail there; when new people come in you have to start again but at least you are in an environment that allows it to happen. It ought to be easier than if you're in an environment that doesn't even have the structure for it to happen. When you have a program that has regular time for staff communication, at least you have the potential for bringing new people in.

Challenge: Overcoming Culture Where Adult Time is Not Valued

On top of feeling underpaid and overworked, childcare workers rarely enjoy a professional culture that supports adult time together away from the children. The first step to overcoming this is learning to understand the power of dialogue and the potential for implementing the principles. Author Janet Gonzalez-Mena talked about this phenomenon:

Everything about the way we work with children says, "This is a sacred place for children." Not for adults. Adults save their conversation for after work, maybe break (if you ever get one) . You put aside your needs. But in full day care you can't do that; it makes people crazy. Yet the whole thing is set up and people are trained to keep themselves out of the program; to not show children any kind of relationships with other people (except maybe nice, happy ones). I think this is a huge issue and a big problem in the field. Children don't see adults behave normally. They don't see adults problem-solving with each other. This is all working against the idea of using each other as resources, because theoretically you can't do it while the kids are around.

Challenge: The Importance of Leadership

Where California Tomorrow did find programs incorporating dialogue about diversity issues on a regular basis, the leadership of the directors was crucial. Directors play a key role in creating the time, opportunities, an open and supportive atmosphere, and commitment that allows productive dialogue to occur.

Directors, along with the whole staff, may feel that they do not have the skills or the information themselves and so do not feel prepared to take on a leadership role in focusing a dialogue on diversity in their program. However, the type of leadership that is needed does not necessarily require that the director know more than the staff about these issues but that they place a high priority on diversity issues and be willing to learn. Ardella Dailey gave a picture of what leadership means in this context:

Many times we are all in the same boat and there is no captain because everyone is struggling at the same level. I think it is more that the person who is in leadership—in terms of focusing on diversity and addressing the needs of the different cultural groups in the program—has to have a commitment to always push at the door. That is almost more important than having more knowledge than another person.

As Dan Bellm, writer and editor on early childhood education issues, put it—directors can make an incredible contribution by saying "I may not know much about this, but I declare that this is important and we will explore it together."

Part Four

Early Childhood Education in the Ivory Tower

CHAPTER TEN

The Stealing of Wonderful Ideas:
The Politics of Imposition and Representation
in Research on Early Childhood

Janice A. Jipson
National Louis University

"Why don't you talk about something interesting, for a change?" the voice of my six-year-old son, calling out from the back seat of the car, reminding my colleague and I that Hey—I'm here, too! Responding to his insistent plea for inclusion, we shift our conversation to the more immediate issue of whether we like Lego pirates or castles better. But just a few miles later, I, cautiously, and with a subdued voice, slide back into my academic interests and begin to talk about how Erik has often provided me with many of the ideas and metaphors for my research and writing (Jipson, 1991, 1992, 1998).

"Yeah," he says as he reinserts himself into the conversation, "you're always stealing my ideas." And so I am, because isn't this what early childhood researchers are supposed to do? To observe (appropriate?) and interpret the experiences of young children?

In responding to Erik's [im]pertinent commentary on the political and impositional nature of early childhood research, I must confront basic questions about why and how we do early childhood research and who it is for. I am forced to consider whether the research process can ever equitably serve the interests of those involved, particularly the interests of young children.

Inherent in the research process is determining what counts as valid and useful knowledge. Erik poses an important question—who determines what is "interesting" to know? Further, who decides how that knowledge is acquired, understood, and textually represented? And whose voice articulates the process each step of the way?

Erik's insistence also prompts me to wonder: What is the nature of the relationship between the researcher and the researched? If we truly believe that knowledge is socially constructed, how can we adequately acknowledge and represent the multiple perspectives and understandings that emerge in a research process that includes young children? How can we address the issues of imposition and power that are so inherent in the traditional research relationship[1] yet are so problematic when working with young children, who, seemingly by chronological and conceptual definition, have less power, less voice? I began to question the political nature of doing research on early childhood.

The importance of these questions was clarified for me as I listened to a recent discussion of "theory of mind."[2] The research on theory of mind is of general interest to me so I paid particular attention to the speaker's anecdotes interpreting the meaning of two children's play dialogue which she had overheard. How, I wondered, does anyone really know what was intended or understood by the children as they played together with their toys? Who could accurately estimate their understanding of what it meant to assume, enact, and discuss the personas of their stuffed animals. Were the scripted interactions between their toys a repetition of a dialogue recalled from television or home? A sign of their understanding of what it meant to assume a role and then talk about it? Or an indicator of their ability to plan and think about their play at a meta-analytic level? How could one ever really know? Had anyone asked the children? Was it of any importance to children? To their parents? Or teachers? To whom did it matter, anyway? Were these researchers actually a lot like me, stealing Erik's wonderful ideas to make my own meaning, prove my own point?

The Politics of Early Childhood Research As-We-Know-It

In redefining relationships within the process of doing educational research in early childhood, the unique developmental and behavioral characteristics of children create a complexity that displaces many of the obvious alternatives to answering the political concerns of power and voice. The traditional models of empirical research[3] applied to early childhood assert that the world exists independently of knowers and that knowledge of the world takes the form of firm and steady truths that can be directly accessed through one's senses—by observation (Beyer & Bloch, 1996). They also assert that human behavior (and thus development) is predictable and measurable. Research conducted within the empirical paradigm further posits a finite, allowable range of research relationships that clearly articulates separations between researcher and researched. These distinctions, created in the cause of "objectivity," have served, according to

Roman & Apple (1989), "to remove, minimize, or make invisible [the researchers] subjectivities, cultural beliefs and practices, while simultaneously directing attention to the subjectivities, beliefs and practices of their research subjects." Empirical research thus can be said to produce knowledge through detachment, knowledge which, because of its genesis, is equated with truth and is assumed to be neutral and apolitical.

The belief that the value of knowledge is characterized by its ability to represent regularities in the Euro-American educational world has provided a seemingly consistent base for early childhood research and the understanding of child development throughout the last half century. The assumptions of empiricism and the political implications of generalizing Western knowledge of child development to the rest of the world, are, however, beginning to be more seriously questioned (Cannella, 1997).

Jeffrey Lewis (1995), in exploring the assumptions underlying research in developmental psychology and early education, challenges these supposed developmental regularities as he points out that the existence of "universal" and "immutable" stages of child development (Bredekamp, 1987; New, 1994) is contradicted by current crosscultural research in psychology and anthropology. He goes on to question the current research focus on individual development, independence, and cognitive learning, citing Levine, (1994) characterization of theories of child development as "cultural scripts" and "folk theories." Valerie Walkerdine (1984) has also critiqued the notion of the universality of research-based developmental psychology, arguing that "developmental psychology is premised on a set of claims to truth which are historically specific and which are not the only or necessary way to understand children" (p. 154).

Critical theorists have constructed the most directly political critique of empirical researchers, noting that because of their assumptions about objectivity and truth, they fail to recognize the social and cultural values inherent in the decision as to what knowledge is of most importance to explore, and they also fail to consider whose interests are served by the knowledge they produce. Their emphasis on observability, predictability, measurability, and generalizability as criteria for the research process also has an obscuring effect on the determination of what is worth knowing, thereby displacing or muffling a recognition of the frequently atypical, unpredictable, and idiosyncratic experiences of children.

Gary Price (1992) has suggested, in an essay on the use of quantitative methods in multicultural research, that "positivism, also know as scientific empiricism, refuses to concede the status of reality to things not directly observable...[resulting in] inattention to the thoughts, customs, and intentions of subjects" (p. 64). As Price points out, this limits consideration to only those behaviors that can be directly observed, that is, those behaviors that happen to occur (and reoccur) in the particular research setting.[4] This repeated focus on recurrence potentially obscures the recognition of the unique and emergent occurrences of lived experience in favor of the identification of the predictable. It also, thereby, disallows the creation of a knowledge that is inexact, unexpected and multifocused, and sometimes peculiar in its appearance. Finally, it positions the child/children/subjects as objects of the researchers' process, thus denying them agency in the understanding of their own activity.

The Politics of the Interpretive Tradition in Early Childhood Research[5]

Providing an alternative to the relational constrictions of observability and objectivity inherent in empirical research are various methodologies within the traditions of interpretivism that deny a strict separation between researcher and researched; encourage a plurality of voices and narratives; affirm a commitment to interactivity that is egalitarian and nonexploitative; promote reflexivity as a strategy shared by all participants in the research process; and take as their method the analysis of the intersubjective processes through which meaning is generated.

Interpretivism is based on the belief that people regularly interpret and make sense of their worlds and that situations can only be understood from the subjective point of view of the participants within their own cultural and interactional contexts. Interpretive research relies on on-site observations where the researcher is free to recognize what is happening, using herself as an instrument to determine what counts or is important.

The interpretive research process is grounded in the researchers' subjective understanding as they account for and explain what they have observed and described and then articulate what it means. Researcher attention focuses on the particular as they attempt to understand the meaning of events and interactions in participants situations from the participants point of view. The expectation of the researcher is that one can explain what has been observed and thereby develop new concepts or elaborate on existing concepts, provide insights that refine knowledge, clarify complexity, and develop theory.

The issues of imposition and representation inherent in the interpretivist paradigm parallel those of the positivist perspective. Interpretivism views explanations of research participants' actions in terms of reasons or motives that are accessible to, and acknowledged by, the participant. The assumption is that the participant can always be made cognizant of such motivations. Missing, however, are effective strategies to reliably ascertain the thinking and motivation of young children who may lack the verbal skills or supportive opportunities to fully articulate their thoughts and desires. Thus, the researchers' representation of the participant creates rather than mirrors the participants' experiences, thoughts, and feelings. The researcher can never actually capture lived experience, in part because as soon as an experience occurs it is gone, except through its reconstruction in memory. It is the researchers' recollection that is imposed upon the participants' experience and representation becomes a narrative production.

Thus, interpretivism, like empiricism, makes assumptions about the relationship between that which is observed and the researchers' interpretive system or analytic scheme. Differences in social, historical, or cultural traditions between the researcher and the participants may create distortions in understanding and, therefore, in representation. It follows then that inseparable from issues inherent in research relationships are a set of concerns questioning the politics of conducting research outside of one's own cultural experience (Hauser, 1998) and of researching other individuals at all (Jipson, 1995; Jipson & Paley, 1997). Central to these concerns are assertions that authentic depictions of subjective experience can only be generated through personal reflection on one's own lived experience and the frequently intuitive examination of one's own ideas and beliefs (Jipson & Paley, 1997).

What does this mean when the research participants are children? Rex and Wendy Stainton Rogers (1992) suggest that:

> One of the deep paradoxes of finding out about childhood lies in our having been children (and therefore having "known" childhood at first-hand), and yet having no direct...only represented...access to that experience. Stories are all that we can ever have...stories compounded out of: the stories we re-tell to ourselves and to others (our childhood memories); stories our caregivers and others (like siblings and childhood friends) told to and tell us; and stories woven around the odd artifact we have retained (like family photos, pictures we drew or a battered teddy still sitting in the cupboard). These autobiographical stories have been produced in ways which define and construct for us what it is that is significant about childhood. (p. 19)

The Rogers (1992) go on to suggest that it is important to understand the nature of childhood from the perspective of the child.

When the "researched" are children, multiple interferences are apparent. In addition to the notions about childhood we bring from our own experiences as children, various social constructions of the young child (Cannella, 1997; James, Jenks, & Prout, 1998) as object of adult attention and care, as developmentally maturing organism, and as unequally able to participate in rational problem solving or adult discourse, may constrain our understandings of what children are able to do and of what meanings their activities have for them. These constructions of childhood, which primarily emanate from Western cultural experience, thus impose both limitations and expectations on children, thereby actively serving to reproduce dominant Euro-American patterns, relationships, and behaviors.

Finally, the relativism implicit in the interpretivist position must be examined. Interpretivism, by its very definition implies the possibility of multiple understandings, multiple meanings for every event. There are, however, often, good reasons for preferring one explanation or interpretation over another. Each alternate impressionistic representation of early childhood inscribes power and privilege in specific ways, thus creating particular social texts and engendering particular possibilities.

The Politics of Critically Informed Early Childhood Research

Many early childhood educators actively engaged in research with young children face the dilemma of balancing their roles as researchers with their personal commitments to social change, their concerns with the "developmental appropriateness" of children's educational experiences, and their acknowledgment of the social construction of meaning. The inherent conflict in being committed to a liberatory, critical research, while not imposing personal values and agenda on others, raises serious political issues for those early childhood researchers striving to employ egalitarian and non-exploitative research methodologies with children.

Critically informed early childhood researchers assert that knowledge is socially constructed and mediated. They also believe that knowledge is invariably culturally and historically embedded in the concrete specifics of the situation. Thus, for critically informed researchers, knowledge must always be [re]viewed in the context of its constitution.

Critically informed researchers also believe that what appears to be "objective reality is actually what ones mind constructs, thereby confronting positivist claims of external truths that can be verified through direct observation. Knowledge is examined from a cultural and historical perspective in terms of its role or potential within social evolution. For example, the concept of "child-centeredness" or developmentally appropriate practice" or "optimal birthrate" can be understood as emerging within privileged Eurocentric cultural systems and societies that can afford to put their children at the center of their lives—as objects of their devotion, upward mobility, and material consumption, rather than as contributors to the family economy (Azhar, 1998).

From a critical perspective, knowledge is valued in terms of its potential to contribute to progressive social change and social justice. Critically informed researchers assert that the knowing individual can shape and reshape the world through instrumental action, through symbolic and communicative activity, and through the dialectical interplay between the two. In the case of research with young children this would involve both their actions, in work and play, and their understandings of their activity (thus bringing us back to the importance of research on theory of mind and questions as to whether young children are able to reflect on their own experiences) within the historical, cultural, and social context in which they live.

Critically informed researchers focus their concern on the emancipatory or repressive potential of knowledge, suggesting, in direct contrast to empiricists, that knowledge and values are fundamentally interrelated. They assert that knowledge can never be neutral or disinterested, and notions of "truth" are always tied to values, with validity emerging only within a dialectical process that serves to illuminate rather than submerge difference.

Furthermore, critically informed researchers recognize that knowledge is unequally distributed and that knowledge-makers inevitably use their knowledge to enhance their own status and to support their own interests. Their point is exemplified by the mechanics of the knowledge-producing industry of academe where research output is inextricably tied to promotion, tenure, and success.

Since critically informed researchers believe that the world is socially constructed and shaped by human action, however, they believe it can also be re-shaped and transformed through human action. The child, from the critical perspective, is a kind of "colonized subject" in western society who lives within and through the codes of parents and teachers, yet is also an active agent able to formulate challenges and create changes (as any parent will attest).

The question then is how can we capture another's reality when it is continually changing and when the other is a child? One possibility for critically informed early childhood researchers is to directly engage children in the process of meaning-making and knowledge producing. But how might we do this, given the inherent positional power and status of the researcher that can readily overwhelm and subvert the child's understanding of his or her own experience and agency? The power of the researcher works in direct and subtle ways in the researcher/child relationship both through the imposition of authority and in the subjective meaning the researcher brings to the interpretation of the interaction—an interpretation that invariably legitimizes the particular versions of social reality.[6]

Critical research begins with intersubjective understanding and commitment between participants. The doing of research, however, constructs boundaries that may enable or constrain relations of power related to discourse, culture, location, and subjectivity. As researchers with young children, therefore, we must identify how children's understanding and subjectivity are shaped through their interactions with us. We must also consider the historical and social situatedness of the discourses that frame and colonize our own experiences and position us as well as the children with whom we work. At a minimum, we must consider the local, partial, and contingent nature of our discourse with and about children.

The challenge, then, is to ground our research in the interpretations of the children with whom we work and to distinguish between the multiple interpretations we consider, recognizing that subjective understandings are partially determined by context. We must develop an awareness of how our understandings may have been distorted or repressed through critical reflection.

Research is also the process of constructing representations of our understandings, representations we call knowledge. How do we choose to represent our understandings if all experience, and therefore all knowledge, is under continual construction/[re]construction. What purposes do our partial, shifting, positional representations serve, particularly if they are representations of our own (the researchers) reality anyway? Or if it is a child's experience like our own/never just like our own?

Early Childhood Research: Is It Only Make-Believe?

And so, we ask, with children as coparticipants in the inquiry process, what counts as research? What matters as data? What procedures are considered legitimate, ethical, for the production of knowledge? And how can children, themselves, contribute to the making of meaning? These questions, with their insistent focus on the place of children in the processes of educational research, are political in that they raise questions about the status of pedagogic, representational, and research authority.

But there are further questions, also political in their challenge to the constituted authority of early childhood education and child development. Why do research at all? Can we assume that there actually is "new" knowledge to discover? And how do we determine what knowledge is of most worth? Is "new" knowledge really just an application of an old story or metaphor to a new situation? Or, since all knowledge is grounded in personal experience, is "new" knowledge just a shifting of interpretations as they are layered on across time?

Parallel with the prior questions, critical theorists urge us to interrogate knowledge itself in terms of the social and historical context of its production: Whose knowledge is it, that is, who is involved in the construction of the knowledge? Whose interests will it serve? And whose needs will it meet?

Similarly, we must ask ourselves: How has our research been constructed and how can it be reorganized or reformulated into an analytic existence that acknowledges the coparticipation of children in its process, including the process of representation? How can we express understanding other than through the conventions of printed language? What power relations does an insistence on print representation reproduce? Empower? Restrict? For whom and in what ways?[7]

Patti Lather (1991) has suggested that "data might be better conceived as the material for telling a story where the challenge becomes to generate a polyvalent data base that is used to *vivify* [original italics] interpretation as opposed to support or prove. Turning the text into a display and interaction among perspectives, and presenting material rich enough to bear reanalysis in different ways bring the reader into the analysis via a dispersive impulse which fragments univocal authority" (p. 91). Her comments suggest additional questions: How do children typically represent their knowledge and experience? And how can children's' representations become part of this display? Become central to the "data base of the display"?

To borrow from Sandra Harding's (1987) search for a distinctively feminist methodology, perhaps what the field of early childhood needs is a rethinking of familiar research methods, a movement beyond replacing objectivism with subjectivism, beyond assessing generalizability and particularity, beyond debating truth and relativism. Needed is a close examination of the constructed and relational nature of early childhood and the invention of a new research where children's understandings of their own experience can flourish, where the voices of children, themselves, can be heard, and where the historical and sociocultural contexts in which children live today can become central to our understanding of their experience and our own.

In addressing issues of subjectivity, voice, power relations, collaboration, and representation in research with young children, we must decenter the binary notion of the mature, rational, and therefore "knowing" researcher and the developing, "innocent" and disem-powered child. We must ask ourselves[8] how research in early childhood can be reconfigured so that children, in their own way, can fully participate in reflecting on how they are historically and socially constructed and so that they can begin to rethink the relationship of themselves to others and to society.

As Usher & Edwards (1994) has suggested, we need to "take account of the dimension of power" and how it "challenges the possibility of disinterested research and value-free knowledge." We need to consider how "values permeate research both in its methods and outcomes" and acknowledge how "research is an enactment of power relations" and is dependent on "sociocultural practices and contexts, unacknowledged values, tacit discourses and interpretive traditions" (p. 29). We need to take seriously the child in early childhood research.

And so my thoughts return to Erik. I take seriously his concerns about my appropriation and misrepresentation of his experiences. How can I give him the last word?

NOTES

I would like to credit the "twist" in my title to Eleanor Duckworth, (1972). The Having of Wonderful Ideas, New York: Teachers College Press.

1   Habermas suggests that the problem of research is in the enscribed power rela-
    tion and its relation to knowledge.

2   Janet Astington, Paul Harris, and David Olson (1988) describe theory of mind
    as an area of cognitive psychology that looks at the emerging understandings of
    perception, action, and language in preschool-aged children as they begin to
    systematically distinguish between the world and representations of the world.

3   Robin Usher (1996), in an essay delineating the assumptions of several research
    paradigms, refers to these models, collectively, as positivist/empiricist.

4   Uri Bronfenbrenner (1979) critiques the laboratory-boundedness of much de-
    velopmental research and theorizing and its related neglect of wider cultural and
    institutional settings. He characterizes the research process as "strange people
    doing strange things to children in strange situations."

5   For examples, see the comprehensive review of qualitative research in early
    childhood settings compiled by Pamela C. Browning and J. Amos Hatch (1995).

6   I recall several years ago when an early childhood student asked if one could be
    oppressed if one did not feel oppressed. The ensuing discussion of the
    imposition of oppression occupied the class for several subsequent sessions.

7   These questions reflect a consideration of similar issues in the author's book, co-
    edited with Nicholas Paley (1997), Dare Devil Research: Rethinking Analytic
    Practice.

8   Assuming, of course, that contemporary theories of children's mind[s] support
    these possibilities.

CHAPTER ELEVEN

Introducing Postmodern Thought in a
Thoroughly Modern University

J. Amos Hatch
University of Tennessee

This chapter is the story of my experiences at attempting to introduce postmodern perspectives into my work at the University of Tennessee. The chapter is grounded in my developing understanding of postmodern and poststructuralist thought. It is a description of my own journey of understanding and of how I have tried to apply my changing perspectives to my work in a conservative college in a conservative university. My own assumptions about research, theory, and practice have been challenged by my reading of postmodern scholars, and I have tried to encourage my students and colleagues to rethink their own assumptions, given the postmodern critique.

It was at the first Reconceptualizing Early Childhood Education conference at the University of Wisconsin that I realized that postmodern thought might influence my own thinking. I had just become editor of *Qualitative Studies in Education* (*QSE*), I had been racing to get a handle on the international state-of-the-art for qualitative research, and I had been traveling to as many conferences as I could. I knew a little about postmodern and poststructuralist ideas, but my overriding impression was captured in a complaint I made to a colleague after a particularly obtuse session at the University of Pennsylvania Ethnography meetings earlier in 1991: "I can't find the thesis; every idea seems to be an aside."

At the Reconceptualizing meetings, Michael O'Loughlin was passionate about not letting this new kind of conference become like other meetings we all attended, and he used comparisons to postmodern architecture to make a compelling case for thinking about conferences in new and unusual ways. I had lunch in downtown Madison with a group that included Robin Leavitt, Marti Power, and Joe Tobin. The three of them began playing a game that I play with my children on car trips: players work their way through the alphabet, naming a world capital, a corporation name, or whatever category is agreed upon. Robin, Marti, and Joe were naming postmodern scholars.

I felt seriously overmatched and strategically stayed out of the game. I left the conference with the impression that folks I admired were into something important that I needed to know more about.

I am not a poststructuralist. Politically and intellectually, I think of myself as a liberal (in the classical sense of that term). I come to my understandings of postmodern thinking from grounding in a research orientation that could be characterized by terms such as constructivism, symbolic interactionism, postpositivism, cultural anthropology, or Chicago-style sociology. My university teaching is driven by the same forces that led me to work for 13 years in early childhood classrooms in communities with high rates of poverty: I want to change the world by working in it. In my research, writing, and teaching, it's not my style to slam folks in the face with what they don't know, don't believe, or don't do. I am much more comfortable respecting where people are and offering alternatives for them to consider. This approach characterizes how I have gone about introducing postmodern thought into my teaching and scholarship.

I have decided to organize this chapter into a series of stories. The stories represent examples of how my own thinking is evolving and how I have tried to influence the thinking of others. It would be easier to organize the chapter around some familiar structures like research, teaching, and program development; but these all run together in real life. The stories presented overlap in time but are roughly chronological. I recognize that, although some are stories of failure, I am the hero of my own stories. Others will have a different take on what happened and why. After telling the stories, I will discuss some problems and paradoxes I have encountered in these experiences.

And the Truth Is Not in Us

Five years ago, our college of education was given the opportunity to reinvent itself. Based on three years of strategic planning, existing departments were "sunsetted" and groups of faculty were invited to join with others who were willing to rethink their work in an effort to create a new college of education at the University of Tennessee. Some of us in the college actually took this opportunity, and I was lucky enough to align with four others to develop what came to be the inclusive early childhood education unit (see Cagle, Coleman, Benner, Hatch, Judge, & Blank, 1997).

The five of us were determined to challenge every assumption we could identify about how early childhood teachers ought to be prepared. The most energy was spent wrestling with basic notions of what teachers need to know and the best ways to "teach" it. We spent months arguing about how we were going to handle the expectation from the state that our students had to demonstrate competency in a long list of "knowledges and skills" in order to be licensed to teach. Two folks (with backgrounds in special education) believed that we should start with the state requirements and build alternative strategies for developing and demonstrating competencies. I argued, with support from another early childhood person and a philosopher of education, that our students should be working alongside us to decide what they want and need to learn. Although Foucault's name was never dropped and the term poststructuralism was not brought up until months later, we decided to radically change the ways knowledge and power were configured in our new program. We outlawed lecturing. We became our students, colleagues, giving them responsibility for their own learning. We did away with traditional testing and grading, and we even found a way around the university's scheduling structure (see Hatch, 1996).

About to start with our fifth cohort of students, we are still uneasy, having given up the absolutes of teacher preparation, we still deal with students frustration when they realize that there is no one correct answer to their questions, and we still pass out the state knowledges and skills so the students can keep track of their own "progress." What seems important is that our acknowledgment that Truth is a social and political construct has led us to operate in a different way in relation to knowledge, students, and the learning process.

United We Stand (and fall)

Reading the poststructuralist critique, editing *QSE*, and attending conferences led me to reexamine my own research in terms of the nature of my findings and especially my relationship to participants in my studies. I did a paper on ethics in qualitative classroom research at the Chicago Reconceptualizing meetings that later was revised as a chapter in *Qualitative Research in Early Childhood Settings* (Hatch, 1995). In the paper, I describe ways to acknowledge and reduce differences between researchers and participants in terms of risk, control, and benefits. About the same time as I was struggling with these ideas, I had the opportunity to work with four experienced preschool and kindergarten teachers who were trying to meet new licensure standards so they could continue teaching. All worked in family resource centers serving children and families from poor, mostly African American communities. As part of our work together, we decided to study ourselves using what we called a "collaborative narrative inquiry."

We audio-taped our conversations about the teachers' daily practices in their local settings. Because the standard for early childhood educators was codified in NAEYC's *Developmentally Appropriate Practices Handbook* (Bredekamp, 1987), it was natural for us to discuss what they were doing in relation to *DAP*. We analyzed transcripts of our conversations and taped more conversations based on that analysis, then did a final analysis together.

We wrote a paper entitled "Developmentally Appropriate for Whom? Perspectives of Inner-City Early Childhood Educators," which we presented at NAEYC in Atlanta (Hatch, Brice, Kidwell, Mason, & McCarthy, 1994). In the postmodern spirit, we did the paper and presentation as a performance piece—a kind of readers' theater. We each played ourselves as we used the words from our transcribed data organized into a script. The presentation was well received, and members of the committee responsible for revising DAP have told us that our paper was important in their deliberations; but the manuscript was never published. Reviewers had difficulty with the unusual research approach and with the fact that the paper didn't look like any report of research that they had ever seen. Our goal throughout was that we would be studying ourselves—not me studying them. I could have reshaped a manuscript that looked like a standard research article, but we had a contract that we would be co-researchers, copresenters, and coauthors. That meant power relations were more equal, ownership was more equal, benefits were more equal, and disappointments were more equal.

You Can't Go Back

The *QSE* editorial board recommended that we do a special issue on life history and narrative. My coeditor, Richard Wisniewski, and I agreed and set about trying to identify someone to guest edit. We talked to some folks about doing it and consulted with others about who should do it, finally deciding (for mostly political reasons) to do it ourselves. We invited papers and received an outstanding set of manuscripts—too many for one issue. We negotiated with Falmer Press to do the special issue as a book, adding three chapters, including one by Richard and myself. The strategy for developing our chapter was to do an open-ended survey of individuals doing life history or narrative work, asking them to answer questions about key issues, and to identify exemplary publications. Analyzing their feedback, searching the literature to connect their responses to a theoretical base, and writing the chapter were very helpful in developing my understanding of important poststructuralist concepts.

The two questions that brought the most interesting responses were: "What are the major issues connected with life history or narrative work?" and "What is the relationship of life history or narrative work to poststructuralism?" Issues included poststructuralist concerns such as authorship, ownership, power, and voice, and both questions elicited discussion of the crisis of representation, the nonlinearity of life, the noncoherence of self, and the place of deconstructivism in narrative analysis. Attempting to theorize these issues and relationships took me into challenging and often troubling intellectual territory. As I read and reread Sartre, Derrida, and Ricoeur (and their interpreters), I confronted issues that called my assumptions about research, text, even reality itself, into question. The following is a quote from the chapter:

First, the act of telling one's story is an act of creating one's self. In *Nausea*, Sartre (1964) asserts that "nothing really happens when you live. The scenery changes, people come in and go out, that's all. There are no beginnings. Days are tacked on to days without rhyme or reason, an interminable monotonous addition" (p. 39). A life (the story of a life) is created in the consciousness to give order and meaning to events that have no "intrinsic or immanent relations" (Freeman, 1993, p. 95). The telling of a story is in a real sense the construction of a life (Hatch & Wisniewski, 1995, p. 129).

The story of my life (as researcher, teacher, person) changes when I take such ideas seriously—and I do. So far, I don't have ways to reconcile the disequilibrium created by such phrases as "Nothing really happens when you live," but pretending that such ideas are unimportant is impossible.

Teaching Is Believing

The first time I had nerve enough to try to formally teach postmodern ideas was with a small doctoral seminar I shared with two faculty colleagues, Susan Benner and Sharon Judge. We organized the content of the seminar as we do the experiences of our undergraduates in the inclusive early childhood unit: we sat down with the students and decided what the group wanted to learn and who would be responsible for taking the lead on particular topics. I announced that I was interested in learning more about postmodernism and poststructuralism and volunteered to identify some common readings and lead a discussion. In addition to the other topics identified for the semester, we all agreed to read David Elkind's (1994) then new book, *Ties That Stress: The New Family Imbalance*, dividing responsibility for certain chapters among students and professors in the group.

For my session on postmodern thought, I chose the following readings: (a) Joe Tobin's (1995) chapter entitled "Post-Structural Research in Early Childhood Education"; (b) Chapter 2, "Two Modes of Thought," from Jerome Bruner's (1986) *Actual Minds, Possible Worlds*; (c) my chapter with Richard Wisniewski, "Life History and Narrative: Questions, Issues, and Exemplary Works," from *Life History and Narrative* (Hatch & Wisniewski, 1995); and several sections from *An Introductory Guide to Post-Structuralism and Postmodernism* by Madan Sarup (1988). To help organize the group's preparations for discussing the Tobin, Sarup, and Hatch and Wisniewski readings, I put together "Ideas to Consider in Preparation for our Discussion" (see appendix A). Members of the group were encouraged to bring to class brief responses to the ideas in the handout (e.g., "Post-structuralism assumes knowledge is partial, power is dispersed, and identity always in flux."). I opened the discussion with an informal, lecture-style presentation in which I tried to give an overview of the development of postmodern thought, place poststructuralism in relation to the broader postmodern movement, provide characteristics of postmodernity, and list some gener-alizations from postmodern thought. I used handouts as organizers for discussing the last two elements and these are included as appendixes B and C.

Larry Coleman, another professor from our unit, joined the seminar for the discussion, and we had an interesting, stimulating time. We struggled together with the content and with our own mostly modern assumptions. While none of us left the experience feeling like he or she finally understood what postmodernism or poststructuralism is all about, all of us, including me, felt like we had a better handle on some basic ideas and a better chance of making meaningful connections when such ideas were encountered in our work.

I had read *Ties That Stress* and recommended it to the seminar because we had all read Elkind's earlier work, and I wanted to check out their reactions to his attempts to apply a postmodern analysis to the family. The consensus of the group seemed to match my own conclusion that the initial chapters comparing the modern nuclear family with the postmodern permeable family were interesting and insightful. We were disappointed that Elkind returned to familiar themes as he tried to reconcile differences by describing what he called the vital family, which I read as a baldly modern approach.

For many of us, the focus on postmodern/poststructuralist thought was the highlight of the seminar. Several students are now doing qualitative dissertations that have been influenced by our readings and discussions; I made myself clarify and organize lots of mostly disconnected ideas (one of the great rewards of teaching at any level); and Susan Benner, one of the professors in the group, used the seminar as a springboard for developing a chapter entitled "The Challenges of Postmodern Thought" in her 1998 book, *Special Education Issues Within the Context of American Society.*

I have also used Tobin's chapter along with Robin Leavitt's (1994) *Power and Emotion in Infant-Toddler Day Care* and Bronwyn Davies, (1989) *Frogs and Snails and Feminist Tales: Preschool Children and Gender* as examples of poststructuralist studies in my early childhood qualitative research classes. I have mixed these with conceptual pieces from Cherryholmes (1988), Flax (1990), and Scheurich (1995) in an effort to encourage potential researchers (and some are pure quantoids in these classes) to think more broadly about what research can and ought to be.

And Master of None

I teach a cycle of master's level early childhood education courses on theory, curriculum, and social change. Some of the students in these classes are experienced teachers returning for advanced degrees, but most are getting a master's degree as part of a five-year teacher preparation program that includes an internship at the graduate level. The background and needs of the latter group dictate a different kind of learning experience than they would get in a traditional graduate class. I am committed to trying to provide learning opportunities that these teachers-to-be see as meaningful and useful, while also trying to build in experience struggling with important ideas, including exposure to postmodern thought.

Although I have done little directly to include poststructuralism in the curriculum course, I have introduced the postmodern critique of grand narratives as a kind of troubling finale to the theory class, and I have assigned a chapter from *Ties That Stress* as a way to get discussion going in the social change class. In the theory course, we read Gesell, Erikson, Piaget, Skinner, Bronfenbrenner, Vygotsky, and

Rogoff directly, and we study examples of program applications of their theoretical principles. The goal is to see what we can learn from these theories and applications that will help us make better decisions as professionals and individuals. I have tried bits of Sarup's (1988) or Flax's (1990) books as readings, but these don't work well for these master's students. I give an overview of the critique of grand theory and, in the Foucauldian spirit, we try to engage in an analysis of the consequences of actions undertaken in the name of theories we've looked at during the semester. In fact, this often turns out to be a pretty hollow activity, with me doing most of the analysis and them wishing the class were over. Next time I teach the theory class, I plan to use readings from Walkerdine (e.g., 1984) or Cannella (1998) to give students a better sense of what a critique of mainstream early childhood theory might look like.

In the social change class, we read about and discuss changes in society and how these affect young children. Ignoring his reliance on the modernist device of binary oppositions, I use the framework Elkind (1994) sets up in *Ties That Stress* (i.e., progress, universality, and regularity versus difference, particularity, and irregularity) as a starting place for exploring postmodernity. Relying mostly on Jameson (1984) and Baudrillard (1988), I provide students with an overview of postmodern ideas and lead a discussion of the impact of postmodernity on their lives as individuals and teachers. Two different discussion guides are included in appendixes D and E. In one, I get students to write brief reaction statements to Elkinds descriptions of modern and postmodern families. In the other, I break out more specific contrasts from *Ties That Stress* and ask students to rank their own experiences on a continuum from fully modern to fully postmodern. Typically, these activities lead to discussions that go much better than those in the theory class. This may be true because these students live in a rapidly changing world and they see value in having ways to understand those changes and deal with what they mean for themselves and the children they will teach.

A Mid-Life Crisis of Representation

I completed my tenure as *QSE* editor, published two edited books, and was promoted to full professor within a six-month period. I was worn out physically and burned out emotionally. My perspective on the value of the academic work that had consumed my time for 15 years was increasingly jaded, so I took time away from going to conferences and cranking out scholarship to try to get some perspective on what I was doing and why. I hit upon an idea that gave me a way to talk directly to teachers about what I had learned about teaching: I would write a postmodern textbook.

The book was a way to bring together an odd assortment of ideas that were influencing my perspectives on teaching, learning, and scholarship. A few excerpts from the cover letter I sent out will give a flavor for what I was trying to do:

> I am writing a book about the real world of contemporary teaching. My target audience is students preparing to be teachers and inservice teachers who are struggling to make sense of classroom life in a world that is vastly different from what they experienced when they were in school.

> The book has a different form and a different message than traditional texts. It is organized around topics that are vital to teaching at all levels, and topics are explored through (mostly autobiographical) stories that take the reader into real situations. The book purposely has no citations or references. It is billed as one story of teaching, and addresses teachers as if I were talking to them face-to-face.

> As I say in my introduction, this book is not meant to replace traditional textbooks. I see this as a "postmodern textbook." The working title is *Teaching in the Real World*. The title works on two levels: first, teachers have always been convinced that professors and textbooks are effective only in a world separate from the real world of classroom teaching (they're right of course); and second, "The Real World" on MTV represents a kind of "postmodern text" that most students currently preparing to teach understand and relate to. The book works hard to be "real" in both senses.

> Several themes are woven throughout the stories, including: (a) the complex, even paradoxical, nature of teaching; (b) the importance of individual integrity and professional decision making; (c) the changing nature of life in postmodern society and the effects on teachers, children, and schools; (d) the importance of meaningful connections among people and between learners and what is to be learned; and (e) the necessity of thinking about teaching-learning settings in new ways. The idea is neither to hammer readers over the head with a treatise on postmodern thought nor to provide the usual cookbook of ways to teach. My goal is to start teachers thinking about what it's like to be out there and what it will take for them to be successful.

I put six months into writing several sections and enjoyed the act of writing in a way that I had forgotten (or maybe never knew). I pulled together a group of four teacher education students from our program who volunteered to read sections one a time, to give me written reflections on the reading, and to meet with me as a group to discuss what they saw as important in what they had read. The idea was not to get a critique from them, but to see how real students might actually use the material in a university setting. We had a great time. Three of the students seemed to get it, using the stories as ways to think more deeply about what they believed or questioned about teaching. The fourth's "reflections" and comments in the group meetings were often complaints that teachers would not know what to do with the stories and only be more confused by the (relativistic) tone and (lack of) content in the sections.

I set my sights high and sent my prospectus and sample sections (revised based on student input) to several top publishers, reasoning that if I wanted to "talk to teachers" I would need a mainstream publisher, not an alternative press that no one would ever find. No one liked the idea. Acquisitions editors who took the time to write back sent the stock "don't see a market for this book" letter. One publisher sent the prospectus out for review, and the reviews were unequivocal pans.

I set about grieving the failure of this project, generating a series of rationalizations: publishers are only interested in making money; no one really understands the idea; this is too avant-garde for the audience; they sent it to the wrong reviewers; I am ahead of my time. Then I turned on myself: this book is an exercise in pure egoism; you didn't work hard enough to pull this off; you're not a good enough writer to make this happen; either this is a bad idea, a poor execution, or both; what makes you think you have anything to say to teachers anyway?

I am closer to accepting this loss, but I had an interesting realization the other day. I was looking at the responses to a survey we conduct to keep track of our graduates. The four students who helped with the postmodern textbook project all finished their internships last spring. One is working for Disney in hotel management, one is in charge of a teen ministry at a local Presbyterian church, one is working on a second masters in computer science and training for the Sydney Olympics in Tae Kwon Do, and one is teaching second grade in a local elementary school. The student whose reaction matched the publishers is the one who chose teaching.

This Bud's for You

I was recently invited to do a chapter on qualitative research for the 1998 *Yearbook in Early Childhood Education*. Bernard Spodek and Olivia Saracho are editing this volume on "research in early childhood education." If patterns from the past hold and my information is correct, mine will be the only chapter on anything other than research from the positivist paradigm. Writing this chapter for what I perceive to be a bright but mostly mainstream audience, I saw it as an opportunity to introduce some poststructuralist thinking to folks not likely to be searching for it in other sources.

I included an "examples of early childhood qualitative research" section in the chapter and identified examples through an inductive analysis of early childhood qualitative studies published since 1989. Among the examples I used were Bill Ayer's (1989) "life-narratives" of six preschool teachers, Deborah Ceglowski's (1994) feminist analysis of interviews with Head Start teachers and administrators, and Bronwyn Davie's (1989) feminist poststructuralist study of preschool children's gender identity socialization. In the chapter, research approaches are described and the examples offered as ways to help those outside the circle of "true believers" to see value in the products of such research and their potential contributions to educational decision making. Again, this strategy reveals my orientation to making change gradually and from within.

Where Are We Going When We Make the Postmodern Turn?

Part of the reason I am attracted to postmodern analyses is that they add complexity that makes modern perspectives seem two-dimensional at best, and they embrace paradox in ways that match up well with my experience of the world. At the same time, my students and I are often overwhelmed with the complexity and are perplexed by the paradoxes in postmodern thought. I will hint at a few of the problems and paradoxes discovered while working with postmodern thinking in a thoroughly modern university. Each would make an inviting topic for a doctoral seminar on postmodern thought.

What comes after a post-everything world? At one level, this could be just a semantic problem: Will a post-poststructuralist social science emerge? But more deeply, is it possible to "construct" a new social science (or new literary criticism, new psychoanalysis, new linguistics...) now that the act of construction has been deconstructed? Many of my students expect scholars they read to offer an alternative to what they tear down; the students see it as unfair to deconstruct the world without offering something to fill the void. They resonate with statements like, "deconstruction without reconstruction is an act of irresponsibility" (Putnam, quoted by Cannella, 1998, p. 2). I point out that they are operating on modern assumptions when they make such claims, but I share their frustration and wonder with them about what follows the postmodern moment.

What would a postmodern text look like, anyway? Even though their writing is dense and sometimes convoluted, all the post-structuralists I read are making their arguments using the logic and structure of modern thinking and writing. The most elegant essays on deconstruction of text are constructed in ways that could not stand the test of their own theses. As Derrida (1991, p. 41) acknowledged, "The enterprise of deconstruction always in a certain way falls prey to its own work." In *QSE*, we tried to experiment with different forms of text (e.g., Meloy, 1993; Tierney, 1993), but these efforts were difficult to get past our reviewers and far from revolutionary in their form. Perhaps a James Joyce for the social sciences will burst onto the scene; but who will publish his/her work?

Isn't poststructuralism another grand narrative? Doctoral students who get into critiquing grand theories, truth claims, and metanarratives understand the paradoxical positioning of post-structuralism as a discourse that deconstructs discourses. Again, in form and intent, it's hard to distinguish poststructuralism from other discourses that systematically organize knowledge and make claims to universal validity. Even appeals to analyze local instances of knowledge and power, for example, are based on a universalized generalization that such analyses are possible and worthwhile. My modern mind gets dizzy trying to follow the spiraling logic here. My postmodern sensibilities are satisfied with the realization that it is indeed a paradox.

Isn't it possible that the terms "critical poststructuralism" and "feminist poststructuralism" are oxymorons? When I first started reading the poststructuralist critique of grand theory, an early thought was: Where does this leave my friends doing feminist research? As I worked my way through Foucault's and Lyotard's deconstructions of Marxism (see Seidman, 1994), I wondered: How will my colleagues doing critical theory work respond? My simple reading was that the poststructuralist critique delivered a heavy blow to generalizing discourses like feminist studies and critical theory. I was not surprised that those applying perspectives already at odds with the mainstream would be the ones most interested in the radical epistemology of postmodern thought. I am still surprised that so much contemporary poststructuralist work appears uncritically to pick and choose from the seminal thinking at the base of the perspective. I would not go so far as Aronowitz (1992, p. 315), who charges that "Foucault's work has been shamelessly appropriated by his universalizing disciples," but I do have questions. For example: Do not feminist and critical discourses include all the elements of a master narrative? If not, how would we recognize the work as feminist or critical? At a recent conference, one of my colleagues explained that of course the discourse of feminism framed her work, "after all, it's *feminist* poststructuralism." I admire her work and know it provides important insights. Ultimately, it may not matter what it is called, but, in spite of the work of Butler (1994) and others, the question persists: Can it, at the same time, be poststructuralist and remain grounded in the decidedly structuralist metanarrative of feminism?

Is there a cure for postmodern malaise? Many of us fought very hard to move beyond positivism; now the postpositivist assumptions at the base of our work are challenged by the poststructuralist critique. Trying to follow postmodern thought to logical conclusions is difficult and depressing. One understandable reaction among scholars is a kind of "poststructural paralysis" that can be debilitating (Hatch & Wisniewski, 1995, p. 130). It may be time to do less reflecting on our work and more of the work itself. One form that such work might take is described by Seidman (1992, p. 70) as "local narratives [that] would analyze a circumscribed social phenomenon in a densely contextual way. This procedure entails analyzing an event...in its particular social setting...while attending to its heterogeneous meanings for different populations." Other university activity (i.e., teaching and service) might benefit from being more local, contextual, and particular as well.

For Lemert (1992), "Postmodernism is an ironic general social theory," which has as its first principle: "Reality is discussible—not much more than this" (p. 23). Dealing with pervasive irony and accepting transient notions of reality is difficult for most of us and deeply troubling for individuals unused to thinking outside the comfort of modern discourses. As I have tried to demonstrate in this chapter, there are ways to introduce students, colleagues, and readers to postmodern thought without creating so much disequilibrium that they dismiss the ideas out of hand. My goal is to help my audiences learn to live with "contradictory discourses" (Kristeva, 1981). My overall approach is to invite others to join me as I seek out, struggle with, and construct my own understandings of postmodern thought. Even in a conservative institutional setting, such an approach can give others new ways to look at and think about the world.

Appendix A

Ideas to consider in preparation for our discussion
Where do you stand on the following?
From Tobin:

- Structuralists are convinced that systematic knowledge is possible; poststructuralists claim to know only the impossibility of this knowledge.
- Foucault advises us to ignore the conscious, stated intentions of do-gooders, and to concentrate instead on the effects of the practices they recommend.
- Jameson's key features of late capitalism are superficiality, the dominance of the signifier over the signified, simulation, commodity reification, and waning of effect.
- Because words have no fixed or stable relationship to the things or concepts they are meant to signify—the meanings of words can only be described with more words—meaning is endlessly deferred.
- A prissy hesitance to write in other than clinical terms about children's interest in the bodily lower stratum contributes to a bowdlerized curriculum that fails to live up to its claim to begin "where children are at."
- Queers can be understood as protesting not just the normal behavior they are accused of not having, but the idea of normal behavior.

From Sarup:

- Postmodernity emphasizes diverse forms of individual and social identity. The autonomous subject has been dispersed into a range of plural, polymorphous, subject-positions inscribed with language.
- Lyotard attacked the legitimizing myths of the modern age (the grand narratives), the progressive liberation of humanity through science, and the idea that philosophy can develop universally valid knowledge.
- In postmodernism, there is a shift from content to form or style; a transformation of reality into images; the fragmentation of time into a series of perpetual presents.
- There is a move to "textualize" everything: history, philosophy, jurisprudence, sociology, and other disciplines are treated as so many optional "kinds of writing" or discourses.
- Scientific knowledge has always existed in competition and conflict with another kind of knowledge: narrative.

From Hatch & Wisniewski

- Poststructuralism questions whether researchers can accurately represent reality or can gain access to an independent reality.
- The postmodern focus is on the text per se, not on life beyond text.
- Poststructuralism situates "subjectivity" and "identity" within multiple competing and conflicting narratives. We inherit narratives already codified and populated by other's meanings. As selves, we narrate our world to give it form and meaning; but at the same time, we are being narrated because the forms we use are not our own—they belong to other times, other places, other contexts.
- Poststructuralism assumes knowledge as partial, power as dispersed, and identity as always in flux.
- A life (the story of a life) is created in the consciousness to give order and meaning to events that have no "intrinsic or immanent relations." The telling of a story is in a real sense the construction of a life.
- Language, in both its written and spoken forms, is always inherently unstable, in flux, and made up of the traces of other signs and symbolic statements. Hence there can never be a clear, unambiguous statement of anything.
- What does the text mean? For the deconstructivist it can only mean: anything or nothing.

IECE 650, A. Hatch, U. Tennessee

Appendix B

Characteristics of Postmodernity
1. Form and style are more important than content and substance.
2. Images are more important than reality.
3. Time is fragmented into a series of perpetual presents.
4. Individual identities have been dispersed into a range of plural selves.
5. Consumption has become the driving economic force, and all aspects of postmodern life are being commodified and sold.
6. Feelings have been separated from experience.

IECE 650, A. Hatch, U. Tennessee

Appendix C

Generalizations from Poststructuralist Thought
1. Truth claims (grand narratives) are social constructions, not universal constants.
2. We should not be concerned with the "truth" of grand narratives but with the consequences of action based on those narratives.
3. Knowledge is always partial, local, and subjective.
4. Knowledge and power are inseparably linked.
5. For deconstructivists, we can never know life itself—only texts of lives are possible; we can never know reality—only textualized discourses are possible.
6. Scientific discourses compete with a fundamentally different discourse: narrative.
7. The telling of a story is the construction of a life.

IECE 650, A. Hatch, U. Tennessee

Appendix D

Discussion of *Ties That Stress*

Elkind describes modern, nuclear families and contrasts them with postmodern, permeable families. What are the key differences?

Do you agree with his description of these two family types? Explain.

What is the impact of postmodernity on Knoxville, Tennessee?

Is it possible to return to modern times and the nuclear family? Is it desirable?

IECE 584, A. Hatch, U. Tennessee

Appendix E

Elkind Reading

MODERN	POSTMODERN
NUCLEAR FAMILY	*PERMEABLE FAMILY*
Sentiments: romantic love	Sentiments: consensual love
maternal love	shared parenting
domesticity	urbanity
Values: togetherness	Values: independence
innocence	competence

Fully Modern	Mostly Modern	Mostly Postmodern	Fully Postmodern
1	2	3	4

Rank the following on the continuum:

m = my family
h = families in my hometown
u = U.S. families overall
p = families of my peers

IECE 584, A. Hatch, U. Tennessee

CONCLUSION

An Early Childhood Dreamspace of Social Justice and Equity

Lourdes Diáz Soto
The Pennsylvania State University

Ants can move a mighty mountain.
Water can drip through stone.
If you do not climb the mountain, you will not see the plain.

Chinese proverbs collected by Ruthanne Lum McCunn (1991)

The nation and the popular media have recently been shocked by incidents of violence in predominantly white schools such as Paducah, Kentucky; Jonesboro, Arkansas; Pearl, Mississippi; Springfield, Oregon; and Edinboro, Pennsylvania. The criminal justice system is debating issues of childhood as it makes decisions about whether the perpetrators should be tried as adults or as children. Should the child's age be the determining factor or should the type of crime determine the punishment?

It is evident that these schools reflect the society, the society that is clinging so to the sacred western lens. One of the minors in the Arkansas shooting was being trained by his own grandfather from his private arsenal of firearms. Some of the school shooters were dressed in camouflaged clothing and were imitating the vision they have seen portrayed in the media (and in their homes?). These perpetrators evidently did not fully understand the consequences of their actions nor have they learned the attributes of peace and compassion.

As the schools are flashed on the screen it becomes clear that western regimented, quantifiable, scientific driven epistemologies have not brought peace and wisdom to the schoolhouse door. Even the architectural designs of the schools reflect more of a prison-like environment than the circular notions of peace and harmony. How do children make sense of a world that bombards them with capitalistic driven notions, violence, and the glorification of the young, the beautiful, the restless? At a time when we are so concerned with our children's welfare shouldn't we begin to examine multiple ways of knowing based upon children's daily realities?

The goal of this concluding piece is twofold, first to critique the sacredness of the western lens while integrating the work of my colleagues (early childhood reconceptualists and critical theorists); and second to provide the reader with the hope and possibility for a collaboratively charted, newly evolving, liberating, "third space": an early childhood dreamspace of social justice and equity. In order to accomplish this I will share with the reader salient issues imfluencing early childhood education in profit-driven cultures, and "other ways" and perhaps "multiple ways" of envisioning childhood.

Early Childhood Education in Profit-Driven Cultures

The economic engine and the capitalistic concerns of our nation have influenced the politics of early childhood education. Williamson (1997), in her call for "The Healing of America," refers to "blood money" and states, "Money is, at heart, the great moral issue of our time. America must have a serious discussion with itself about the wisdom of allowing the market to drive us" (p. 216).

The fact that our nation is so concerned with Wall Street profits has meant that our familiar visions of childhood are disappearing and being replaced by a different kind of childhood. We have seen young persons in sophisticated Calvin Kleins, the Disneyfication of children's toys and media, Internet-literate second graders, the appeal of the Spice Girls, Joe Camel's reach for our children, and the recent release of the Tweety Bird stamp.

Do you remember how the phrase, "It's economy stupid" drove Bill Clinton's presidential campaign? Newt Gingrich has even tried to draw connections among notions of family values and the income tax system. It is clear that legislators in Congress have undertaken a mean-spirited agenda that disregards the needs of children and families when their coded words include "welfare reform," "English-only," "law and order," "immigration reform," and "private school vouchers." Much of this agenda ultimately punishes vulnerable families, the poor, the working class, single head of household families, children, and families of color. The rewards in the capitalistic system are for a small privileged elitist few. Have you ever wondered what would happen if families had as much clout as the well-funded lobbying arms of the tobacco industry or the firearms industry? Are the rewards in the capitalistic system only for a small privileged elitist few?

The capitalist system has also meant that childcare teachers are among the lowest paid workers in the nation. Only 15 occupations pay lower median wages, according to the Bureau of Labor Statistics. A typical childcare teacher earns $6.12 an hour while a parking lot attendant earns $6.38 and a bus driver earns $11.58. The U.S. Treasury Department has documented the importance of childcare to the economy and its value to business as it increases productivity and reduces absenteeism. Marcy Whitebook of the Center for the Child Care Workforce notes, "To be focused on getting mothers to work, without focusing on quality care for their kids, is shortsighted, and stupid at best, and criminal at worst" (Gardner, 1988).

Profits reaped by our country have been made on the backs of our childcare teachers and children. Childcare teachers are victimized by the system as they search for jobs from center to center in order to obtain the best possible hourly wage. Most of these centers do not provide health insurance for their workers. The "glamorous" lifestyle of childcare teachers includes washing toilets and scrubbing floors. The children are the ones who lose out in centers where there is a high worker turnover. It is apparent that in order to be a childcare teacher in America you must truly love children and families because there are no economic incentives or health care benefits.

This profit-driven perspective is also affecting the health of our children. The environmental pollution of the industrial waste site installed in the South Bronx (see National Public Radio, May 1996) is just one example of the health dangers our children endure on a daily basis. The thick fumes, the pollution, the odors, the war–torn–like housing, the rats and cockroaches continue to affect the wheezing, the breathing, and the opportunity for a healthy future. Shouldn't our whole nation be outraged by the unhealthy conditions our children are experiencing? Or will the bottom line, the profit, the big industrial giants, the privileged few continue to reap the profits on the backs of our poor and neglected children? The children of the South Bronx, the children of Appalachia, the children in the housing projects of Chicago, the children in reservations throughout America struggle in an American nightmare, as the industrial giants and the privileged few sleep in their plush mansions and travel to their summer playgrounds.

Beth Blue Swadener, in her piece, asks us to critically analyze the political shift to the Right that is being referred to as the "new federalism" or "devolution." Relying on Valerie Polakow's work, Swadener describes the Republican vilification of mothers as "breeding mules," "alligators," and "monkeys" during the debate of the "Personal Responsibility Act." Swadener asks us to think about "who benefits from this growth of poverty?" as we continue to blame the victims and disregard the economic and societal forces and dynamics.

The media has also disregarded children's daily realities as it hungers for profits and thinks little about the effects of violence in children's lives. Recent research continues to document that young children will imitate what they see on the screen. David Walsh of the National Institute of Media and the Family conducted a simple experiment in a Minneapolis day care center. He observed that when two- to five-year-olds watched "Barney," the purple dinosaur, they sang, held hands, marched together, and laughed. When children watched the aggressive avengers of the "Mighty Morphin Power Rangers," they initiated karate chopping and high kicks with one another. In addition, Dale Kunkel of the University of California at Santa Barbara recently conducted a three-year study and concluded that the way violence is portrayed as desirable, necessary, and painless poses a serious risk to children (Marks, 1998).

The obsession with profits has even led to the commodification of early childhood education by our own professional organizations. Glenda MacNaughton and Patrick Hughes (this volume) in their brilliant piece "Take the Money and Run?: Toys, Consumerism, and Capitalism in Early Childhood Conferences," ask us to examine the ethical dilemmas posed by this continued trend. They ask us to debate the issues and to critically reflect on the place these toys should have in our conferences when we meet to deliberate the important issues in our field.

Bloch and Popkewitz, in their illuminating and provocative piece, point to the role of foundations and institutions of higher learning in the historical evolution of early childhood education. Their piece helps us to understand how we came to be in this place with sacred heroes and sacred child development ways of viewing children and families.

The making/remaking of the teacher, the child, and the parent that are embodied in these pedagogical discourses are, following Rose (1989), "governing the soul" and effects of power. These effects of power historically need to be continually scrutinized and examined historically as to their paradoxes and ironies.

It is clear that it will be crucial for the field to continue to critically analyze how privileged ones and more powerful elements have influenced the direction of the field toward the scientific-driven epistemologies and the sacred western lens. Who stands to benefit from the overreliance on western ways of seeing the world? Why has it been so difficult for the field to examine the western canon? Where are our ethical concerns ?

Are There "Other Ways" and
Perhaps Multiple Ways of Envisioning Childhood?

The lingering question for us is how issues of power have affected the politics of early childhood education. Abundant evidence indicates that decades of western ways of early childhood education have not led us to a safe and peaceful society. Is there knowledge and wisdom that we can gain from the other, from the feminist, from the critical?

We have, for too long, in the field of early childhood education, relied on scientific-Cartesian driven epistemologies. Smith (1994) notes that in many ways science, although necessary, is also the "winnowed wisdom of the human race." Capra (1991) in his book, "The Tao of Physics," calls for a shift from an attitude of domination and control to one of cooperation and nonviolence. In addition, he states

> The Cartesian paradigm was based on a belief in the certainty of scientific knowledge...In the new paradigm it is recognized that all scientific concepts and theories are limited and approximate. Science can never provide any complete and definitive understanding (p. 333).

If the scientists themselves are indicating that scientific-driven epistemologies need to be tempered, are limited, are approximate, and "never provide any complete and definitive understandings," then why is the field of early childhood education clinging so to outdated, outmoded paradigms?

Social justice and equity have not been uppermost in the minds of the child development experts who use yardsticks and measuring tapes to decide what is a "normal" childhood and who falls within the purview of the standard norms. Issues of power, issues of language, and culture are rarely discussed and when they are included, children and families are essentialized and categorized. Are there other ways of framing early childhood education?

The sacred western lens along with the sacred heroes and texts has meant that it has often appeared almost impossible to begin to critique the field. Jan Jipson, Sally Lubeck, Mimi Block, Shirley Kessler, Beth Swadener and others valiantly began the discussion on a variety of levels, including the historical perspective, the notion of developmentally appropriate practices (NAEYC), and how to begin the dialogue (Kessler & Swadener, 1992). Gail Sloan Cannella (1997) in her book describes how "childhood discourses actually conceal and even disqualify certain forms of knowledge, generating power for particular groups and subjugating others" (p. 42).

Cannella adds that the universal child discourse has generated positions of power including colonialist power perspectives. This discourse has been grounded in the belief in universal human development and predetermined experiences.

As the field of early childhood education critically and honestly examines the sanctity of the single western lens, it can begin to move beyond existing and outdated paradigms toward a newly evolving and liberating "third space." It will mean that we can move toward the critical, toward the multicultural, toward the dialogic, toward the feminist, toward the personal, with others, with the silenced, and in solidarity with multiple players. This can also reflect the vision for our journey that is our early childhood critical multicultural dreamspace of social justice and equity.

In their book, Brendtro, Brokenleg, and Van Bockern (1990) depict examples of Native American childrearing practices that provide one possible "other" perspective. These writers describe the optimism of the Swedish sociologist Ellen Key who envisioned "the century of the child" and the need for the "reclaiming" environments that are needed in order to restore, to recover, and to redeem. The concepts of generosity, belonging, independence, and mastery are illustrated within a circular depiction by the Native American artist George Bluebird. They state that "members of the dominant culture who define success in terms of personal wealth and possessions are usually unable to view positively the Native values of simplicity, generosity and nonmaterialism" (p. 45).

In the book *Shaman's Circle* (Wood & Howell, 1996) life is also depicted as a series of circles where harmony, continuity, the bonds with nature, and the need for personal meaning are evident. An excerpt from this beautifully illustrated book can help to remind us about other ways of envisioning early childhood education.

> "From my grandmother I learned courage, the kind needed to fight in what I believe in. From my grandfather I learned patience, the winter he went hungry so that our family could eat... I was given the opportunity to exchange self importance for wisdom." (p. 33)

Nila Rinehart describes how tribal children are taught to not only honor tribal practices but also to view themselves as connected to one another and to the greater universe. When children are taught that balance is important in their lives it can lead to a sense of belonging. Can you envision how much of a healthier, happier life you would have, our nation's children would have, and our country would have, if we all learned how to lead more balanced lives?

Eastern traditions may also hold valuable knowledge for the field of early childhood education. Capra (1991) notes how "the Chinese mind was not given to abstract logical thinking and developed a language which is very different from that which evolved in the West" (p. 103).

Capra in his discussion of the traditional Chinese writings notes how many words (characters) can be used as adjectives, verbs, or nouns so that the word order of a sentence is determined not so much by the grammatical rules but rather by the emotional content. The speaker, in this case, is more interested in influencing the listener than in expressing ideas. The Taoist learn about the interplay and the dynamics of polar relationships, yin and yan. For Western thinkers the idea of unity within a field of opposites is extremely difficult to comprehend.

Many early childhood educators (Beth Blue Swadener; California Tomorrow researchers, Nila Rinehart; Soto, 1997a, b; Soto, Paul, & Gutierrez, 1997) have asked us to think about how we might learn to collaborate and work in solidarity with what Lisa Delpit (1993) refers to as "other people's children," the families, and the children that our society has learned to somehow deem "less valuable," "non-traditional," "those others." Lisa Delpit (1993) in her work describes how teachers need to examine their practices in light of the children they are serving. She states that "appropriate education of poor children and children of color can only be devised in consultation with adults who share their culture" (p. 138).

Beth Swadener (in this volume) sees the need for building authentic alliances with families. The work from California Tomorrow asks us to engage in dialogue and reflection about race, language, and culture on an ongoing basis. Ivy Goduka (1998) from South Africa calls for the healing perspectives that envision teachers as cultural workers and healers. Alice Paul, Cathy Gutierrez, Antonia Lopez, and myself have presented collaborative sessions at annual professional conferences (National Association for the Education of Young Children and National Association for Bilingual Education) asking early childhood educators to dream about the possibilities and to integrate non-Western perspectives into the field. We refer to these nontraditional concepts as "wisdom" by integrating notions of early childhood teachers as "architects," early childhood teachers as "wisdom keepers," early childhood teachers as "dream keepers," and early childhood teachers as "healers."

At a recent conference of the National Association for the Education of Young Children, the larger than life-sized posters of Piaget and the total celebration of Piaget were quite evident. I counted one session in the entire conference from a postmodern perspective and that was a session Janet Gonzalez Mena and I put together along with Jan Jipson and one panel presenter at the Conference for Early Childhood Teacher Educators. One of my dearest colleagues teased me at that conference since that was the year I ventured at critiquing Piaget. "Don't look at the posters!" she would say.

On many levels I felt awkward and foolish as my own students warned me, "Don't do it Dr. Soto!" But at the same time as I involved myself in the research and thought about Piaget's initial biologically driven work with *limnaea stagnalis* (snails), I found myself becoming quite passionate and inserted a quip that perhaps we are not all snails, perhaps some of us are jellyfish, or perhaps others are lobsters (Soto, 1997b)! It was heartwarming for me to receive such a warm and positive reaction from my colleagues. I learned that it is indeed possible and that together we can continue the critique of the sacred heroes and the sacred Western lens. As we pass the rod on to our younger colleagues I know that we have only just begun.

I feel that this is an opportune time in many ways. Opportune because children and families are calling out for equity based upon their daily realities and opportune because our colleagues in the field are searching for alternate models. I was reminded of this at the California Tomorrow meeting. Scholars from around the country sat at a table to discuss a document and research that California Tomorrow was about to release. The issue of "quality child care" became controversial when one of the researchers claimed that the phrase could not be inserted as a part of the document because "quality child care" referred to her quantifiable research only. The question became how can you talk about quality without viewing issues of language and culture? It is obvious that we live in different worlds and that we need to find that "third space" lest we continue to rely on the quantifiable scientific-driven epistemologies that speak with one winnowed voice.

Even privileged early childhood scholars who do not fall within the taken-for-granted child development perspective are themselves shunned by the quantified, quantifiable elitist club and struggle to have their voices heard. The reconceptualist early childhood scholars have begun to initiate their own conferences, their own sessions, and their own writings in order to find a safe space to examine the critical, the postmodern, and the feminist. A word of caution needs to be inserted so that in our attempt to initiate other views and other perspectives that another exclusive club is not initiated that leaves out players representing the others, the culturally and linguistically diverse, the poor, and the very real needs of American families and children.

Our own vision needs to differ from the sacred Western lens and the cultural invaders. Freire (1970) reminded us that cultural invasion helps to explicate the struggle that colonized and oppressed people face within a climate of disregard.

> The invaders penetrate the cultural context of another group, in disrespect of the latter's potentialities; they impose their own view of the world upon those they invade and inhibit the creativity of the invaded by curbing their expression (p. 150).

The western lens has attempted to define the norm, the acceptable, while at the same time excluding the culturally and linguistically diverse, the poor, the personal, the feminist, and the other.

Freire (1985) also indicated that "it would be extremely naive to expect the dominant classes to develop a type of education that would enable subordinate classes to perceive social injustices critically" (p. 102).

It is vital to remember that the cultural invaders are armed with newly invasive tools that influence the daily realities of children and families. When critical theorists such as Steinberg and Kincheloe (1997) and Giroux, Steinberg, Kincheloe, and McLaren ask us to consider the popular construction of childhood via the Disney movies, the Barbie dolls, the trips to McDonalds, and television's violent Mighty Morphin Power Rangers, it becomes clear that invasive practices come from the media from toys and from children's everyday interactions in a complex postmodern context.

Our children are not growing up with the Dick and Jane basal readers or with the *Brady Bunch* television series. For some these were idealized images, e.g., Bob Keeshan, the creator of Captain Kangaroo:

> Childhood for every child, should be as close as possible to the ideal world of Dick and Jane. Sometimes the ugliness of our surrounding gets in the way. With love and security—an occasional ice cream bar—our children will turn out like Dick and Jane. (Kismaric and Keiferman, 1996, preface)

Children growing up in postmodern America are not a part of Dick and Jane's world, populated by white people, or in families that are necessarily headed by two parents. Whole language proponents are no doubt glad to see Dick and Jane leave children's classrooms, while critical multiculturalists find no solace in the exclusive monocultural, sexist, racist, Western lens of the Dick and Jane readers. It is clear that in postmodern America children growing up in the housing projects of Chicago, Philadelphia, Los Angeles, and the South Bronx neighborhoods have no grassy fields to play in, no backyard to run in, and most likely no Spot or Puff. I have seen too many of our children restrict themselves to small areas of their apartment or homes because the outside world frightens them.

We have for too long disregarded the idea that children can lead us toward greater wisdom. Lucinda and Anita are two daughters of inner-city Philadelphia that reminded me of this fact during a recent visit to the city. Their childcare teacher introduced them to me, and I learned that their friendship is quite remarkable. Evidently both families struggle economically, with Lucinda's family engaged in seasonal migrant activities, while Anita's family pursues multiple part time jobs in the city and outside the city. I observed how these two children interacted and how they reached out to each other in compassionate ways. The children have learned a kind of sharing that includes snacks, turn taking, dramatic experiences, walking trips, and generally sharing and caring.

The clothing was what first caught my attention. Lucinda owns two basic faded outfits that are washed and pressed for her on a daily basis so she can take turns with a dark rose skirt and its matching top and a dark green skirt with a striped top. Anita, on the other hand, comes to the center with what appear to be hand-stitched cotton outfits in multiple florals and sometimes patched together mixed patterns. One day Anita arrived with a new velour tiger fabric jumper. Lucinda asked Anita if she could touch the jumper and Anita complied. I later overheard Anita whisper to Lucinda, "I'll bring it so you can wear it after tomorrow." Sure enough the next day Anita brought the jumper neatly folded in a brown paper bag. Lucinda took it home and wore it the following day. Both children seemed to beam that day as they continued on their journey of friendship, sharing and caring. I wonder if as adults we may not be able to learn from Anita and Lucinda about creative ways to share and to care?

As we struggle with the multiple issues of power in the field, it may be useful for us to continue to consider how the field will benefit from postmodern thought. Maher (1987), for example, proposed the need for a synthesis among models of liberatory pedagogy and feminist perspectives, since in her analysis, the gender models tend to ignore power while the liberation models have tended to ignore the personal domain. Maher finds that the "aspiration for a life of 'completeness'" cannot be solved at the level of theory, but must be worked out in practice "in our muddled daily lives" (p. 99).

How might we begin "in our muddled daily lives" to take the onus off the oppressed players and take a good clear picture of invasive practices? Moraes (1996) provides us with a possibility with her call for a dialogic-critical pedagogy.

> A dialogic critical pedagogy that makes the possibility for voices to be heard within a dialogic social awareness in which the voice of the oppressed reaches the oppressor (who is another oppressed) and both agents must engage toward a reciprocal freedom (p. 118).

The call for a dialogue of social multivoicedness sees the Freirian perspective as providing the impetus from the margins to the center while the Bakhtinian movement exemplifies a move from the margins and from the center. The notion of a dialogue of social multivoicedness also provides additional space for possibility for the players who are systematically silenced, forcing them to struggle with disrespect of their knowledge and wisdom.

Conclusion

It is possible for us to begin to anticipate "other ways" and "multiple ways" of envisioning early childhood education. As we dream our dreams and foresee our newly liberating "third spaces," we will need to ensure that children and families are an integral part of the chart making, and map making that help us to understand the emerging daily realities in this postmodern world. As ethical early childhood professionals we can work in solidarity and as collaborators ensuring equity and social justice. The *consejo* and advice from families in Steeltown, Pennsylvania (Soto, 1997a) is timely as they remind us that educators are not the only knowledge brokers. Collaborative power models hold the promise of affording us a view from the mountain top in solidarity with multiple players, toward the dialogic, with the other, with the silenced, toward the personal, toward the feminist, toward our critical early childhood dreamspace of social justice and equity.

We already have much wisdom and much knowledge. We are not traveling alone. Many have come before us. We have multiple choices and yet we may choose to forge paths that we are only just imagining. Hatch asks us to consider introducing postmodern thought without creating so much disequilibrium that people will dismiss our ideas. Is there a combination model that will feel comfortable for all of us?

How might we pursue liberating, anti-racist, feminist, critical, revolutionary models?

Can we envision an early childhood education that is liberating, anti-racist, feminist, critical, and revolutionary?

We can no longer afford to allow the sacred Western lenses to "govern our very souls." Our experimental and newly evolving paradigms will mean that we are traveling creative paths, as architects, as builders, as wisdom keepers, as healers who discover, build, and chart newly liberating spaces of hope and possibility. Only when we collaboratively envision an early childhood education that is built on a theory of cultural democracy and acknowledges the issues of power and the political nature of the field can we begin to hope. Only then will we find ourselves in our multiple roles and as cultural workers invested in healing. Only when we dream our dreams in solidarity with multiple voices will diverse children, families, and communities experience social justice and equity in our lifetimes. Only when we garner our greatest courage and wisdom will we find the light and the peace in our dreamspace. Our goal in solidarity can mean the emancipation and liberation of children, families, childcare teachers, our field, and ultimately America.

Ants can move a mighty mountain.
Water can drip through stone.
If you do not climb the mountain, you will not see the plain.

Chinese proverbs collected by Ruthanne Lum McCunn (1991)

BIBLIOGRAPHY

Allen, R. (Ed.). (1990). *The concise Oxford dictionary*. Oxford: Clarendon Press.

Allen, R. (1997). Disney's ready to read with Pooh. *Focus on Early Childhood, 9*(4), 2.

Ames, L., & Ellsworth, J. (1997). *Women reformed, women empowered: Poor mothers and the endangered promise of Head Start*. Philadelphia: Temple University Press.

Aptekar, L. (1996). *Street children in Nairobi, Kenya*. Unpublished manuscript. San Jose State University. (Project report to National Science Foundation)

————. (1994). Street children in the developing world: A review of their condition. *Cross-cultural Research, 28*(3), 195–224.

Arnold, M. S., & Swadener, B. B. (1993). Savage inequalities and the discourse of risk: What of the white children who have so much green grass? *The Review of Education, 15*, 261–272.

Aronowitz, S. (1992). The tensions of critical theory: Is negative dialectics all there is? In S. Seidman and D. G. Wagner (Eds.), *Postmodernism and social theory* (pp. 289–321). Cambridge, MA: Blackwell.

Ayre, E. (1996). *They won't take no for an answer: The Relais Enfants-Parents*. Early Childhood Development: Practice and Reflections Series, Number 11. The Hague: Bernard van Leer Foundations.

Ayers, W. (1989). *The good preschool teacher: Six teachers reflect on their lives*. New York: Teachers College Press.

Azhar, R. (1998). Children: A cost-benefit analysis. Paper presented at the International Conference on Reconceptualizing Early Childhood Education. Honolulu, Hawaii.

Baker, B. (1998). Childhood-as-rescue in the emergence and spread of the U.S. public school. In T. Popkewitz & M. Brennan (Eds.), *Foucault's Challenge: Discourse, knowledge, and power in education* (pp. 117–143). New York: Teachers College Press.

Baudrillard, J. (1988). *Selected writings*. Stanford, CA: Stanford University Press.

Beatty, B. (1995). Preschool education in America. New Haven: Yale University Press.

Benner, S. M. (1998). *Special education issues within the context of American society.* Belmont, CA: Wadsworth.

Bernstein, R. (1988). *Beyond objectivism and relativism: Science, hermeneutics, and praxis.* Philadelphia: The University of Pennsylvania Press.

Beyer, L., & Bloch, M. (1996). Theory: An Analysis (Part 1). In *Advances in Early Education and Day Care*, Volume 8, p. 39. JAI Press.

Bledstein, B. (1976). *The culture of professionalism: The middle class and the development of higher education in America.* New York: Norton.

Bloch, M. N. (1987). Becoming scientific and professional: An historical perspective on the aims and effects of early education. In T. S. Popkewitz (Ed.), *The formation of school subjects* (pp. 25–26). Basingstoke, England: Falmer Press.

Block, A. (1995). *Occupied reading: Critical foundations for an ecological theory.* New York: Garland.

————. & Choi, S. (1990). Conceptions of play in the history of early childhood education. *Child and Youth Care Quarterly, 19*(1), 31–46.

————. (1992). Critical perspectives on the historical relationship between child development and early childhood education research. In S. Kessler, & B. B. Swadener (Eds.), *Reconceptualizing the early childhood curriculum: Beginning the dialogue* (pp. 3–20). New York: Teachers College Press.

————. (1996, October). *Age, stage and grade: Transitions in development and schooling in Russian early schooling.* Paper presented at the International Conference on Vygotsky and Education, Moscow.

————. Seward, D., & Seidlinger, P. (1989). What history tells us about public schools for four -year olds. *Theory into Practice, XXVIII*(1), 11–18.

Bourdieu, P. (1972). *Outline of a theory of practice.* Cambridge, UK: Cambridge University Press.

Bredekamp, S. (Ed.). (1987). *Developmentally appropriate practice in early childhood programs serving children from birth through age 8.* Washington, DC: National Association for the Education of Young Children.

————. & Copple, C. (Eds.) (1997). *Developmentally appropriate practice in early childhood programs* (Rev. ed.). Washington, DC: National Association for the Education of Young Children.

Brendtro, L. K., Brokenleg., M., & Van Bockern, S. (1990). *Reclaiming youth at risk: Our hope for the future.* Bloomington: National Educational Service.

Brown, A., Ash, D., Rutherford, M., Nakagawa, K., Gordon, A., & Campione, J. (1993). Distributed expertise in the classroom. In G. Salomon (Ed.), *Distributed cognition: Psychological and educational considerations* (pp. 188–228). New York: Cambridge University Press.

Brown, J. S., Collins, A., & Duiguid, P. (1989). Situated cognitions and the culture of learning. *Educational Researcher, 18*, 32–42.

Brown, R. H. (1978). Bureaucracy as praxis: Toward a political phenomenology of formal organizations. *Administrative Science Quarterly, 23*(3), 365–382.

Bruner, J. (1986). *Actual minds, possible worlds.* Cambridge, MA: Harvard University Press.

Burchell, G., Gordon, C., & Miller, P. (1991). *The Foucault effect: Studies in governmentality.* Chicago: The University of Chicago Press.

Burman, E. (1994). *Deconstructing developmental psychology.* London: Routledge.

Butler, J. (1994). Contingent foundations: Feminism and the question of postmodernism. In S. Seidman (Ed.), *The postmodern turn: New perspectives on social theory* (pp. 153–170). New York: Cambridge University Press.

Cagle, L., Coleman, L. J., Benner, S. B., Hatch, J. A., Judge, S., & Blank, K. (1997, March). *Building a teacher education program from scratch.* Paper presented at the North East Wales Institute International Conference on Reforming Teacher Education, Wrexham, Wales.

Cannella, G. (1997). *Deconstructing early childhood education.* New York: Peter Lang.

———. (1998). *Deconstructing early childhood education: Social justice and revolution.* New York: Peter Lang.

———. (1999). Post-formal thought as critique, reconceptualization, and possibility for teacher education reform. In J. Kincheloe, S. Steinberg, and L. Villaverde (Eds.), *Rethinking intelligence: Confronting psychological assumptions about teaching and learning.* New York: Routledge.

Capra, F. (1991). *The Tao of Physics.* Boston: Shambhala.

Carlsson-Paige, N., & Levin, D. E. (1990). *Who's calling the shots? How to respond effectively to children's fascination with war play and war toys.* Gabriola Island, BC.: New Society Publishers.

Castel, R. (1991). From dangerous to risk. In G. Burchell, C. Gordon, and P. Miller (Eds.), *The Foucault effect.* (pp. 281–298) Chicago: The University of Chicago Press.

Ceglowski, D. (1994). Conversations about Head Start salaries: A feminist analysis. *Early Childhood Research Quarterly, 9,* 367–386.

Ceglowski, D. (in press). *Policies from practice: The stories of the Whitewater Head Start program.* New York: Teachers College Press.

Cherryholmes, C. H. (1988). *Power and criticism: Poststructural investigations in education.* New York: Teachers College Press.

Children's Defense Fund (1994). *The State of America's Children.* Washington, DC: Children's Defense Fund.

Cook, D., & Fine, M. (1995). "Motherwit": Childrearing lessons from African American mothers of low income. In B. B. Swadener & S. Lubeck (Eds.), *Children and families "at promise": Deconstructing the discourse of risk* (pp. 118–142). Albany, NY: State University of New York Press.

Cupit, C. G. (1996). Educative care and the media. *Every Child, 2*(1), 4–5.

Danziger, K. (1990). *Constructing the subject: Historical origins of psychological research.* New York: Cambridge University Press.

Davies, B. (1989). *Frogs and snails and feminist tales: Preschool children and gender.* Sydney, NSW: Allen & Unwin.

Delgado-Gaitan, C. (1990). *Literacy for empowerment: The role of parents in children's education.* London: Falmer Press.

Delpit, L. (1988). The silenced dialogue: Power and pedagogy in educating other people's children. *Harvard Educational Review, 56,* 280–298.

——— (1993). The silenced dialogue: Power and pedagogy in education of other people's children. In L. Weis & M. Fine (Eds.), *Beyond silenced voices* (pp. 119–139). Albany: State University of New York Press.

DeParle, J. (1994, November 13). Momentum builds for cutting back welfare system. *New York Times,* p. A1, (front page) A30, column 1.

Derrida, J. (1991). Of grammatology. In P. Kamuf (Ed.), *A Derrida reader: Between the blinds.* New York: Harvester Wheatsheaf.

deVries, M. & Lubeck, S. (1998, April). *Parent involvement in Head Start.* Poster presented at the annual meetings of the American Educational Research Association. San Diego, CA.

DeYoung, A. (1993). The natural man and the virtuous woman: Reproducing citizens. In C. Jenks (Ed.), *Cultural reproduction.* New York: Routledge.

Dodd, A. (1992). *War and peace: Toys, teachers and tots.* Paper presented to the Annual Conference of the Southern Association on Children Under Six, March 23–28, Tulsa, OK.

Donzelot, J. (1991). Pleasure in work. In G. Burchell, C. Gordon, and P. Miller (Eds.), *The Foucault effect: Studies in governmentality* (pp. 251–280). Chicago: University of Chicago Press.

Duckworth, E. (1972). The having of wonderful ideas. *Harvard Educational Review 42*, 217–231.

Dyson, A. H. (1990). Research currents: Diversity, social responsibility, and the story of literacy development. *Language Arts, 67*, 193–205.

Elkind, D. (1994). *Ties that stress: The new family imbalance*. Cambridge, MA: Harvard University Press.

Ellsworth, E. (1989). Why doesn't this feel empowering? Working through the repressive myths of critical pedagogy. *Harvard Educational Review, 59*, 297–324.

Ellsworth, J., & Ames, L. (Eds.). (1998). *Critical perspectives on Project Head Start: Re-visioning the hope and challenge*. Albany, NY: SUNY.

Evans, J. L., Karwowska-Struczk, M., Korintus, M., Herseni, L., & Kornazheva, B. (1995). *Who is caring for the children? An exploratory survey conducted in Hungary, Poland, Bulgaria and Romania*. Washington, DC: Consultative Group on Early Childhood Care and Development, Report to the World Bank.

Farrell, A. (1997). *Children's rights in a consumer society*. Paper presented to the Australian Early Childhood Association Conference—Children in the Balance, September, Melbourne.

Fernandez, M., & Bloch, M. N. (1993). *Cross-national analysis of existing childcare programs in Bulgaria, Hungary and Poland*. Final Report. Washington, DC: U.S. Agency for International Development.

Flax, J. (1990). *Thinking fragments; Psychoanalysis, feminism, and postmodernism in the contemporary West*. Berkeley, CA: University of California Press.

Foucault, M. (1979). *Discipline and punishment: The birth of the prison*. New York: Vintage.

————. (1979/1991). Governmentality. In G. Burchell, C. Gordon, & P. Miller (Eds.), *The Foucault effect: Studies in governmentality,* (pp. 87–104). Chicago: University of Chicago Press.

————. (1980). *Power/knowledge: Selected interviews and other writings, 1972–1977*. New York: Pantheon Books.

————. (1983). Afterword. In H. Dreyfus and P. Rabinow, *Michelle Foucault: Beyond structuralism and hermeneutics.* (pp. 229–264). Chicago. The University of Chicago Press.

Fraser, N., & Gordon, L. (1994). A geneology of "dependency": Tracing a keyword of the U.S. welfare state. *SIGNS, 19*, 309–336.

Freeman, M. P. (1993). *Rewriting the self: History, memory, narrative.* New York: Routledge.

Freire, P. (1970). *Pedagogy of the oppressed.* New York: Seabury.

————. (1985). *The politics of education: Culture, power, and liberation.* South Hadley: Bergin & Garvey.

Frost, J. O., & Klein, B. L. (1979). *Children's play and playgrounds.* Boston: Allyn and Bacon.

Funiciello, T. (1993). *The tyranny of kindness.* New York: Atlantic Monthly Press.

Gallas, K. (1997). Your mother squeezes your brains out your ears: The social construction of gender and race in a primary classroom. Paper presentation, American Educational Research Association, Chicago, IL.

Gardner, M. (April 23, 1988). Low day-care salaries undervalue children as well as providers. *Christian Science Monitor*, p. 12.

Gee, J., Hull, G., & Lankshear, C. (1996). *The new work order: Behind the language of the new capitalism.* Boulder, CO: Westview Press.

Geertz, C. (1983). *Local knowledge: Further essays in interpretive anthropology.* New York: Basic Books.

Goduka, I. (1998). Ubuntu. Discussion at the Annual Conference of the American Educational Research Association. San Diego, California.

Goffin, S. (1996). Introduction to the special issue on child development knowledge and teacher education. *Early Childhood Research Quarterly, 11*(2), 117–133.

Goldberg, G. S., & Kremen, E. (1990). *The feminization of poverty: Only in America?* New York: Greenwood Press.

Gordon, L. (1990). The new feminist scholarship on the welfare state. In L. Gordon (Ed.), *Women, the state and welfare.* Madison, WI: University of Wisconsin Press.

————. (1994). *Pitied but not Entitled: Single mothers and the history of welfare.* Cambridge: Harvard University Press.

Gould, S. J. (1977). *Ontogeny and phylogeny.* Cambridge: Harvard University Press.

———. (1981). *The mismeasure of man.* New York: Norton Press.

Grace, D., & Tobin, J. (1998). Carnival in the classroom. In J. Tobin (Ed.), *Making a place for pleasure in early childhood education*, pp. 119–158. New Haven, CT: Yale University Press.

Greene, M. (1986) In search of a critical pedagogy. *Harvard Educational Review, 56*, 427–441.

———. (1994). Epistemology and educational research: The influence of recent approaches to knowledge. *Review of Research in Education, vol. 20* (pp. 423–464). Washington, DC: American Educational Research Association.

Grubb, W. N., & Lazerson, M. (1982). *Broken promises: How Americans fail their children.* New York: Basic Books.

Hacking, I. (1991). How should we do the history of statistics. In G. Burchell, C. Gordon, and P. Miller (Eds.), *The Foucault effect: Studies in governmentality.* Chicago: University of Chicago Press, 181–196.

Hall, G. S. (1911). The pedagogy of the kindergarten. *Educational Problems, I.* New York: D. Appleton.

———. (1969). *Adolescence: Its psychology and its relation to physiology, anthropology, sociology, sex, crime, religion and education (Vol. I).* New York: Arno Press and the *New York Times.* (Originally published 1905)

Harding, S. (1987). *Feminism and Methodology.* London: Routledge.

Hatch, J. A. (1995). Ethical conflicts in classroom research: Examples from a study of peer stigmatization in kindergarten. In J. A. Hatch (Ed.), *Qualitative Research in Early Childhood Settings* (pp. 213–223). Westport, CT: Praeger Publishers.

———. (1996). Walking the talk: An example of inclusive early childhood teacher preparation. *Educating Young Children* (Australia), *2*, 46–49.

———. Brice, D., Kidwell, M., Mason, M., & McCarthy, B. (1994, November). *Appropriate practices in non-mainstream settings: Perspectives of inner-city early childhood educators.* Paper presented at the Annual Meeting of the National Association for the Education of Young Children, Atlanta, GA.

———. & Wisniewski, R. (1995). Life history and narrative: Questions, issues, and exemplary works. In J. A. Hatch and R. Wisniewski (Eds.), *Life history and narrative* (pp. 113–135). London: Falmer Press.

Hauser, M. (1998). In our own backyards: Whose view? In M. Hauser & J. Jipson (Eds.), *Intersections: Feminisms/early childhoods* (pp. 137–145). New York: Peter Lang.

Heath, S. B. (1989). *Ways with words: Language, life and work in communities and classrooms*. New York: Cambridge University Press.

Herman, E. (1995). *The romance of American psychology, political culture in the age of experts*. Berkeley: University of California Press.

Hinchey, P. (1998). *Finding freedom in the classroom: A practical introduction to critical theory*. New York: Peter Lang.

Hindess, B. (1996). Liberalism, socialism and democracy: Variations on a governmental theme. In A. Barry, T. Osborne, and N. Rose (Eds.), *Foucault and political reason: Liberalism, neo-liberalism and rationalities of government* (pp. 65–80). Chicago: University of Chicago Press.

Holmes, B. (1991). *War toys: Preparing your child for war*. Paper presented to the Toys, Triggers and Television Violence and Youth in the 1990s Conference, Melbourne.

Horton, J., & Freire, P. (1990). *We make the road by walking: Conversations on education and social change*. Edited by B. Bell, J. Gaventa, and J. Peters. Philadelphia: Temple University Press.

Hughes, P., & MacNaughton, G. (1998). *Fractured or manufactured? Gendered identities of culture in the early years*. Paper presented to the Early Childhood Education Reconceptualizing Conference, January 11–13, Hawaii.

Hughes, F. P. (1995). *Children, play, & development*. Boston: Allyn and Bacon.

Hultqvist, K. (1998). A history of the present on children's welfare in Sweden. In T. S. Popkewitz & M. Brennan (Eds.), *Foucault's challenge: Discourse, knowledge, and power in education* (pp. 91–117). New York: Teachers College Press.

Hunter, I. (1994) *Rethinking the school: Subjectivity, bureaucracy, criticism*. New York: St. Martin's Press.

James A., Jenks, C., & Prout, A. (Eds.). (1998). *Theorizing Childhood*. New York: Teachers College.

Jameson, F. (1984). *Postmodernism: Or, the cultural logic of late capitalism*. Durham, NC: Duke University Press.

Jipson, J. (1991). Developmentally appropriate practice: Culture, curriculum, connections. *Early Education and Development, 2,* 120–136.

———. (1992). The emergent curriculum: Contextualizing a feminist perspective. In S. Kessler and B. Swadener (Eds.), *Reconceptualizing the Early Childhood Curriculum* (pp. 149–164). New York: Teachers College Press.

————. (1992). Midwife and mother: Multiple reflections on curriculum, community, and change. *Journal of Curriculum Theorizing 10*(1), 89–116.

————. (1998). *Postmodernism/deconstruction: What does it say about childhood?* Paper presented at the International Conference on Reconceptualizing Early Childhood Education. Honolulu, Hawaii.

————. Munro, P., Victor, S., Froude Jones, K., & Freed-Rowland, G. (1995). *Repositioning feminism and education: Perspectives on educating for social change.* Westport, CT: Bergin & Garvey.

————. & Paley, N. (Eds.). (1997). *Daredevil research: Re-Creating analytic practice.* New York: Peter Lang.

Johnson, A. (1999). Teaching as sacrament. In J. Kincheloe, S. Steinberg, L. Villaverde (Eds.), *Rethinking intelligence: Confronting psychological assumptions about teaching and learning.* New York: Routledge.

Kearney, R. (1988). *The wake of imagination.* Minneapolis: University of Minnesota Press.

Kessler, S. (1991). Alternative perspectives on early childhood education. *Early Childhood Research Quarterly, 6,* 183–197.

Kessler, S., & Swadener, B. (1992). *Reconceptualizing the early childhood curriculum: Beginning the dialogue.* New York: Teachers College Press.

Kilbride, P., & Kilbride, J. (1990). *Changing family life in East Africa: Women and children at risk.* University Park, PA: Pennsylvania State University Press.

Kincheloe, J., & Steinberg, S. (1993). A tentative description of post–formal thinking: The critical confrontation with cognitive theory. *Harvard Educational Review, 63*(3), 296–320.

King, N. (1992). Play in context. In S. Kessler and B. Swadener, Reconceptualizing the early childhood curriculum: Beginning the dialogue. New York: Teachers College Press.

Kismaric, C., & Keiferman, M. (1996). *Growing up with Dick and Jane. Learning and living the American dream.* New York: Harper Collins Publishers.

Kliebard, H. (1986). *The struggle for the American curriculum 1893–1958.* Boston, MA: Routledge & Kegan Paul.

Kline, S., & Pentecost, D. (1990). The characterization of play: marketing children's toys. *Play and Culture, 3,* 235–255.

Kotlowitz, A. (1991). *There are no children here: The story of two boys growing up in the other America.* New York: Doubleday.

Kozol, J. (1991). *Savage inequalities: Children in America's schools.* New York: Crown Publishers.

———. (1996). *Amazing grace.* New York: Crown Publishers.

Kretzmann, J., & McKnight, J. (1993). *Building communities from the inside out.* Chicago, IL: ACTA Publications.

Kristeva, J. (1981). Women's time. *Signs, 7*(1).

Ladson-Billings, G. (1992). Culturally relevant teaching: The key to making multicultural education work. In C. A. Grant (Ed.), *Research in multicultural education: From the margins to the mainstream* (pp. 106–121). London: Falmer Press.

Lather, P. (1991). *Getting smart: Feminist research with/in the post modern.* New York: Routledge.

Lears, J. (1981). *No place of grace: Antimodernism, and the transformation of American culture, 1880–1920.* New York: Pantheon.

Leavitt, R. L. (1994). *Power and emotion in infant-toddler day care.* Albany, NY: SUNY Press.

Lemert, C. (1992). General social theory, irony, and postmodernism. In S. Seidman and D. G. Wagner (Eds.), *Postmodernism and social theory* (pp. 17–46). Cambridge, MA: Blackwell.

Levin, D. (1996). Disney, Mattel ink three–year deal. *Variety.* April 8–14.

Levine, R. (1994). *Child Care and Culture: Lessons from Africa.* Cambridge: Cambridge University Press.

Lewis, J. (1995). *Critiques and Alternatives to Child Development Theories.* Unpublished manuscript.

Lorde, A. (1984). The masters tools will never dismantle the masters house. In *Sister outsider* (pp. 110–113.) Freedom, CA: The Crossing Press.

Lubeck, S. (1987). Nested contexts. In L. Weis (Ed.), *Class, race and gender in American education* (pp. 43–62). Albany, NY: State University of New York Press.

———. (1994). The politics of developmentally appropriate practice. In B. L. Mallory, and R. S. New (Eds.), *Diversity and developmentally appropriate practices* (pp. 17–43). New York: Teachers College Press.

———. (1996). Deconstructing "Child development knowledge" and "teacher preparation." *Early Childhood Research Quarterly, 11*(2), 147–169.

———. (1998). Is DAP for everyone? *Childhood Education, 74*(5), 283–292.

Lubeck, S., deVries, M., Nicholson, J., & Post, J. (1997). Head Start in transition. *Early Education and Development, 8*(3), 219–244.

Lyotard, J. F. (1984). *The postmodern condition: A report on knowledge.* Minneapolis: University of Minnesota Press.

Macdonald, L. (1988). Curriculum, consciousness, and social change. In W. Pinar (Ed.), *Contemporary curriculum discourses* (pp. 156–174). Scottsdale, AZ: Corsuch Scarisbrick.

Maher, F. (1987). Toward a richer theory of feminist pedagogy: A comparison of "liberation" and "gender" models for teaching and learning. *Journal of Education, 169*(3), 91–100.

Mallory, B. L., & New, R. S. (Eds.). (1994). *Diversity and developmentally appropriate practices.* New York: Teachers College Press.

Marcus, G., & Fischer, M. (1986). *Anthropology and cultural critique: An experimental moment in the human sciences.* Chicago: The University of Chicago Press.

Marks, A. (April 17, 1998). What children see and do: Studies of violence on TV. *Christian Science Monitor,* p. 3.

Martin–Baro, I. (1994). *Writings for a liberation psychology.* Edited by A. Aron and S. Corne. Cambridge, MA: Harvard University Press.

Matusov, E. (1996). Intersubjectivity without agreement. *Mind, Culture, and Activity, 3*(1), 25–45.

McCormick, M. (1995). Preschool video comes of age. *Billboard.* July 1.

McIntosh, P. (1988). *White privilege and male privilege: A personal account of coming to see correspondences through work in Women's Studies.* Working paper No. 189. Wellesley, MA: Wellesley College Center for Research on Women.

McKey, R. H., Condelli, L., Garrison, H., Barrett, B. M., McConkey, C., & Plantz, M. (1985). *The impact of Head Start on children, families, and communities.* Washington, DC: CSR, Inc.

McLaren, P. (1993). Border disputes: Multicultural narrative, identity formation, and critical pedagogy in postmodern America. In D. McLaughlin and W. Tierney (Eds.), *Naming silenced lives* (pp. 201–235). New York: Routledge.

Meloy, J. M. (1993). Problems of writing and representation in qualitative inquiry. *Qualitative Studies in Education, 6,* 315–330.

Moraes, M. (1996). *Bilingual education: A dialogue with the Bakhtin circle.* Albany, NY: SUNY Press.

Munyakho, D. (1992). *Kenya: Child newcomers to the urban jungle*. New York: UNICEF.

Muraya, J. (1993). *Street children: A study of street girls in Nairobi*. Monograph, Center for Development Studies. University College of Swansea, Wales.

Napoli, D. (1981). *Architects of adjustment: The history of the psychological profession in the United States*. Port Washington, NY: Kennikat Press.

New, R. S. (1994). Culture, child development and developmentally appropriate practices. In B. L. Mallory, and R. S. New (Eds.), *Diversity and developmentally appropriate practices* (pp. 65–83). New York: Teachers College Press.

Nightingale, C. (1993). *On the edge: A history of poor black children and their American dreams*. New York: Basic Books.

Oakes, J. (1988). Tracking in mathematics and science education: A structural contribution to unequal schooling. In L. Weis (Ed.), *Class, race and gender in American education*. Albany, NY: SUNY Press.

O'Donnell, J. (1985). *The origins of behaviorism: American psychology, 1876–1920*. New York: University Press.

Pearce, D. (1978). The feminization of poverty: Women, work and welfare. *The Urban and Social Change Review, 11*(1 & 2), 28–36.

Pecora, N. O. (1998). *The business of children's entertainment*. New York: The Guildford Press.

Perkins, D. (1995). *Outsmarting IQ: The emerging science of learnable intelligence*. New York: The Free Press.

Polakow, V. (1982, 1992). *The erosion of childhood*. Chicago: University of Chicago Press.

———. (1993). *Lives on the edge: Single mothers and their children in the other America*. Chicago: University of Chicago Press.

———. (1997). Family policy, welfare, and single motherhood in the United States and Denmark: A cross-national analysis of discourse and practice. *Early Education and Development, 8*(3), 245–264.

———. & Swadener, B. B. (1993, September). *Lives on the edge: A conversation with single mothers*. Symposium presented at the Third Reconceptualizing Research, Policy and Practice in Early Childhood Conference, Ann Arbor, Michigan.

Popkewitz, T. S. (1996). Rethinking decentralization and the state/civil society distinctions: The state as a problematic of governing. *Journal of Educational Policy, 11*, 27–51.

————. (1997). A changing terrain of knowledge and power: A social epistemology of educational research. *Educational Researcher, 26*(9), 18–29.

————. (1998a). The culture of redemption and the administration of freedom in educational research. *Review of Educational Research, 68*(1), 1–35.

————. (1998b). *Struggling for the soul: The politics of education and the construction of the teacher.* New York: Teachers College Press.

————. & M. Brennan (1998). *Foucault's challenge: Discourse, knowledge, and power in education.* New York: Teachers College Press.

Price, G. (1992). Using Quantitative Methods to Explore Multicultural Education. In Grant C., (Ed.), Research and multicultural education: From the margins to the mainstream (pp. 58–70). London: Falmer.

Quintero, B., & Rummel, M. K. (1995). Voice unaltered: Marginalized young writers speak. In B. B. Swadener & S. Lubeck (Eds.), *Children and families "at promise": Deconstructing the discourse of risk* (pp. 97–117). Albany, NY: State University of New York Press.

Ramsey, P. (1995). Growing up with the contradictions of race and class. *The Web Journal of the Culturally Relevant Anti–Bias Early Childhood Educators Network*, December 11–15.

Reed, A. (1992). The underclass as myth and symbol: The poverty of discourse about poverty. *Radical American, 24*(1), 21–40.

Reynolds, G. & Jones, E. (1977). *Master players: Learning from children at play.* New York: Teachers College Press.

Rogers, R., & Rogers, W. (1992). *Stories of childhood: Shifting agendas of child concern.* Toronto: University of Toronto Press.

Rogoff, B. (1990). *Apprenticeship in thinking.* New York: Oxford University Press.

Rogoff, B., Matusov, E., & White, C. (1996). Models of teaching and learning: Participation in a community of learners. In D. Olson & N. Torrance (Eds.), *The handbook of education and human development* (pp. 388–414). New York: Blackwell.

Roman, L., & Apple, M. (1989). Is naturalism a move away from positivism? Materialist and feminist approaches to subjectivity in ethnographic research. In E. Eisner and A. Peshkin, Qualitative inquiry in education: The continuing debate. New York: Teachers College Press.

Rorty, R. (1979). *Philosophy and the mirror of nature.* Princeton, NJ: Princeton University Press.

Rose, N. (1989). *Governing the soul.* New York: Routledge, Chapman & Hall.

———. (1996). *Inventing ourselves: Psychology, power, and personhood.* New York: Cambridge University Press.

Rose, N., & Miller, P. (1992). Political power beyond the state: Problematics of government. *British Journal of Sociology, 43,* 173–205.

Rothman, S. M. (1980). *Women's proper place: A history of changing ideals and practices, 1870 to the present.* New York: Basic Books.

Salomon, G. (Ed.) (1993). *Distributed cognition: Psychological and educational considerations.* New York: Cambridge University Press.

Samuels, A. (1993). *The political psyche.* New York: Routledge.

Sartre, J. P. (1964). *Nausea.* Norfolk, CT: New Directions. (Original published in 1938.)

Sarup, M. (1988). *An introductory guide to post-structuralism and postmodernism.* New York: Harvester Wheatsheaf.

Scheler, M. (1980). *Problems of a sociology of knowledge* (M. Frings, Trans.). Boston: Routledge & Kegan Paul. (Original work published 1924).

Scheurich, J. J. (1995). A postmodernist critique of research interviewing. *Qualitative Studies in Education, 8,* 339-352.

Schleifer, R., Con Davis, R., & Mergler, N. (1992). *Culture and cognition: The boundaries of literacy and scientific inquiry.* Ithaca, NY: Cornell University Press.

Schlossman, S. (1981). Philanthropy and the gospel of child development. *History of Education Quarterly,* 275–299.

Schön, D. (1983). The reflective practitioner: How professionals think in action. New York: Basic Books.

Schubert, W. (1986). *Curriculum: Perspective, paradigm, and possibility.* New York: Macmillan.

Sears, R. (1975). Your ancients revisited: A history of child development. In E. M. Hetherington (Ed.), *Review of Child Development Research, 5,* 1975, 1–73.

Seidman, S. (1992). Postmodern social theory as narrative with a moral intent. In S. Seidman and D. G. Wagner (Eds.), *Postmodernism and social theory* (pp. 47–81). Cambridge, MA: Blackwell.

———. (Ed.) (1994). *The postmodern turn: New perspectives on social theory.* New York: Cambridge University Press.

Seiter, E. (1992). Toys are us: Marketing to children and parents. *Cultural Studies,6*(2), pp. 232–248.

Shotter, J. (1993). *Cultural politics of everyday life.* Toronto: University of Toronto Press.

Sidel, R. (1992). *Women and children last: The plight of poor women in affluent America.* New York: Penguin Books.

Smith, H. (1994). *World's religions: A guide to our wisdom traditions.* New York: Harper San Francisco.

Soto, L. D. (1993). Success stories. In C. A. Grant (Ed.), *Research in multicultural education: From the margins to the mainstream* (pp. 153–164). New York: Falmer Press.

———. (1997a). *Language, culture, and power. Bilingual families and the struggle for quality education.* Albany: State University of New York Press.

———. (1997b). Constructivist theory in the Age of Newt Gingrich: The post formal concern with power. *Journal of Early Childhood Teacher Education, Proceedings Issue, 18*(2) 43–57.

———. (1998). The multicultural worlds of childhood in post-modern America. In C. Seefeldt (Ed.), *Early childhood curriculum: A review of current research.* New York: Teachers College Press.

Soto, L., Paul, A., & Gutierrez, C. (1997). Wisdom keepers: Part II. Presentation at the Annual Conference of the National Association for the Education of Young Children. Anaheim, California.

Steinberg, S., & Kincheloe, J. (Eds.). (1997). *Kinderculture.* Boulder, CO: Westview Press.

Swadener, B. B. (1990). Children and families "at risk": Etiology, critique and alternative paradigms. *Educational Foundations, 4*(4), 17–39.

———. (1995). Stratification in early childhood social policy and programs in the United States: Historical and Contemporary Manifestations. *Educational Policy, 9*(4), 404–425.

Swadener, B. B., Dunlap, S. K., & Nespeca, S. M. (1995). Family literacy and social policy: Parent perspectives and policy implications. *Reading & Writing Quarterly: Overcoming Learning Difficulties, 11,* 267–283.

Swadener, B. B., & Jagielo, L. M. (1997). Politics at the margins: Feminist perspectives on early childhood social policy and programs. In J. Jipson & M. Hauser (Eds.). *Intersections: Feminisms and early childhood education.* New York: Peter Lang.

Swadener, B. B., & Lubeck, S. (Eds.). (1995). *Children and families "at promise": Deconstructing the discourse of risk*. Albany, NY: State University of New York Press.

Swadener, B. B., & Niles, K. (1991). Children and families "at promise": Making home-school-community connections. *Democracy and Education, 5*(3), 13–18.

Swadener, E. B., & Kessler, S. (Thematic Issue Eds.) (1991). *Early Education and Development, 2*(2).

Swadener, E. B., & Bloch, M. N. (1997). Children and families in transition: Cross national perspectives. *Early Education and Development, 8*(3), 207–217.

Swiniarsky, L. B. (1991). Toys: Universals for teaching global education. *Childhood Education.* (Spring), 161–163.

Taylor, D., & Dorsey-Gaines, C. (1988). *Growing up literate: Learning from inner city families*. Portsmouth, NH: Heinemann Educational Books.

Thompson, J. (1990). *Ideology and modern culture*. Stanford: Stanford University Press.

Tierney, W. G. (1993). The cedar closet. *Qualitative Studies in Education, 6*, 303–314.

Tobin, J. (1995). Post-structural research in early childhood education. In J. A. Hatch (Ed.), *Qualitative research in early childhood settings* (pp. 223–243). Westport, CT: Praeger.

Toner, R. (1995, September 20). Senate passes bill to abolish guarantees of aid for the poor. *New York Times*, A1 (front page), B9 column 1.

UNICEF (1995). *The state of the world's children 1995.* Oxford: Oxford University.

U.S. Department of Health and Human Services (1993, December). *Creating a 21st century Head Start*. Washington, DC: US Department of Health and Human Services; Advisory Committee on Head Start Quality and Expansion.

U.S. General Accounting Office (1997, April). *Head Start: Research provides little information on impact of current program*. Washington, DC: Report to the Chairman, Committee on the Budget, House of Representatives.

Usher, R., & Edwards, R. (1994). *Postmodernism and education.* New York: Routledge.

Veroff, J., & Goldberger, N. (1995). What's in a name: The case for an intercultural psychology. In N. Goldberger & J. Veroff (Eds.), *The culture and psychology reader.* New York: NYU Press.

Wagner, P. (1994). *Sociology of modernity: Liberty and discipline.* New York: Routledge.

Walkerdine, V. (1984). Developmental psychology and the child-centered pedagogy. In J. Henriques, W. Hollway, C. Urwin, C. Venn, & V. Walkerdine (Eds.), *Changing the subject: Psychology, social regulation, and subjectivity* (pp. 153–202). London: Methune.

————. (1988). *The mastery of reason: Cognitive development and the production of rationality.* London: Routledge.

Washington, V., & Bailey, U. (1993). *Project Head Start: Models and strategies for the twenty-first century.* New York: Garland Publishing.

Weisner, T. (1987). Review of J. Wertsch, Vygotsky and the social formation of mind. *American Anthropologist, 89,* 479–480.

Wertsch, J., Del Rio, P., & Alvarez, A. (1995). Sociocultural studies: History, action, and mediation. In J. Wertsch, P. Del Rio, and A. Alvarez (Eds.), *Sociocultural studies of the mind.* New York: Cambridge University Press.

Williamson, M. (1997). *The healing of America.* New York: Simon and Schuster.

Willis, S. (1996). Play for profit. In C. Luke (Ed.), *Feminisms and pedagogies of everyday life,* 188–203. Albany, NY: State University of New York Press.

Wittgenstein, L. (1966). *The philosophical investigations: A collection of critical essays.* (G. Pitcher, Ed.), Notre Dame, IN: University of Notre Dame Press. (Originally published 1953).

Wittrock, B., & Wagner, P. (1996). Social science and the building of the early welfare state: Toward a comparison of statist and non–statist Western societies. In D. Rueschemeyer and T. Skocpol (Eds.), *States, social science and the origin of modern social policies* (pp. 90–114). Princeton, NJ: Princeton University Press.

Wood, N., & Howell, F. (1996). *Shaman's Circle.* New York: Delacorte.

Woods, P. (1983). *Sociology, and the school: An interactionist viewpoint.* London: Routledge and Kegan Paul.

Wrigley, J. (1991). Different care for different kids: Social class and childcare policy. In L. Weis, P. G. Altbach, G. P. Kelly, and H. G. Petrie (Eds.), *Critical perspectives on early childhood education* (pp. 189–209). Albany, NY: State University of New York.

Zigler, E., & Muenchow, S. (1992). *Head Start: The inside story of American's most successful educational experiment.* New York: Basic Books.

Zweigenhaft, R., & Domhoff, G. (1991). *Blacks in the White establishment.* New Haven: Yale University Press.

RETHINKING CHILDHOOD

JOE L. KINCHELOE & JANICE A. JIPSON, *General Editors*

A revolution is occurring regarding the study of childhood. Traditional notions of child development are under attack, as are the methods by which children are studied. At the same time, the nature of childhood itself is changing as children gain access to information once reserved for adults only. Technological innovations, media, and electronic information have narrowed the distinction between adults and children, forcing educators to rethink the world of schooling in this new context.

This series of textbooks and monographs encourages scholarship in all of these areas, eliciting critical investigations in developmental psychology, early childhood education, multicultural education, and cultural studies of childhood.

Proposals and manuscripts may be sent to the general editors:

> Joe L. Kincheloe
> 637 W. Foster Avenue
> State College, PA 16801
>
> *or*
>
> Janice A. Jipson
> 219 Pease Court
> Janesville, WI 53545

To order other books in this series, please contact our Customer Service Department at:

> (800) 770-LANG (within the U.S.)
> (212) 647-7706 (outside the U.S.)
> (212) 647-7707 FAX

Or browse online by series at:
> www.peterlang.com